Communicatio
Editor: Jerem

The sociolog

In the same series

SIMON FRITH

The sociology of rock

CONSTABLE
London

Published in Great Britain 1978
by Constable and Company Ltd
10 Orange Street London WC2H 7EG
Hardback ISBN 0 09 460220 4
Paperback ISBN 0 09 462290 6
Reprinted 1979

Set in Monotype Times
Printed in Great Britain by
REDWOOD BURN LIMITED
Trowbridge & Esher

Contents

List of tables

Preface

I was a rock fan long before I was a sociologist, and when I first had the idea of writing this book it was as an easy way of combining work and pleasure. I soon discovered that what was involved was not the simple application of sociological terms to my rock experience, and preparing this book has been a hard, if enjoyable, research grind. I am very grateful to Jeremy Tunstall and to Elfreda Powell of Constable for giving me the chance to do the work in the first place and for tolerating my broken deadlines with grace, patience and encouragement.

My fan's knowledge turned out to be a confusion of fact, myth and wishful thinking and my major concern in writing this book has been to get things right in a field bedevilled by commercial hype, loose talk and instant expertise; I have deliberately used the full academic battery of footnotes to support my own assertions. In the text my emphasis is on published sources, but my rock knowledge derives ultimately from the people at all levels of rock culture who have talked to me, given me access to their records, and, in general, allowed me to see how the rock world works for them.

Other debts are more specific. I have learnt about youth culture from my friends and fellow-sociologists, Paul Corrigan, Trev Jones, Angie McRobbie, Graham Murdock, Paul Willis, and Kevin Buckley, from whose research in Coventry I have drawn extensively, and, above all, from Gill Frith, who has shared with me her knowledge and insights and been an astringent critic of my own work. And I am very grateful for the amused cooperation of my Keighley youth sample.

I have learnt about rock culture from my friends and fellow-writers, Lester Bangs, Bob Christgau, Phil Hardy, Ian Hoare, Dave Laing, Dave Marsh, Greil Marcus and John Pidgeon; I am especially grateful to the editors of *Creem* magazine who have, over the years, given me complete freedom to develop my ideas in public. And this book would have been impossible without the work I was able to do for *Let It Rock*.

I have tried to write a book which will make sense simultaneously to sociologists who know nothing about rock and to rock fans who know nothing about sociology; the result is bound to irritate both sorts of reader but I intend it also to educate them. It is an introductory text, raising as many questions as it answers, and I hope that a more sophisticated sociology of rock will follow, but I must emphasise that this is a sociological study and not an exercise in rock criticism – I do not discuss individual rock works. My aim has been to provide an analysis that has general validity, that is not confined to particular rock styles or to particular rock moments, and in developing this approach I have incurred two debts in particular: Simon Clarke has helped me to clarify and tighten my arguments, Charlie Gillett has given me free access to his knowledge of the rock business and a detailed commentary on every stage of my own work; I hope that between them they have spotted my worst errors and muddles. Those that remain are, of course, all mine.

S.F.

1
Introduction

When I went to university in 1964 I assumed that I'd reached the end of my teenage bopping days and I didn't even take my records with me. Three years later I had an Oxford degree, entrance ticket to high bourgeois culture, it was 1967, and I didn't feel particularly eccentric setting out for California under the inspiration of a pop song, Scott McKenzie's 'San Francisco'. My own use of music hadn't changed much but pop's cultural power was now publicly realised, and in Berkeley I found a culture in which rock and politics, music and the Movement, pleasure and action were inextricably linked. They have been linked for me ever since, and by the time I came back to England again I was sure that rock was the most interesting and the most encouraging of the contemporary mass media.

In the heyday of counter-culture and student organisation this was a widely shared (if rarely examined) assumption, but in the 1970s sociologists turned their attention back to traditional academic matters and the learned tomes on the significance of rock that once seemed likely never appeared. In order to pursue my interests I had to live a double life: on the one hand going through the paces of an academic sociological career – respectable research on the history of education, on youth as a social phenomenon – and on the other hand ringing the changes as a semi-professional rock writer, contributing my obstinate prejudices and enthusiasms to the thousands of words that accompany the release of every new rock record, the discovery of every new rock star.

My two careers have rarely been good for each other. Rock writing is not considered suitable for inclusion in an academic curriculum vitae; 'sociology' is a term of abuse among rock writers. But I have never lost the convictions that link the two worlds – that rock is a crucial contemporary form of mass communication, and that sociological analysis can contribute to the understanding and appreciation of this form. Hence this book.

My belief in the importance of rock is supported, at its most obvious level, by the statistics. In 1974 well over $4 billion was spent annually in the world on musical products; in America, at least, music was by far the most popular form of entertainment – the sales of records and tapes easily outgrossing the returns from movies or sport – and in

Britain alone more than 160 million records were pressed. The steady expansion of the British record industry since 1955 (when 60 million records were pressed) shows little sign of stopping, economic crises notwithstanding.[1]

The problem is what these figures mean. Sociologists of mass media usually include records in their lists of mass communications, but this is usually also the only mention that records get. Media analysis continues to be dominated by terms and problems derived from studies of television and the press, and records cannot easily be fitted into the subsequent sociological conclusions. The statistics that I've cited are certainly those of a highly profitable industry, but they don't directly establish records as a mass medium (similar figures could probably be unearthed for blue jeans or yoghurt). To get at the power of rock we must go beyond the account books and the sales returns, and in this chapter I want to make clear the assumptions that underpin my treatment of music as mass communication.[2]

Records are the result of complex formal organisations. If in other musical experiences the musicians and their audiences are joined by the speed of sound, for recorded music the link is an elaborate industry. Between the original music and its final listener are the technological processes of transferring sound to tape and disc and the economic processes of packaging and marketing the resulting product; like the other mass media, records rely on capital investment and specialised technical equipment, on the organisation of a variety of skilled roles. The basis of any sociological analysis of records must be an analysis of the record industry and this will be my focus in Part Two. But there is an immediate question to be asked about record production which in the light of the statistics may seem silly, though it is, in fact, crucial for an understanding of records as a mass medium: are they directed at a large audience?

Large is a relative term in media studies. Mass media have large audiences relative to other media and relative to the number of communicators involved; there is not a given size of audience to which a communication must be addressed to reach mass status. But the position is especially complicated in the case of records by the distinction we can make between the record industry as a whole and its products, individual records. The recording industry is geared to capital accumulation and its profits depend on the numbers of records sold. Initial recording costs are one-off expenditures, unaffected by the number of records resulting, while the costs of manufacture and distribution are proportionately reduced as the numbers involved increase. The record business is ruled by the logic of mass production and a large market is its overriding aim.

This market is, however, made up of different audiences buying different records and listening to different kinds of music. And the sales of a particular record can be anything from a handful for an avant-garde recital of electronic blips to millions for the latest platinum smash from Rod Stewart. Should we take all records, whatever their type or success, as directed at a large audience? Or should we assign some (random?) sales figure which a record must reach before it can be classified as a mass communication?

Both approaches are wrong. We can, more constructively, make a distinction between music of which the original conception, composition and purpose had nothing to do with a mass market, and music for which the mass market has been inseparable from its conception, composition and purpose. The former category includes classical music, all folk music and most jazz; the latter category consists of pop music. Pop music is created with the record industry's pursuit of a large audience in mind, other music is not. That classical or folk music can be listened to on records is accidental; only pop music is *essentially* a music which is communicated by a mass medium. This is true even though some classical records sell tens of thousands of copies and many pop records are bought by nobody. Pop music is created for a large audience and is marketed accordingly by the record industry – pop records get the bulk of the attention of the advertisers, distributors and retailers. Classical music, folk music, and the other 'special' forms are believed to be confined to a relatively small and stable audience. At most, classical music accounts for 10% of record sales – pop accounts for 85 to 90%.[3]

Pop music doesn't have to be in record form by this definition – Tin Pan Alley was marketing songs for mass consumption long before the recording industry was flourishing – but at least since the Second World War pop music has meant pop records. To define pop as music aimed at a large market is also, these days, to define it as music aimed at record sales. I will return to the effects on the industry and on the music of the shift from songs to records as the basis of pop.

Pop records are, at any rate, public, accessible to everyone. Once a record has been issued there is nothing to stop anyone listening to it except its price or the lack of access to a gramophone. Radio stations can ban a record from the airwaves but they can't stop people buying it – Judge Dread's rude reggae records continue to be Top Twenty hits and the Sex Pistols' 'God Save the Queen' topped the charts; the mechanisms of record distribution are not such final controllers of choice as they are, for example, in the cinema. Pop records, indeed, have a wider public than any other medium because their availability is not limited by considerations of literacy or language. They can and do cross all national and cultural boundaries. The

Beatles were a mass medium phenomenon in nearly every country in the world and there is a continuous interplay between English and American and, more recently, continental European pop; if anything, Anglo-American mass music dominates the world more effectively than does any other mass medium.[4]

It follows obviously that the record-buying public is heterogeneous, coming from a variety of social conditions. But this brings us to the central peculiarity of records as a medium. If pop interest is not exclusive to any country or class, to any particular educational or cultural background, it is connected to age: there is a special relationship between pop music and youth. The bulk of record buyers (over 80%) are under 30 and more than 75% of pop sales are to 12- to 20-year-olds.[5]

The significance of this becomes clear when we consider the question of the simultaneity of record listening. In general terms the pop public is dispersed: if people do listen to the same records it is independently of each other as well as of the original musicians. In what sense is their listening simultaneous? The relevance of this concept for other mass media is obvious: radio listening and television watching are exactly simultaneous activities and even reading daily newspapers or weekly magazines can be judged as approximately simultaneous – most people read Tuesday's *Daily Mirror* some time on Tuesday. But there are no technological or topical reasons why record listening should be so time-bound. People can listen to their records when they choose and their value is not obviously limited to a particular date. On the other hand, there are good economic reasons why records should be dated. The record industry requires constant consumer turnover and exploits notions of fashion and obsolescence to keep people buying.

British record companies issue about 3,000 singles and 3,000 pop albums every year (the American figures are 7,000 singles and 5,000 albums) and while a proportion of these are re-releases or repackages of old recordings the majority are new. A good part of the record business revolves around the attempt to make records time-bound, to persuade an audience to buy a record at the moment of its release, to get bored with it after a few weeks, to discard it for a yet newer release, and so on. Records are released with a fanfare of publicity, advertising, plugging on the radio, articles in the press. They are aimed directly at the hit parade, which symbolises simultaneous listening by listing the records which attracted the most purchasers the previous week. They have a definite and limited active life (for singles it's 60 to 180 days, depending on success), during which time they can be heard on the radio, on juke-boxes, in discothèques. After that they become 'out of date' and cease to be played. Most pop singles are eventually deleted only to be revived in the future as 'oldies', their appeal now resting on their precise nostalgic connection with a particular past date. The individual listener is encouraged by the pressure of the market, novelty and fashion to echo this pattern in his or her own listening. For him or her, too, records tend to have a brief active life of incessant listening before being placed at the bottom of the pile when something new comes along, to be brought out again only to revive memories.[6]

Of all the dating mechanisms involved in the pop process the hit parades – charts of current best sellers – are the most important. For the British Market Research Bureau, which compiles the British charts, they are simply an analysis of record sales, not much different as an exercise in sampling from the market analyses the Bureau supplies to many other industries. On those charts, however, depend radio stations' play-lists, artists' performance fees and A & R men's careers; what is special about record market research is that a measure of previous sales can determine future sales, through its effect on radio play and promotion and retailers' stocks. One bizarre result is that in an industry which is paying a considerable amount of money for an accurate measure of record sales there are people employed to make this measure inaccurate by 'fixing' the returns – there are various ways of planting false sales on BMRB sample shops.[7]

Although only 7–8 % of a year's record releases are hits the importance of the charts is reflected in the fact that the majority of records sold – singles and albums – come from the Top Thirty. The chart suggestion of continuous musical sensation and change is reinforced by the music press which, by turning pop music into news, makes the dating of records even more precise. The result of the whole process is that at least part of the pop audience does buy and hear its records simultaneously.[8]

The simultaneous part of the pop audience is youth. This is suggested not just by the appeal of the chart records themselves but also by the appeal of the trappings of chart pop. At least 70 % of the readers of the music press are under 24, for example, and the predominant appeal of both Radio 1 and Radio Luxembourg is to young listeners. I will be discussing these findings in detail in later chapters; the point I want to make here is that in its simultaneous aspect 'young pop' can be distinguished from 'old pop'. The latter, equally produced for a mass market, by and large lacks the former's hit parades, magazines and juke-boxes. It takes the form of 'standards' with the 'timeless' appeal of 'quality'. Quality pop is broadcast on Radio 2 and featured on the bills of working men's clubs and TV variety shows; it is eternal film-score and background music and difficult to date.[9]

The distinction between chart pop and quality pop is not clear cut. Quality pop stars get into the hit parade; chart toppers achieve standard status; musicians move from one type of music and audience to the other. And, of course, the chart audience is not exclusively young, nor is the quality audience exclusively old. Nonetheless, in this book I'm going to call young pop *rock*. By my definition rock music is music produced for the simultaneous consumption of a large youthful market. This is not the way rock is usually defined, but then the usual use of the word is confused, carrying implications not just of youth but also of the form of music involved and of the intentions of the musicians. In particular, rock is often opposed to pop as being less single-mindedly commercial. This contrast makes no sense of today's money-making rock profession even if it did once have hippy validity, and the musical definitions of rock are woefully imprecise. But it is true that there are rock musicians who are not making their music for a mass market (the various self-proclaimed avant-garde groups, for example) and there are also signs that as the rock audience ages its values and tastes are informing a new form of quality pop, a new genre of hip easy listening.

I will return to these issues later. The point I want to stress here is that rock's meaning as a mass medium depends on its relationship to youth culture. In most respects rock's consumers make up just another impersonal and anonymous mass public – the rock market is not, in any organised sense, anything more than a collection of individuals. And yet, because of their shared youth, its members do have a sense of being part of a common audience – whether a general sense of generation or a specific sense of a particular cult – and rock stars become, however impersonally, a part of this identity; they are also young. The sociology of rock is inseparable from the sociology of youth and I will begin this book with an analysis of this relationship.

This is, admittedly, an oblique way into the study of rock, and readers may well be tempted to skip straight to the account of record production. I am certain, though, that any sociology of rock must begin with a study of its consumption. The record industry has developed its rules of production from its interpretations of the youth market, and the ideology of rock is riddled with untested assumptions about youth culture and about music's meaning for youth culture – the sociologist's first task must be to strip away the resulting accumulation of myths and false certainties. Indeed, it is within the sociology of youth (rather than within the sociology of culture or the media) that we find what academic theories of rock there are. These, too, need an early critical consideration.

Finally, though, what most clearly distinguishes rock from other mass media is not its audience but its form: Rock is *musical* communication and its ideology as a mass culture derives not just from the organisation of its production, not just from the conditions of its consumption, but also from the artistic intentions of its musical creators and from the aesthetics of its musical forms. Rock's meaning as music, art and culture will be my theme in Part Three, but there is one last introductory comment to be made. This book began as a study of British rock. Although I have, where possible, made comparative reference to American material, and although I'm sure that the arguments in Parts One and Two are equally applicable to us rock, the bulk of my 'hard' data on record production and consumption, on youth culture and record companies is drawn from British studies and British sources. But in interpreting rock's meaning as music even this working notion of British rock broke down. Britain occupies an extraordinarily influential place in the world record market – its musical sounds, styles and genres continue to feature in the charts of every continent, and its record companies, notably EMI, have a significant share of world trade – but, equally, American and European records feature in British charts and American and European record companies have a significant share of British trade. A study of British rock cannot just be a study of British music. Indeed, as I will argue in Chapter 10, the musical roots of British rock are almost all American. In short, this analysis of 'British Rock' is intended to contribute to the understanding of rock as a mass medium which is *general* to contemporary capitalist culture.

PART ONE
The consumption of rock

2
Youth

Rock is the music of youth, and the question I want to answer in this chapter is straightforward: what's so special about the young? In the sociological literature there are two different approaches to this problem and two different descriptive categories: teenagers and youth (or Elvis Presley and the Beatles). These different terms partly reflect different historical moments, partly different concerns, though they often overlap. Teenager is a fifties concept, youth and youth culture come from the sixties; 'teenager' refers mostly to the working-class young, 'youth' suggests the irrelevance of class distinctions at this age but is usually, if implicitly, applied to the middle-class young. Both concepts must be examined in detail.

Teenagers

> This teenage ball had had a real splendour in the days when the kids discovered that, for the first time since centuries of kingdom come, they'd money, which hitherto had always been denied to us at the best time in life to use it, namely, when you're young and strong, and also before the newspapers and telly got hold of this teenage fable and prostituted it as conscripts seem to do to everything they touch. Yes, I tell you, it had a real savage splendour in the days when we found that no one couldn't sit on our faces any more because we'd loot to spend at last, and our world was to be our world, the one we wanted and not standing on the doorstep of somebody else's waiting for honey, perhaps.[1]

The important thing about 'teenager' as a concept was that it described a style of consumption. In his 1959 study of the teenage consumer, Mark Abrams, having defined teenagers as young people from the time they leave school until the time they are married or reach 25, turned immediately to the teenage market and showed that this market was dominated, in money terms, by young male workers: the aesthetic of the teenage market was a working-class aesthetic. J. B. Mays, writing in 1965, made a clear distinction between 'a culture largely based on working-class peer-group solidarity and the commercialised entertainment world, on the one hand, and the

individualistic, middle-class, high school and university career system
on the other.' The former world was that of teenagers.[2]

But if it was agreed that teenagers were working-class youngsters,
it did not follow that their activities were analysed by reference to
their situation in the world of work. 'Teenage' referred to consumption, to leisure, and this stress on leisure and pleasure has been retained in accounts of working-class youth ever since. Jeremy
Seabrook, for example, in his angry 1971 study of Blackburn,
suggests that the only real difference between the life of Blackburn's
teenagers today and that of previous generations 'is a greater sense of
hedonism, a commitment to enjoying life'. He describes the young's
'preoccupation with self-gratification' and argues that:

> The only really new feature in the lives of the young is the intensity
> and resolution of their devotion to pleasure, a commitment to
> enjoyment and consumption.[3]

A teenager is the conspicuous consumer par excellence, and certainly
for the intrigued public of the 1950s the teenage world was the world
of teenage consumption objects, 'the world of coffee-bars, motor-
scooters and jazz-clubs', to quote the blurb of *Absolute Beginners*.
But once this world had been described, once its basis in the relative
affluence of young workers had been established, once the teenagers'
lack of obligations (especially after the end of National Service) had
been stressed, the questions remained: why did these teenagers
consume the way they did? What was the basis of their leisure choices?

It is in the responses to these questions that we can see how fearful
a phenomenon the teenager originally was. One fear was that teenagers
consumed without any values at all: in this interpretation they were
victims of the sorts of market manipulation documented by Mark
Abrams. 'Teenager' was a commercial creation and the result of that
creation was a nihilistic culture, a generation without any values
save those of flashy, instant pleasures. Professionals concerned with
young people, teachers and youth workers, worried about the consequences; conservatives pointed to the 'private hedonism and lack
of public and community sentiment' of the young; socialists feared
a generation of depoliticised, 'never-had-it-so-good' workers. 1960
was marked, appropriately, by the publication of the Albemarle
Report on the Youth Service.[4]

For the media the problem wasn't the banality of teenage life, it
was its apparent possibilities for sex and violence. Fears of a world
of youth unpenetrated by adult interests and dominated by peer-
group norms had been around at least since the beginning of the
century (the boys clubs movement was one result), and the image of

the adolescent gang had long had blood-chilling potency; what the notion of the teenager did was to blur the distinction between the ordinary and the violent kids:

> Here is a frightful indictment of youthful crime and vice in the U.S.A. It shows how the violent and sex-crazed teen-age cult exists in a living nightmare of ruthlessness and depravity.
> These are the ordinary kids you read about every day of your life – 'ordinary', that is, until they shoot a store-keeper, assault a girl, torture a bum or wind up dead in a ditch.
> (blurb for *Teenage Jungle*, a 1957 paperback.)

Teddy boys were Britain's first symbols of the fearful possibilities of the teenage condition (I can remember praying each night that I wouldn't meet a teddy boy on my way to primary school). If it was not their delinquency that was new, but their aggressive and exclusive sense of youthful style, the effect was still to identify the style with the delinquency. 'Teenager' and 'delinquent' became associated terms and have in many ways remained so. When the occasional study does appear to remind people of the ordinariness of most teenagers it gets its own media treatment as sensational news.[5]

This was as true of the sociological literature as of the mass media. The most studied teenagers were the most publicly deviant teenagers – from teds through mods and rockers to skinheads and now punks. The assumed identity of teenagers and deviants led to a number of sociological conventions. Firstly, teenage behaviour was seen in sensationalist terms: the groups sociological research focused on and the activities it worried about were the same as those of the headline writers. Secondly, as teenagers were seen as a leisure group, the assumption was made that consumption determined identity, that style determined behaviour. Thirdly, teenagers were seen in static terms: being a teenager was a state rather than a process or a relationship. Fourthly, attention was focused almost entirely on boys and on boys in relationship to other boys. The consequence of these conventions was that when theorists of deviance sought to account for the difference between delinquent teenagers and the rest, they did it in terms of values – the problem was wrong choices, reflecting wrong attitudes. There is a huge body of literature exploring delinquents' values, and even when an attempt was made to relate these to the material aspects of young people's lives the link was made through their attitudes to work. The successful working-class teenager, the 'college boy', was portrayed as interested in and satisfied by his working life. His leisure time was consequently used responsibly and without any big deal, he was conformist, quietist, integrated into his society. The unsuccessful teenager, the 'corner boy', was degraded and demoralised at work and burst out into delinquency in leisure in order to compensate for his alienation and achieve a sense of status.[6]

Youth

Even before the Beatles the more astute observers of the teenage scene were remarking on the development of a culture that was specifically young but not specifically working class. The hero of *Absolute Beginners* commented that:

> the great thing about the jazz world, and all the kids that enter into it, is that no one, not a soul, cares what your class is, or what your race is or what your income, or if you're boy, or girl, or bent, or versatile, or what you are – so long as you dig the scene and can behave yourself, and have left all that crap behind you, too, when you come in the jazz club door. The result of all this is that, in the jazz world, you meet all kinds of cats, on absolutely equal terms, who can clue you up in all kinds of direction – in social directions, in culture directions, in sexual directions, in racial directions . . . in fact, almost anywhere, really, you want to go to learn.[7]

And George Melly, analysing the significance of dialects and the use of language in 1963, claimed:

> Scratch the rebel, art student, beatnik, CND supporter, jazz musician, and you'll usually find a lower-middle-class background. The suburbs have thrown up most of the young people who are in conscious revolt. . . . Their only sin, and it's a minor one, is some- times to lie about their origin. They pretend to be working class.[8]

These were early intimations of what was to develop as 'youth culture', a culture that was apparently classless and rebellious, but which rested on the gradual middle-class adoption of the trappings of working-class teenage life. In the words of one historian:

> The lack of a firm class sense was one of the most notable things about a great many of the young. The working-class lad was no longer swallowed up into the beery fug of the working-class pub. In the new coffee bars, jazz cellars and youth clubs, grammar school and modern school rubbed Italianate shoulders; 'fish-and-chip' girls and Acacia Avenue girls alike embraced the new in- formality of 'separates' and drove holes into the floor with stiletto

heels of approximately the same sharpness. A teenager was a
teenager.[9]

Youth was an ideological concept; it reflected the observation that
middle-class children were deliberately adopting lower-class values –
'toughness, excitement, chance-taking, indulgence, "conning",
autonomy and hardness' – and were thus making a conscious decision
to oppose the values of their parents (unlike working-class teenagers,
who were simply indulging themselves on their way to a life of
conformity).[10]
The development of youth culture in the sixties became associated
with the development of the student movement and the 'counter-
culture'. The great symbolic event happened in France in May '68,
as students and young workers joined together in an act of political
and cultural opposition to the state. Even usually hard-headed
sociologists were carried away. Norman Birnbaum proclaimed a
crisis of industrial society and found politics even in the commodities
of youth culture:

> The entire new generation experimented with new forms for its
> own sensibilities, and were critical of an elder generation which
> seemed to demand only compliance with an unrewarding routine.
> For once, mass culture had as its content neither total escape from
> routine nor an ignoble capitulation to it, but a modicum of
> criticism of it [11]

As late as 1972 John Rex was arguing that:

> The power of the British ruling class is being challenged, both in
> defensive and offensive terms, in the seventies. Its legitimacy is
> denied as a new generation of highly educated young men and
> women comes into existence outside the power class, bearing its
> own counter-culture and values.[12]

Sociologists devoted more time to the deviant middle-class young
than they had even to deviant teenagers. Journals, conferences and
text books were devoted to 'Alienated Youth', to 'Youth Culture – a
New Social Force', to the 'Death of the Protestant Ethic' and the
'Greening of the Western World'. A lot of this literature reads
strangely now that the youth 'revolt' of the late sixties has become
the hedonistic apathy of the mid-seventies. It is hard not to agree
with Bottomore's sour point that its connection with 'youth culture'
was one of the student movement's weaknesses: pop music and drugs,
he notes, 'have very little radical significance at all'.

It is true that these phenomena have sometimes been regarded as forming part of a general movement of liberation, but this is largely a misinterpretation of them. Pop music expresses, generally in the most banal language, the universal doubts and uncertainties of adolescence. It has little critical content, and what it had at the outset has diminished with the growth of commercial interests.[13]

But this is glib, and even from a *post hoc* position of righteousness it doesn't take account of the serious attempts student radicals made to show *why* youth culture could be a political force. The basic questions raised by the sixties youth movements must be considered seriously: was there such a thing as *youth* culture, a set of actitivies and attitudes and values which, on the one hand, distinguished young people from adults and, on the other hand, gave young people an identity that transcended their class differences? Did such a youth culture have any political significance? How did it relate to the commercial interest in youth?[14]

The affirmative answer to the question whether youth existed in the sixties as a specific social group rested on an argument originally developed by Mannheim. He suggested that young people find themselves in a particular set of occupations and roles in most societies and consequently develop a consciousness of themselves as an age-group, but only rarely is this consciousness of shared age developed not just with respect to the immediate problems of self-definition but also with respect to history, as the consciousness of a generation. In certain historical situations – Mannheim referred to periods of profound social change and situations of political instability – an age-group becomes a generation and youth culture becomes political. The positive accounts of sixties youth culture therefore involved an analysis of the historical reason why youth had become a generation. The focus was the capitalist boom of 1952 to 1968 and the effects on the young of full employment, the expansion of secondary and higher education, the developing importance of tertiary and scientific workers, the decline of unskilled labour. The object was to show why the youth experience of the sixties was something new and why the young were consequently politically important.[15]

The accounts of generational conflict, however radical, rested on Mannheimian assumptions about 'age spans': peeking out from even the most glorious proclamations of the power of youth was the concept of 'adolescence'. Being young, it was implied, meant occupying a particular structural position in modern capitalist societies; when it came down to it, youth and youth culture could be explained in functional terms – by reference to the need of society to incorporate youth into the social system and to the need (or refusal) of the young to be so incorporated. Youth culture could be understood as a solution to the social, emotional, and sexual problems of adolescence. The grand structural-functionalist account of youth is S. N. Eisenstadt's *From Generation to Generation*. Its argument can be summarised as follows. In all societies children have to go through a process of socialisation before they can be afforded full adult status. In primitive societies the values which inform the life of a child are so similar to those he will have as an adult that the change of status is non-problematic and is marked only by a ritual moment – a puberty or initiation rite. There is no transitional period and youth doesn't exist as a socio-structural category. In modern industrial societies, by contrast, there is a basic structural discrepancy between the family in which a child is brought up and the economic and social system in which he must eventually take his place. The shift of status is neither instant nor easy but involves a transitional structural position – adolescence. Youth culture has, then, to be understood by reference to the process by which a modern industrial society detaches children from their families and socialises them into the wider social system.[16]

Eisenstadt emphasises two aspects of this process. Firstly, the young have a marginal social status. Young people at school or college, in apprenticeships, in and out of work at the bottom of the unskilled job market, are not integrated fully into the economic structure; they have emerged from one family but not yet formed another, they are not integrated fully into the social structure. For Eisenstadt the end of youth is not marked by legal symbols but by the real experience of adult values and status. He gives theoretical support to the market researchers' empirical assumption: youth is ended by marriage and a steady job, by 'settling down', whether this occurs at 18 or 30.

His second point is that societies have a series of formal preparatory institutions to control the transition period: not just schools, apprenticeships and other overt forms of training, but also youth clubs and other such organisations which provide training in 'adult orientations'. Whatever the other differences between them, young people share the experience of preparatory institutions and they share the experience of powerlessness – these institutions may be for the young but they are controlled by adults.

Shared experiences make for shared needs: adolescents seek a stability to balance against their time of change, they seek a sense of autonomy, status and self-esteem to balance against their time of insignificance. Hence the role of peer-groups (something between the family and society) and their symbols of pride and self-assertion.

Eisenstadt himself is most interested in how peer-group values ease the transition from 'particularism' to 'universalism', but his general point is that youth groups are transitional institutions; young people have to move through them. Youth culture cannot be the basis of a counter-culture because its values are not opposed to those of adults but a preparation for them. It is a social problem if people freeze into a youthful outlook, refuse to adopt an adult approach, but the refusal to grow up is not a political act but an Oedipal one.

Although structural functionalism is at present unfashionable, much radical sociology is actually the same theory in different words. Certainly Eisenstadt's account of youth, with its analysis of adolescents' marginality and powerlessness, its explanation of youth culture as the solution to the resulting problems, is echoed (with an added social critique) in the radical accounts of youth. Even the explicit critics of the concept of adolescence accept the basic argument. Their quarrel is with the consequences: they see adolescence as a fraught and unhappy state, and adolescents as a repressed status group developed by society for its own purposes.[17]

The problem of the Eisenstadt approach (and of other analyses which retain the notion of adolescence) is their abstraction. As Sheila Allen has argued, in capitalist societies the experiences of different class groups, occupying different economic situations, having different amounts of power, with different access to educational rewards, can't be similar, subjectively or objectively, whatever their age. We can't understand youth in a class system without reference to that system, and we can only find what all youth have in common – which was as much the concern of the youth ideologists of the 1960s as it is of structural-functionalists – by reaching to a level of theoretical abstraction (the psycho-social needs of a group in transition) at which the material basis of youth culture vanishes from view.[18]

An attempt to bring class back into the analysis of youth has been made by the so-called 'new' deviancy theorists. In 'labelling theories' of teenagers the question becomes not why do they do the things they do, but why these things freak out their elders, and research attention is shifted from teenagers to labellers of teenagers – media, police, schools, courts, etc. The suggestion is that the battle of definitions is a power struggle, but the class basis of teenagers remains obscure.[19]

Sub-cultural accounts of teenagers try to explain their behaviour as the rational response to their teenage situation. Teenagers are problem solvers; to understand their solutions we just have to understand their problems. But sub-culturalists go beyond youth theorists in trying to interpret the teenage problem as a class problem. Teenage values are derived from the problems of survival in a class position and don't determine behaviour but articulate it. What is crucial for teenage culture, then, is not the process of cultural transmission or the presence of a specific cultural tradition (both arguments popular in American literature on deviancy) but a shared experience leading to a shared problem leading to a collective solution. Values are shared because experiences are. The difficulty in this approach is to decide what is meant by a working-class teenage experience/situation/position. What is noticeable about the answers given by sub-cultural theorists is that class is not defined in relation to production. It is either defined culturally (hence the common use of a concept of working-class 'community') or else by reference to specific state and leisure institutions – school, football, etc. Sub-cultural theory does not get away from the conventional deviancy focus on sensational, leisure-based males. The teenager remains the teenage consumer and Allen's point remains unheeded. If we are to treat youth seriously as a social group we must have an understanding of its material circumstances. The basic question has still to be answered: what is the relationship of the young to the organisation of production?[20]

Youth and work

Mark Abrams' *The Teenage Consumer* was, obviously, concerned to analyse teenage expenditure rather than the sources of teenage income. His teenagers, young people who had left school, were workers by definition but that was as far as the analysis went. Abrams' purpose was to demonstrate the affluence of the teenage consumer and his relative freedom to indulge in hedonistic expenditure. The teenage market was dominated by working-class boys, who had the largest share of teenage spending power, and Abrams stressed the absence of constraints – such teenagers were unencumbered with the expense of running a home and raising a family. His empirical analysis thus fits into the theoretical approaches that I've been discussing. The teenage problem is one of choice and the sociology of youth is a sociology of choice, whether youth culture is explained in terms of class values, sub-cultures, psycho-social needs, or commercial manipulation. But teenage income is the result of the sale of teenage labour power and this sale puts limits on leisure as well as work. The differences between youth cultures reflect not just consumer choices but also forces in the labour market.[21]

Students

The first thing to point to in this context is the increasing number of young people who are not at work at all but still engaged in full-time education. The accompanying table indicates the extent of the

change between 1964 and 1974 (the school-leaving age was raised
from 15 to 16 in 1973). As recently as 1938, only 38% of 14-year-olds,
4% of 17-year-olds and 2% of 19-year-olds were involved in any type
of full-time education. By 1973, even before ROSLA, the figures were
49·8% for 15- to 17-year-olds, 15·7% for 18- to 20-year-olds, and
5·5% for 21- to 24-year-olds. In absolute terms the number of
students rose from 373,000 in 1963/4 to 638,700 in 1973/4.[22]

Table 1:
Percentage of age-group in school

Age	1964	1974
15	56·50	98·68
16	24·48	48·53
17	13·27	20·31
18	5·92	7·79

Source: CSO, *Annual Abstract of Statistics,* 1975, p. 123.

There are several things to be said about students as a youth group.
The first, perhaps, is that the general statistics conceal particular
differences – for example, between the home-based experience of
school and Further Education colleges and the campus-based experience of residential colleges and universities. They also conceal
the class divisions that are involved in education after the school-
leaving age. But the points I want to stress here are these: firstly,
involvement in full-time education effectively segregates students
from young workers socially; the segregation can be observed in
leisure activities and is illustrated, for example, by the rarity of cross-
educational marriages. Secondly, being a student means being subject to a different form of control, discipline and freedom from that
facing a worker. Thirdly, students, whatever their class backgrounds
or career prospects, are considerably less well off than young
workers. The National Children's Bureau study of 16-year-olds found
that the majority received less that £1·50 per week pocket money and
although more than half the sample had spare-time jobs most earned
from £1 to £3 per week – only about a tenth earned £6 per week or
more. A DES survey of student income and expenditure in 1974–5
found that the average term-time income from all sources was £575
for men and £580 for women, supplemented by vacation earnings of
£225 for men and £139 for women. Average expenditure for all
students during the thirty weeks of term time was £704, well over half
of which went on board and lodging and only £37 of which was
available for entertainment. To understand student leisure we have

to understand the constraints on student life as well as its possibilities.[23]

Young workers

The clearest indicators of the different forces acting on young people in the labour market are the entry statistics (see Table 2) which suggest a number of distinctions.

Table 2:
Percentage of young persons entering employment

Class of employment	boys		girls	
	1965	1974	1965	1974
Apprenticeship or learnership to skilled occupation	40·56	43·0	6·18	6·52
Employment leading to recognised professional qualifications	1·51	1·27	1·71	1·77
Clerical employment	9·99	6·99	40·3	40·5
Employment with planned training apart from induction training	12·7	17·1	12·6	17·2
Other employment	35·2	31·6	39·3	34·0

Source: Dept. of Employment, *British Labour Statistics Year Book*, 1974, Table 96.

Girls

The most striking feature of the 1974 figures (and I include the data from 1965 as a comparative reference to confirm that this is not an accident or an effect of ROSLA) is the extraordinarily different patterns of girls' and boys' occupations. Girls are a special case of young worker: 75% of those girls who do get apprenticeships get them in hairdressing; 75% of those who get recognised professional qualifications get them in 'professional and scientific services', mostly nursing; 40% of girl clerical workers are in 'insurance, banking, finance and business services'; 50% of their 'other employment' is in the 'distributive trades'.[24]

What is most apparent about female job opportunities is their limited career possibilities – very few girls are involved in occupations or training schemes which have a long-term future; indeed, it is the lack of training among girl workers, rather than unequal incomes, that has been of most concern to investigators of sexual inequality. The incomes figures themselves are only another aspect of the sexual differentiation of *opportunity*.[25]

Table 3:
Average earnings of full-time employees not affected by absence (G.B.,1974)

Gross weekly earnings, £

	age	men	women
Full-time:	under 18	18·2	15·7
	18–20	28·7	20·8
	21–24	38·6	25·9
	All	45·8	26·2
Manual:	under 18	18·6	16·9
	18–20	30·7	22·2
	21–24	40·7	24·0
	All	41·9	23·2
Non-manual:	under 18	16·4	15·2
	18–20	24·4	20·3
	21–24	35·6	26·3
	All	52·4	27·6

Source: CSO: *Annual Abstract of Statistics*, 1975, pp. 174–5.

Table 3 shows the continuing inequality of income between boys and girls (which partly reflects the fact that boys work slightly longer hours and rather more overtime) but it also shows that women reach their maximum earning capacity young – by age 24 girl manual workers are already earning more than the average for all women and even non-manual workers are earning only marginally less than the average. For a large proportion of girls, marriage is the only career choice available and the only source of economic opportunity; girls, in the words of one researcher, 'regard homemaking as their vocation'. Girls marry younger than boys (the 1971 Census showed that in the 15–19 age group 8·4% of the girls were married, 2·0% of the boys; in the 20–24 age group 59% of the girls and 37% of the boys) and despite the increasing number of working wives, unmarried girls still form a higher proportion of the female work-force than do unmarried boys of the male.[26] The suggestion that marriage is girls' primary occupational role is confirmed by a number of researchers. In Carter's Sheffield sample girls had reached their final position in the job hierarchy by the age of 20 and marriage (for those girls who had not yet achieved it) was now the only ambition. A government survey of fifth-form girls, specifically concerned to find out why girls have lower educational and occupational aspirations than their abilities warrant, revealed the extent to which marriage and work aspirations are complementary – on the other hand, low aspirations for the future went with a commitment to early marriage and the traditional female role; on the other hand, marriage was seen as a way out from educational failure and work dissatisfaction (a way out not available to boys); girls' job decisions are short-term, made in the long-term context of marriage. Spittles has shown that even the spare-time jobs done by children reflect these different perspectives – the girls are involved in casual, home-based tasks like baby-sitting or light shop work, the boys go into the more systematic work of newspaper rounds and market stalls.[27]

At first glance, a comparison of the occupations of girls in 1974 with their situation before the war suggests marked changes (this was one of Abrams' points). In 1931, for example, almost a quarter of the 14- to 17-year-old girls at work were still indoor domestic servants, though this had been a declining source of occupation since 1900. In 1974 few girls became servants of any sort – hence the belief that this century has meant a steady increase in teenage girls' freedom and independence. But the basic pattern of girls' employment – their lack of involvement in training schemes, their exclusion from skilled jobs and careers – remains similar. Just as much as in 1900, for girls who do not go into higher education marriage is the crucial occupation. Teenage girls regard marriage as their most significant and vital career choice. I will be discussing the effects of this on their leisure in the next chapter.[28]

Skilled boys

The largest group of young male workers are apprentices. There are distinctions within this category, notably between apprentices in manufacturing industries preparing for careers as skilled workers in factories (the largest number are in mechanical engineering) and apprentices in non-manufacturing crafts (such as construction, gas, plumbing) preparing for careers as self-employed artisans (the largest number are in motor repair), but some general points can be made. Firstly, apprentices, whatever the length of their indentures, are involved from the outset in a lifetime career – their future is known. Secondly, the importance of formal training in their jobs means that they experience forms of work discipline and control which resemble those of school as much as those of the adult workplace. In some ways apprentices seem worse off than their untrained peers – they are paid less, have low status at work, are subject to more authoritarian control – but, on the other hand, they are also much more stable in their jobs, and their situation is regarded as desirable by fellow-workers and blends more easily into the work habits and attitudes of adult workers.[29]

The distinction of apprentices from other young workers, and the resulting social distinctions between skilled and unskilled labour have a long history. The pre-industrial labour hierarchy survived the industrial revolution, if in changed form, and in the latter part of the nineteenth century the differentiation of labour became more rigid. Gillis, in his history of youth, suggests that the effect of the 'second industrial revolution' at the turn of the century was not only to increase the number of unskilled jobs for teenagers ('boy labour' in distribution and transport, for example) as the number of apprenticeships available declined, but also to establish the pattern in which unskilled jobs were, immediately, much more financially rewarding than skilled jobs. The young unskilled worker could expect something approaching an adult wage at a time when an apprentice was getting little more than a pittance. This reinforced differences within the working class – the poorer section needed as good wages as their children could get at once, the better off could afford to invest against the future. The apprentice/non-apprentice labour division became associated with the respectable/rough cultural distinction.[30]

Investigation of the effect on young workers of the skilled/unskilled division is now commonplace in the sociology of work. In a review of the literature, Cyril Smith notes, for example, the 'striking difference' between the unskilled and other young workers in their degree of commitment to their jobs. Apprentices are 'stabilised' by their employment situation, by their appreciation of the importance of their apprenticeship, and by their immediate involvement with adult work institutions such as unions; white-collar workers make a similarly realistic assessment of the value of their job and its career prospects; but for the young unskilled the pressure to be a 'steady worker' comes only with marriage.[31]

Unskilled boys

Although this percentage is falling, about half of Britain's school-leavers still leave without any qualifications and these leavers make up the bulk of the 40% of young male workers who enter jobs below craft level and the 30% who enter jobs without any training facilities at all. The unqualified and unskilled have a special relationship to production. Job-changing is frequent and boys, with their greater freedom of occupational choice, change occupations as much as jobs – unskilled girls are less mobile and tend to move within an occupational category. The highest job level is reached by age 20, even if maximum wages are not, and unskilled workers are always at risk of being replaced by younger, cheaper labour. The job mobility of unskilled boys reflects both their own readiness to leave when 'fed up' and their employers' readiness to sack them for 'disciplinary problems'.[32]

It is from this sector of the young work-force that 'trouble' has always been seen as coming – theirs are the occupations of the young 'roughs', from the nineteenth-century scuttlers to the 1970s skinheads; it is here that the criminological analysis of teenage deviants merges with the transition-from-school-to-work analysis of the difficult worker. Both types of analyst come up with accounts of anomie: the young unskilled worker has not yet settled down at home or at work, he is aimless, floundering around for job satisfaction, a prey to bad influences (whether criminal or commercial), a problem for social workers. Sociologists from both camps try to link work 'failure' with school 'failure', suggesting that it is the 'poor self-image' developed in the classroom that is brought by the unqualified young to the labour market. The distinction between school and work is thus dissolved into a distinction between the attitudes and ambitions of two broad groups of children – the integrated and the alienated. We're back to college boys and corner boys.[33]

Although there can be no doubt that the skilled/unskilled work distinction is relevant to the use of leisure, there are problems with these value explanations. It is not clear that there really is a difference in job attitudes between apprentices and the unskilled. Research in Coventry suggests that

> the apprentices' attitudes to their work are not essentially different from that which the literature so often attributes to 'unsuccessful' youth in dead-end jobs. They realise the futility of any struggle from their subordinate position, understand the disinterest of trade unions until they are 'of age' and, therefore, look to leisure for their fun, thrills and excitement, while they await the day when they finish their apprenticeships.[34]

There is similar evidence of the realism of the unskilled. They understand the implications of their job choices, have always realised the relationship between educational achievement and job possibility, and their occupational floundering is, in fact, often perfectly controlled – from their point of view, being young and having a good time is a part of the process by which they know they will marry and settle down. It is a good interlude rather than a bad one.[35]

In short, the different leisure patterns reflect different opportunities as much as different values. In the 1960s, developmental theories of occupational choice began to be replaced by theories of opportunity-structure and the latter have received clear empirical confirmation in the 1970s. Young unemployment, which dwarfs all others as the current youth problem, is clearly a problem of the labour market and not of individuals' attitudes. The young unemployed and the young unskilled cannot be treated as separate categories, they are part of the same statistic.[36]

Unemployed youth

As one of its last acts before being swallowed up by the Manpower Services Commission, the Youth Employment Council set up a working party to investigate the *Unqualified, Untrained and Unemployed.* The subsequent report, which appeared in 1974, argued that whereas from 1945–68 the labour demand for young people was greater than the supply, from 1968–71 there was a complete reversal – the supply outstripped the demand. The evidence suggests that what was happening was not simply the result of a boom/recession trade cycle but also reflected a long-term downward trend: the jobs that were going were those traditionally available to the young unskilled. The report calculated that between 1966 and 1971 there was a job loss of 25% for boys and 27% for girls. Loss was concentrated in unskilled jobs – nearly half of the boys' losses, for example, came in construction, distribution and agriculture. The government's attempts to solve the problem of the unskilled by encouraging employers to 'skill' them (through the Industrial Training Boards) have not been a success; the facilities have been used mainly to consolidate apprenticeship training or to provide opportunities for white-collar staff:

> Operative training for unqualified young people is further limited by the fact that many employers do not have young operatives at all. They recruit their semi-skilled workers at age 18–22 or later, and offer short, specific practical training then. The consequence of this practice is that some unqualified young people, unable to obtain apprenticeships, drift from one unsatisfactory job to another until they are old enough to enter a semi-skilled job.[37]

The report suggested that a number of economic changes have had an effect on the jobs of the young unskilled (in this context a young worker means a worker aged from 16 to 24 – 10% of the males in this group and 7·3% of the females were unemployed in July 1976). What is involved is not just a change in the type of job available but also in the type of worker demanded. In the past the 'casual' intermittent employment pattern of young workers was possible because there were plenty of jobs to be done by such workers, some of which could only be done by them, because of their very irregularity and toughness. But employers are increasingly looking for a quality of 'steadiness' that is not the same thing as 'skill' but may be achieved by a similar process of 'training'. There has always been evidence that jobs with training made for more stable workers than jobs without, and it now seems that employers are 'skilling' jobs only by adding 'training programmes' as a form of work discipline.[38] What is being demanded is a 'responsible' attitude to work as much as a specific task skill, and there is no particular reason to suppose that the right attitudes won't be forthcoming if they are necessary for employment. In the long run we can expect these changes to have a profound effect on youth leisure. On the one hand, the steady decline of casual unskilled labour means a decline in the group that has traditionally been seen as forming the core of the hedonistic youth culture; on the other hand, the increasing sector of the young who suffer long-term unemployment means an increasing number of young people who have no leisure at all! Being unemployed and having leisure are not the same thing. The effects of youth unemployment on youth culture are still unclear, but by the summer of 1976, when nearly two-thirds of school leavers were unemployed, the fearful possibilities were beginning to be voiced. In the words of the President of the National Association of Headteachers, the unemployment figures were

tragic for the individual, shameful for our society, and politically explosive. This vast army may not be as organised as the National Union of Students, but I can assure you they are a far more fertile breeding ground for revolution than all the sociological departments of our universities rolled into one.[39]

The state itself seems more concerned with the economic than the political consequences. Its fear is of the unemployed becoming unemployable – the immediate problem is to inculcate the discipline of work itself, clocking in and turning up, rather than to develop particular job skills. In 1934 the Ministry of Labour, faced with similar problems of youth unemployment, set up Junior Instruction Centres

to give the boys and girls a real interest in life, to keep their minds and fingers active and alert, and their bodies fit, to teach them something that will be of real use to them whether at home or work, and without trying to train them for specific occupations to give them the type of mental and manual instruction which will help them to become absorbed or reabsorbed into employment as soon as opportunity may occur.[40]

The present government's schemes for the young unemployed are similar. Their object is to give the young work experience, to keep them busy. In the long run it may well be that the counter to permanent youth unemployment is a permanent increase in the number of young people continuing in education (particularly in the 'relevant industrial education' that is being demanded). But even without this development a large number of young unemployed must have an effect on our notions of teenage culture – if only from an economic point of view. In 1976 unemployed school-leavers got £7·70 in dole per week; in April 1975 the average gross weekly earnings for manual male workers under 18 were £25·2 and for manual female workers £24 (£23·1 and £21·7 for non-manual).[41]

It has been suggested that punk rock is the consequent expression of these 'dole queue kids', but before examining the relationship of the various youth groups to music I want to make one final point about the teenage 'boom'. The 'affluent teenagers' of the 1950s and 1960s were affluent because their parents were; what was involved was disposable income. Before that time youngsters who were earning did so to help their families stay above the breadline, to pay their parents back for their 'kept' years. One reason for teenagers' good times from 1950 to 1970 was that their parents were fully employed and relatively well off. Teenage 'freedom' was allowed in the context of the constraints of family income. Such freedom is not necessarily permanent.[42]

3

Youth and music

A lively, regular and varied social programme is vital to the building of Young Socialist branches. Every branch should aim to hold a regular discothèque to attract hundreds of youth in the area . . . (*Young Socialist*, 3 April 1976.)

Young people's interest in music is taken for granted by everyone these days, and although post-war sociologists were initially surprised that teenagers should 'frequently and spontaneously' express a love of music, they already knew that young people had their own leisure pursuits and that one of the most popular was dancing. A 1951 survey of British leisure, commenting on 'the importance of dancing as a means of spending leisure', added that

a large majority of dancers are young people, mostly between the ages of 16 and 24 . . . drawn from the working and lower middle classes.

These authors went on to voice familiar fears of teenage hedonism:

Modern ballroom dancing may easily degenerate into a sensuous form of entertainment, and if self-control is weakened with alcohol it is more than likely that it will do so, which might easily lead at least to unruly behaviour and not infrequently to sexual immorality.[1]

Concern for the young at play can be traced back to the nineteenth century, when a variety of institutions appeared to regulate the leisure of proletarian youth. By the 1930s remarks on the 'independence' and even 'affluence' of young workers were commonplace, but although jazz, particularly as a form of dance music, was seen to have a special appeal to the young, neither it nor any other form of popular music was seen as an expression of a youth culture.[2]

The full integration of pop music and youth culture was a development of the 1950s and was symbolised by a new form of music, rock 'n'roll, and a new form of youth, teddy boys. If the young had always had idols – film stars, sportsmen, singers such as Frank Sinatra and Johnnie Ray – the novelty of rock'n'roll was that its performers

were 'one of themselves', were the teenagers' own age, came from
similar backgrounds, had similar interests. The rise of rock'n'roll
was accompanied by the development of a generation gap in dancing,
as dance halls advertised rock'n'roll nights or became exclusively
rock'n'roll venues. In 1954 it was estimated that nine-tenths of
London's teenagers spent some of their leisure time listening to
records, and among the more visible features of the new world of
teenage consumption were the self-service record 'Browseries' and
'Melody Bars'. When Abrams' teenage consumer report came out in
1959 its statistics on music reflected findings that were being made
simultaneously by sociologists.[3]

Abrams showed that music and activities involving music absorbed
a significant part of young expenditure, and in 1961 Coleman's
mammoth survey of American adolescents confirmed that music was
their most popular form of entertainment and that rock'n'roll was
their most popular form of music. The importance of rock in young
people's lives became an axiom of British youth research. In her
1964–5 survey of 15- to 19-year-olds in Glasgow, Jephcott noted that
'pop in any form was an almost universal interest . . . the word
"pop" brought a sigh of relief – "Here's something we *want* to talk
about".' The young's interest in pop determined the television programmes they watched, the magazines they read, the cafés they went
to, the 'necessary tools' – transistor, record player, tape recorder,
guitar – they sought to own.[4]

Jephcott did her research at the time of the beat boom (Lulu and
the Luvvers were a local community group!) but there is no evidence
to suggest that her findings should be confined to the mid-sixties.
Researchers in the 1970s have replicated Coleman's findings that pop
is central to the teenage social system, and a recent survey of the
British literature on adolescent leisure concluded that 'music is in
many ways the central activity of the British youth culture, from
which many subsidiary activities flow'. White's account of young
workers in Wembley is a good illustration of this point. He shows
that it is the presence of 'their music' that attracts young people to
pubs and discos and youth clubs, and that:

> Home-made entertainment means only one thing – music. Front
> rooms are occasionally leased from parents for planned parties,
> but generally this home music-making involves an impromptu
> visit, a couple of young people going round to a friend's house.
> Baby-sitting provides a good opportunity for listening to new LPs.
> And the young workers do listen. This is quite different from the
> overpowering musical wallpaper of the Village Inn [a pub], almost
> an act of worship.[5]

Abrams' 1959 study has never been repeated in so clear a form, but the importance of youth's consumption of musical products has continued to be emphasised in market research. A national teenage survey in 1974 confirmed that the majority of 15- to 24-year-olds go dancing and buy records regularly, own their own record players and radios, and have an overwhelming musical preference for rock music and Top Thirty pop. This pattern of music use is not confined to British youth or even to capitalist youth, although if in America and Britain it was the advent of rock'n'roll that signalled the arrival of musical youth culture, for most European countries it did not emerge clearly until the success of the Beatles in the 1960s.[6]

While there can be no doubting the importance of music for the young, these surveys, sociological or not, are descriptive: music's presence in youth culture is established, but not its purpose. Jephcott suggests that if music is a universal teenage interest, it is also a superficial one – the impression left by her research is of a culture in which music is always heard but rarely listened to.[7] This impression is given statistical support by this finding in the Schools Council's 1968 survey of young school-leavers:

Table 4:
Percentage saying that pop music was important to themselves/to their children/to their pupils

	boys	girls
Children	20	35
Parents	41	64
Teachers	38	71

Source: Schools Council (1968), pp. 167–90.

These figures suggest that young people assess the music in their lives as much less significant than its constant noise makes it sound to outsiders, and it is time now to examine youth's use of music in more detail.

The use of music

In 1972 I conducted a survey of 14- to 18-year-olds at a comprehensive school in Keighley, Yorkshire, and I want to begin this section with a brief summary of the results.[8]

In general terms, the pupils in my sample were all in much the same situation: as school children, they were not affluent – pocket money averaged from 50p for the 14-year-olds to £1·50 for the sixth-formers, supplemented by varying part-time earnings – but most had their own rooms, and most owned the basic tools for music playing – radios, record players and/or recorders. The children were similar, too, in their general attitudes to music: they were 'quite' rather than 'very' interested in it; devoted 'some' time, but not 'a lot', to talking about it; spent a proportion of their income on it, but not an overwhelming one. On the whole, though, they all listened to music as a normal part of their daily lives, and the shared knowledge involved was reflected in the ease with which all my sample could comment on all genres of rock – a question on T. Rex, for example, was answerable by everyone, fan or not, and even the two classical-music devotees knew what T. Rex records sounded like. A basic experience of rock was common to all these young people, whatever their class or academic background, and the findings that most interested me were the different patterns of music use and taste *within* this framework.

Firstly, there was a distinct sixth-form culture, a pattern of rock use shared by all the sixth-formers to whom I spoke (mostly but not necessarily middle-class in background) which merged into student culture and was already being adopted by the academic pupils below them. These pupils bought albums rather than singles, had 'progressive' rather than 'commercial' tastes, were not involved in the trappings of rock (if they did, in a desultory way, watch *Top of the Pops* and listen to Radio 1, *The Old Grey Whistle Test* was the only show they made a special effort to see), and went to performance-based gigs – folk clubs, rock concerts – more than to discos or dances. The ideological essence of this culture was its individualism. Typical replies to questions about influences on taste were:

I like what I like, no one changes my opinions on music . . .
I like what I like, not what I'm told or influenced to like . . .

Choosing records was an individual decision of some importance: albums were never bought spontaneously or on spec and sixth-formers rejected the idea that records were chosen to fit an image or group identity; they didn't accept that they had an image ('I am myself') or else accepted it only reluctantly ('I suppose I have, although I don't readily admit it'; 'I hope not'; 'I do not *want* an image'). The role of the musically knowledgeable in informing and stimulating rock interest was acknowledged – boys were more likely than girls to play the role of opinion leader – but, in the end, musical taste was individual. Records were listened to, appreciated and criticised in terms of their meaning – lyrics were an important but not the only source of such meaning – and music was praised in terms of its originality, sincerity and beauty, or condemned for its triviality, banality, repetition. 'Rubbish' was the favourite pejorative word for 'commercial trash which gets in your head and you can't escape and it does nothing for you except make you puke'.

Such sixth-formers experienced youth culture as a culture with an articulated set of values different from those of an older generation; they saw themselves as 'rebelling against unreasonable ideas and conventional ways of doing things'. Their fear was that even youth culture was not a true or meaningful expression of individuality:

Rock music is unfortunately fashionable and its followers are exploited. It is very hard to separate true opinion from 'conditioned response'.

In sharp contrast to this was the lower-fifth culture of the pupils who bought singles and watched *Top of the Pops*, were regulars at youth clubs and discos but rarely went to concerts, who emphasised beat and sound in their tastes rather than meaning, who identified with a specific youth style and its music, and whose standard mode of criticism of other tastes was abuse:

T. Rex are shit. I've heard kids whistle better than that group. Music, it's all the same, no difference in rhythm or sound. They're all a set of puftas, Bolan with all his make-up and god knows what his wife thinks about wearing glitter under his eyes. Other groups wear it but don't go round talking like a puff. T. Rex ARE CRAP.

But having established that there were distinct rock cultures, I must be careful not to misinterpret the differences. What was involved was ideology, the way people talked about music, more than activity, the way they actually used it. The apparent lyric *vs* beat difference, for example, conceals the fact that the sixth-formers did dance! They danced the same sort of self-taught 'freak' and 'mod' and 'bop' styles as the other pupils and shared their appreciation of the standard dance music like Motown.[9]

If sixth-formers used music for dancing and background as often as for concentrated listening, so the lower fifth-formers were aware of lyrics, could remember and appreciate them, had some notion of songs' meanings – 'love is much better to sing about than a football team' – and responded to the messages and stories of rock and soul singles.

Similarly, I don't want to exaggerate the difference between the individualism of the sixth-formers and the group identities of the lower fifth. The latter were aware of the playfulness of their groups – 'the image changes – it's just for laughs' – and conscious of their individuality within them. Group styles were a matter of convenience and all the pupils could make an instant equation of group and music even when they did not fit themselves *into* such groups:

> I have assorted friends – some hairies, some crombie boys and girls. I can sit and listen to both sorts of music and don't mind either. . . .

> I'm in between a skinhead and a hippie. I wear 'mod' clothes but I listen to both kinds of music. . . .

> I wear skinhead clothes, but I don't just like that type of music. . . .

And consider these two more extended comments from lower-stream fourth-formers:

> I don't know what youth culture means. I think it means what you are – skin, grebo, or hairie. I am none of these. Beat that, I think. The groups have different outlooks on sex, drugs and politics. The lot of it is different views to that of my parents. My brother was a skinhead gang leader for three years. Music is not important to any group, to me music is what I like, not everybody else's opinion.

> I think that music makes up for 75 % of youth culture and that the music you like depends on the cult you're in. This idea of cult is taken too far. Teenagers can't be split into hating each other with a few in the middle just because they have different viewpoints. But they are.

On the other hand, one of the most militant groups among 15- and 16-year-olds was that of the future sixth-formers, the self-identified hairies and hippies, with their missionary zeal for progressive rock and a hatred of commercial pop:

> Rock music, progressive and heavy are fantastic. If they were not there life would not be worth living. They are the backbone behind music as a whole – showing us what it should really be like.

It was from this group that the most assertive statements of image and shared tastes came. If group identity is part of teenage culture for conventional reasons – 'if you like soul or reggae music and they like rock you will both wear different clothes and you may split up to go with your own group' – then even people with an ideology of individual taste become a group of individualists and need the symbols and friends and institutions to assert themselves as a group:

I listen at home most of the time, in my room. I don't often go to parties. Don't go to clubs 'cos I haven't anyone to go with and the clubs round here aren't the places which I enjoy going to. Dances are a bit like clubs, the people that go aren't the sort of people I mix with well. Discos are the same, my sort of people don't go there. I love concerts but it's difficult for me to get to them or get tickets. I go when I can. I listen alone or with a friend most. There's not a lot of people in our village which like progressive music.

One of the paradoxes in my survey was that the group which most stressed individual musical choice also most stressed the importance of shared musical taste for friendship – music served as the badge of individuality on which friendship choices could be based. One of the ironies was that because music was taken as a symbol of a cluster of values, the most individualistic groups were the ones most thrown by their musical heroes changing direction. This was particularly a problem for the hairies because they differentiated themselves from the masses as a self-conscious elite by displaying exclusive musical tastes. When one of their acts went commercial ('sold out') and became part of mass taste there was great bitterness:

What do you think of T. Rex? I do not usually think of them. It puts me off my meals whenever I think about T. Rex. They were once good when called Tyrannosaurus Rex – Next Best Thing to Beatles and Stones. T. Rex are very bopperish. It's all the same music like Tamla. N.B. Marc Bolan and Micky Finn are *Two of a kind*. Puff Puff Puff.

There are two other points I must make about different uses of music. Firstly, there were some pupils whose musical cultures were quite different from those I've described, either because they were not essentially youth-cultural (a small group of Pakistani pupils whose tastes were entirely for Pakistani performers, a brass-band fanatic, the two classical musicians) or because they were subscribers to a musical cult that really was the centre of their lives – there was a soul freak in my sample, and a couple of rock'n'rollers, who had quite distinct patterns of record buying, dancing and magazine reading.

Secondly, the class/academic cultural differences were interwoven with age and sex differences. One aspect of the difference between sixth-form and lower-fifth culture was that sixth-formers were older. It was clear in my survey that the maximum involvement in youth groups and their symbols occurred in the fourth year, when most pupils had some such identity; by the fifth year most were claiming non-membership and by the sixth there were no admitted group members at all. There were also distinctions between the sexes. Girls were more interested in dancing and tended to be more concerned with rock lyrics, especially with the words of love. They were all aware of the special female features of pop culture – fan clubs, *Fab 208*, star personalities – even if only a small minority were interested enough to get involved in them. I shall return to the sex division in youth cultures in the next chapter.

I want to conclude this section with a qualitative description of the pupil cultures I found in Keighley. Alison and her friends were a group of sixth-formers and students who had a busy and self-contained social life, meeting weekly at the folk club (most of them picked at guitars themselves), at parties in each others' houses, at concerts or the bar at the local universities, at selected pubs. The group tended to come from middle-class backgrounds (the local professional and management class) and this had some effect on the material basis of their leisure – they had access to cars, for example, which made them mobile – but they were not particularly well off in terms of income, spent a large proportion of non-school time studying and were consequently at home a lot. Working-class sixth-formers fitted into this culture without much difficulty.

Music was used as a background to their lives, radio and records were always on. The records were LPs, chosen carefully and individually and often saved for after hearing a friend's copy; there was much mutual listening and temporary exchanging of records and few people in the group had a large record collection, although a crucial musical role was played by older brothers and sisters and friends who had more records, knew what was happening and turned the group on to new sounds. The overall result was an eclecticism of taste, with individuals developing their own specialisms – folk, heavy, singer/songwriter; they were aware of general rock trends but not particularly interested in them.

This group was conscious of itself as a group and differentiated itself clearly from the culture of its parents, but what really dominated its members' lives was a sense of possibility. They were all preparing to move on – to universities and colleges, to new towns and opportunities, to new sexual and social experiences; they were all aware that the group itself was transitional and temporary, that individuals had to maintain their individualism within it. They were articulate and self-aware and valued these qualities in music, to which they turned for support as well as for relaxation. They most valued music that was most apparently 'artistic' – technically complex or lyrically poetic – and tastes here went with other interests, in the other arts, in politics, in religion. There were few direct restraints on the activities of this group except the members' shortage of money;

they were successful at school and at home and rarely clashed with
authority. But their life was already a career and the importance of
exams and qualifications was fully realised. The resulting tensions
made music all the more important – as the context for bopping,
relaxing, petting, falling in love and shouting a temporary 'Fuck the
world!'.

Craig and his friends were in their last year at school, fifth-formers
itching to get out. They would leave school without skill or qualifica-
tion but had been used to failure for years and school was not so
much oppressive now as irrelevant. Their lives already revolved
around the possibilities of (unskilled) work – most members of the
group were already working part-time – and their leisure reflected
this expectation. The group went out (no bother about studying) to
the youth club, to the pubs that would take them, to the chippy and
the bus station and the streets. None of this group were militantly
members of any particular gang, but they had skinhead friends and
relations, could run casually with them and with the emerging groups
of mods and crombies and smoovies and knew which side they were
on in a bundle; Friday night, for example, was the traditional time
for a trip to Bradford, the boys for a fight, the girls for a dance at the
Mecca.

This group had plenty of free time but little money or mobility and
their leisure was consequently focused on public places, putting them
in constant confrontation with the controllers of those spaces –
police and bus conductors and bouncers. But home wasn't much
freer and so the boys went out most nights, doing nothing, having a
laugh, aware that this was their youth and that their future would be
much like the past of their working-class parents. Music was a per-
vasive part of their lives, in their rooms and clubs, on the juke-box,
at the disco. Sometimes, when they had the money, they'd buy that
single that was really great. They knew the big names and what was
in the charts and what was good to dance to, though they didn't really
follow it. The point was that when they were in their group they had
their music and knew what it was without thinking much. And they
knew what they hated, that hairy stuff, heavy rock – 'it's crackers the
way it's arranged – isn't it?' – though that mattered more at school
than on the streets, where they were grown up already, went drinking
with their brothers and their mates. Music was for the girls really,
wasn't it? It was the girls who stayed home and listened more, who
even had their favourites pinned on the wall still and sometimes told
the boys what to buy for their girl friends.

David's and Peter's friends were younger, in the fourth form, but
committed to the academic route. They saw their futures stretching
out through the sixth form and college – which was how David's

parents and teachers saw it too, though Peter's had their doubts. They were young yet, lacked the resources and the mobility and the permission for student life. In chafing about this they were more aggressively hip, at school, in the youth club and most of all at home, where they'd gather their friends and sit round the record player like it was Moses or something, bringing messages from on high. It was important for this lot to distinguish themselves from everybody, teachers, parents, peers. They were hippies, hairies, in their clothes and attitudes and tastes and drugs, and they worked at it, read the music press, got passionate about their records and about the evils of commercialism. They were an élite, a group apart from the masses even if they were in the same school and youth club and street.

Most of these kids made it into the sixth form, no sweat, and entered that culture easily, the greater freedom and success accompanying a looser hipness so that their interests remained but their expression was less aggressive. Some, though, did not. Peter failed his O-levels. The school wouldn't have him in the sixth and wouldn't even give him a reference for the tech. He found his life-style incompatible with the unskilled work his father and brothers did, so he lived on the dole mostly, not articulate enough to say what he really wanted but hearing it in the music, which seemed like the right life if he could get it together. He dreamt about that in the cafés by day and the hippie pub by night, did a little dealing and always turned on his friends, still at school or home for the vac. He knew everything that was going on and believed more than ever what they'd all once believed, that 'rock is a real boost from reality', and he needed to believe it too, now more than ever.

Sociological explanations

I have presented a general and a particular description of young people's use of music and I want next to consider the existing sociological explanations of the importance of music in youth cultures. The first comes from adolescence theorists. With their concern for the problems of socialisation and transition, they focus on peer-groups as the social context in which children learn to be adults. Music is seen to be important to peer-groups for two reasons: it is a means by which a group defines itself, and it is a source of in-group status.[10]

The most vivid example of music functioning to define group identity is in Colin Fletcher's account of how rock'n'roll transformed Liverpool street gangs into beat groups, as every gang nurtured its own musicians, provided its own fans and started to fight its battles on stage with the 'wild and basic sound' of Mersey Beat:

This thumping sound made the clubs relatively complete as the new adolescent world, a whole new source of status within them selves. Adolescents had a music, a number of dances, a 'place of their own'.[11]

This quote brings out the two aspects of musical identity: it distinguishes young from old, but it also distinguishes one peer-group from another:

What about me? I dig mod clothes but I don't wear them. I like the Beatles but don't rave over them. I listen to Blue Beat music but don't dance the Blue Beat way. I wear my hair long and sometimes use hair lacquer, but I don't sport a Blue Beat hat. I dig everything a mod raves over but I don't hunt with a mod pack. Recently I asked a typical mod boy what title I should come under. Sizing me up he said, 'You're not one of those in-between mods and rockers called mids. There's an Ivy League style about your suits and your appearance differs from the mid. I would put you under the title of – a Stylist.'[12]

Teenage styles reflect the need of all adolescents to 'belong' and one aspect of group identity is its stylistic precision:

True skinheads look neat. Their clothes are smart and expensive. Their boots are always polished to perfection. Their favourite clothes are Levi Sta-Prest, Harrington jackets, Jaytex (shirts), Bens (shirts), Crombies (coats), Blue-beats (hats), Doc's (Dr Marten's boots), Royals' (shoes), Monkey boots (girls' boots), Fred's (Fred Perry shirts), Toniks (two-tone suits).[13]

Another is that everyone gets put into a group, even if only negatively; *Sniffin' Glue*, the punks' magazine, refers to other groups as 'footballs' and 'discos', for example. Each group has its music, which can and must reflect the finest nuances: 'as skinheads become smoothies and skinhead girls begin to go out with smoothies they start to like T. Rex and Slade better than Motown'.[14]

This is a description of the Halloween dance in her village from one of my Keighley sample:

Just as in the youth club the two rival gangs sit at opposite ends of the room. The band will begin to play and everybody is waiting for everybody else to get up and dance. Then some girls will get up and dance and gradually the floor will fill up with people dancing. Suddenly the record will change to a rock record and everybody makes their way back to the seats as the rockers get up and stand in a circle ready to start their dance. The older folk stand and look amazed as they start to dance, they most probably never seen anything like it before because they are doing cartwheels and splits in the middle of the circle. As their type of music dies away into the background, a Tamla Motown record comes on and all the mods get up and go into a circle and begin to dance. This carries on for most of the night, it's like one big dancing contest, trying to be better than the other. They have nothing against each other, they do it for fun and everybody enjoys themselves either laughing at them or laughing at the people's faces.

And after supper there are old-time dances for older people and the kids join in and 'pretend that they are on *Come Dancing*'.

In such a village the division into groups seems random (indeed, the groups fought together against neighouring skinheads and rockers) and in general adolescent identities can be based on a variety of symbols, including fine musical differences within a single musical taste – Elvis *vs* Cliff, the Beatles *vs* the Stones, Donny Osmond *vs* David Cassidy. Even the slightest differences between groups can be matters of passionate argument and musical identity takes on a variety of references – one of the most visible is the phenomenon of everyone at a rock concert dressing like the star.[15]

The second use of music-as-identity is to distinguish the young from the old, to identify a place or occasion or time as youth's property. Music – played on transistor radios, record players, portable cassettes – becomes the easiest way for the young to maintain and display their control of their rooms, clubs and street corners, of their pubs and discos. The demands made of it – in terms of noise and beat and flash – are general rather than specific. If the noise is right, any noise will do – although familiarity is valued, hence the use of the charts. Music is the context for rather than the focus of youthful leisure. This is most noticeable in the central institution of teenage culture, the dance. It may be true, as Patterson has argued, that the impact of black dancing records – ska and soul and reggae – has reflected the needs of a newly violent and hedonistic white youth culture, but it is also true that the real focus of dances is the youthful displays and interactions which revolve around the 'exchange and mart' of sexual partners, and such displays long pre-date rock'n'roll. The music is the accompaniment of an activity, not its expression, or, as a 15-year-old in my sample put it:

And if the older people want to begin looking for a wife or husband, they have to go to Bradford Mecca.[16]

Although adolescent theorists claim to understand the functions of youth music they are not sanguine about its effects. Do teenage symbols express teenage concerns or do they manipulate them? There has always been a fear that the teenageness of teenage culture has rested on false idols, that the posters and the stars, the beat and the love lyrics and the rest of this world of teenage fantasy are a false expression of real needs. Teenage culture is seen as filling a need, but not really fulfilling it.[17]

My own research suggests that teenagers are much hipper about themselves and their world than the traditional adolescent image allows. They know how commercial rock works, even as they enjoy it. My sample's comments on T. Rex revealed an awareness (no doubt informed by the sneers of the hairies) of the relationship between record-making and money-making. In response to a question asking if they would like to be rock stars, there was only one fantasy along the lines of 'Yes, because you could enjoy yourself, you would be on TV and you would get lots of girl friends and fans.' Mostly there was realistic assessment of rock as a job something like the army – hard work but plenty of travel!

Adolescence theorists' evaluation of teenage culture rests on their understanding of adolescent needs. If the use of music can be explained as answering a need, it can also be judged according to how well it does so. The problem with this model, as I suggested in the last chapter, is that adolescent needs are defined in social-psychological terms, and related to the abstract difficulties of social transition. Leisure is not related to work or, indeed, given any material setting – school leaving, for example, does not, according to these theorists, have any major effects on youth's leisure needs; rather, 'it is leisure that provides the continuity between school and work'. Similarly, although most of the studies of adolescence are studies of working-class teenagers, the suggestion is that the analysis is classless; all adolescents have the same needs and create the same peer-group systems, music therefore fulfils the same purpose for all of them.[18]

This conclusion has been strongly criticised by Graham Murdock. In his own subtle interpretation of the use of music by secondary-school pupils, Murdock emphasises the sharp class differences within youth's use of similar musical symbols. He suggests that, as a source of peer-group status and identity, music must be contrasted with working-class street culture as well as with conformist school culture. He describes a pattern of music use similar to the one I found in Keighley: middle-class children interested in the 'underground' and concerned with lyrics, 'the source of those values, roles and meanings which the school undervalues'; working-class children interested in dance music and concerned with the beat – they got their 'alternative meanings from street peer groups rooted in the situational cultures of working-class neighbourhoods' and music served them simply as a background and 'small coin of social exchange'. From such taste differences sprang the different media uses – *Top of the Pops* vs *The Old Grey Whistle Test* – and Murdock builds up a convincing picture of class differences maintained and even exaggerated by the different uses of a supposedly common youthful means of expression.[19]

There are difficulties, however, in the very neatness of Murdock's conclusions. Obviously I don't doubt the significance of class-based differences in rock use – my own research has similar implications and American sociologists have come up with the same general findings – but I do doubt the precision of Murdock's relationships. The evidence that working-class pupils are less interested in music than their middle-class colleagues, for example, can equally support findings that their taste choices are completely random! Whatever the differences within youth culture, the statistical evidence of an interest crossing class boundaries remains impressive. The readership of the music press, for example, whether the *New Musical Express* and *Melody Maker* or *Fab 208*, includes a roughly similar percentage of readers from each class, as does the audience for Radio 1. Age remains a much better indicator of music use than class.[20]

The problem is to explain the differences within a broadly similar pattern of music use, and Murdock misinterprets some of the differences he found. His research, like mine, was based on a survey of school children, young people in a very particular situation. His sample was poor, for example, and in terms of pocket money working-class children are certainly poorer than their middle-class peers – to what extent is their lesser involvement in music a matter of resources? Some of Murdock's distinctions, as he himself suggests, were related to sex rather than class differences, and how should the argument that middle-class pupils lack the freedom of the streets and base their leisure on the home be extended to students? But the central claim of Murdock's argument is that youth cultures get their meaning from their class base rather than from a universal state of adolescence. In the end, criticism must focus on the definition of class involved.

Murdock classified his pupils according to the occupations of their parents. While this is a good indicator of their likely class futures, it does mean that for the children themselves class was defined as a matter of family culture rather than of productive role: their class characteristics were the results of values and attitudes learnt at home and shaped by school, community and mass media; they were not the results of their own roles in production or in the labour process. Murdock's explanation of class differences in music use is in terms of how class *values* structure responses to adolescent problems. Murdock brings class into the sociology of youth via the notion of youth sub-cultures: if all young people have a need for status and autonomy, how these needs are expressed and experienced depends on their different class-cultural backgrounds. I want to turn now to sub-cultural explanations of youth music.

Sub-cultural explanations

Characteristically, the teds' association with rock'n'roll came to public attention with the outbreak of rock'n'roll riots, disturbances in cinemas featuring rock'n'roll films. In the public mind teds and nastiness merged together in an uneasy blur of primitive rhythms and primitive behaviour. The sub-cultural account of rock takes off from this lead: youth's use of music is related to the behaviour of specific deviant groups. Sub-cultural theorists take teds, for instance, as an example of 'Lumpenproletariat youth'. Their lack of job satisfaction, their 'status frustration', made their leisure important – 'they seek from it the excitement, self-respect and autonomy which are so conspicuously absent from work'. But in their preoccupation with 'toughness, excitement, fate, autonomy and status' the teds were no different from other lower-class adolescents – it was just that their dependence on this culture was more 'intense and comprehensive' and their use of cultural symbols, clothes and music, was thus more jealously defended."

The thrust of the sub-cultural approach is that youth music is a symbol which expresses the underlying leisure values of the group which uses it. The first difficulty with this explanation of rock is that the symbolic objects involved are usually provided by commercial interests rather than generated by the youth groups themselves. If the teds responded to rock'n'roll with passion, it was hardly teddy-boy music by either origin or even style (that connection only developed later with rock'n'roll revival and rocker culture). To interpret music as symbol, it is no good looking at how music is produced; the sociologist must show how youth groups give music its real meaning in the act of consumption, and the mods, the ultimate consumer group, have been taken as the model of a youth sub-culture.

It was the mods who first used music as an exclusive symbol, something with which to distinguish themselves from the conformist young:

They met at the Scene in Ham Yard off Great Windmill Street in London's West End, an all-night club where groups played, but whose main attraction was Guy Stevens' record sessions. Stevens' collection of obscure black American records was the basis of mods' musical tastes and a cornerstone of the soul boom of the mid-sixties. At a time when it was commonplace to hear the Beatles and hip to listen to Jimmy Reed, John Lee Hooker and Howlin' Wolf, Stevens was playing James Brown and Otis Redding, Don Covay, Solomon Burke, the Miracles, the Impressions and Major Lance.[22]

The mods' sociological image is confusing: on the one hand the moral-panic-inducing thugs of Margate and rocker-bashing, on the other hand the pill-popping all-night dancers and all-day consumers of Carnaby-Street style. Sub-culturalist theories seek to focus this double image. The description of the frustrated prole, pouring his needs into leisure, remains, but emphasis is put on the resulting mod style, a more self-conscious and creative mode of expression than ted style, more arrogant, narcissistic, cynical and tense. The mods came on like winners and consumption for them was as much a play-ground as a last resort; if sociologists have failed to ask the obvious questions (Why the scooters? Where did the money come from?) they have been able to make an elaborate reading of the nuances of mod style.[23]

But the second difficulty with sub-cultural accounts of music is that, as a symbol, it becomes completely subsumed in the much more general notion of style. This is most obvious in the analysis of the skinhead sub-culture. They were rough kids again, displaced from working-class communities and occupations and seeking the 'magical recovery of community' through leisure, but they weren't much interested in musical expression – ' "Reggae" was important for only a few months in 1969, but it was soon rejected as "West Indian music".' This doesn't appear to faze the sub-cultural theorists one bit, they simply replace music in their analysis with football![24]

Teds, mods and skins are the three teenage groups that have been examined in the most detail by sub-cultural sociologists. Their find-ings rest on the theories outlined in the last chapter: these kids' uses of leisure are understood by reference to their lack of job satisfaction, their alienation from the community. Music (or foot-ball) is a symbolic expression of this dissatisfaction and alienation, and the particular styles adopted, rock'n'roll, soul, reggae – even when provided by commerce – can be read for their signs of youthful 'cultural space winning'. By their very nature the members of these sub-cultures are rarely articulate about their lives but the good sociologist can extrapolate the true meaning of their activities and styles.[25]

The trouble with this approach is the narrowness of its focus. In interpreting music as a *symbol* of leisure values, sub-culturalists fail to make sense of it as an *activity*, one enjoyed by the vast number of non-deviant kids. The error is clear in the suggestion that for some young people football is a substitute for music. The only way football could be such a substitute is at the symbolic level of group identity – via badges, heroes, talking-points; it can't be the same as an activity. Skinhead identity may not have been based on musical taste, but that didn't stop skins listening to music and enjoying all the usual music-based activities. Indeed, football-based identity soon became a part of rock as Slade, for example, and even David Cassidy made effective use of football chants and songs.[26]

Sub-cultural theory rests on a false freezing of the youthful world into deviants and the rest. As my Keighley survey made clear, the fact is that kids pass through groups, change identities and play their leisure roles for fun. Observing sociologists are wrong to elevate the most visibly different leisure styles above the less apparent sexual and occupational differences in leisure activities. The exact role of music for these sub-cultures remains unclear and it is worth contrasting them with deviant groups which are truly focused on music.[27]

[margin handwritten: choice passing]

Jock Young has argued that whereas 'delinquent youth culture' is centred on leisure because its members are marginal to the labour market in terms of skills and opportunities, bohemian youth culture is centred on leisure because its members have deliberately rejected the rewards of work:

> Like the delinquent he focuses his life on leisure, but unlike the former his dissociation is a matter of choice rather than a realistic bowing to the inevitable. Moreover, his disdain for society is of an articulate and ideological nature. He evolves social theories which uphold subterranean values as authentic guides to action, and which attempt to solve the problem of the domination of the ethos of productivity.[28]

Music had a special importance for hippie culture ('pop music is an essential element of the "underground" and a central preoccupation of most adolescent hippie groups') and because of its ideology, hippie rock was more than just hippie music by adoption. In Richard Mills's words, music was given a 'missionary purpose', it could carry hippie values into the heart of the commercial beast, it could spread

> the ubiquitous notion of 'turning on', the sudden intuition, the transcending of rational standards and structured judgements – there was mystical illumination or there was nothing – and the

explicit linking of mental and physical dimensions – to be 'smiling and bopping about and not questioning, to know what it is to be alive'.

In seeking to transform the experience and use of rock music, hippie culture also sought to transform its production: for hippie groups music came out of the community, the distinction between performer and audience was blurred even in the experience of performance – music was an experience of community as well as its expression:

Pop groups thus held a key position within the culture. They helped minister and uphold that experience of transformation which underlay it, provided the forms and rituals through which its goals and values found expression, and, in the process, established the minimal degree of social and economic organisation necessary to sustain them. All these factors gave them a position of leadership which partly strengthened, and partly itself flowed from, their final role, that of negotiating between the different realities of the hip and the straight.[29]

In the long run this role, as missionaries in the commercial world, proved almost impossible for hippie musicians to sustain. In California, where hippie ideology was most powerful, the violence of the Altamont Festival of 1969 was taken as the final sign that a community could not be based on music use alone – the world of the hip could only be the world of the commercial hip. Nevertheless, in a more politicised form, the hippie argument still inspires many a struggling revolutionary rock band.[30]

My purpose at this stage is not to criticise the hippie ideology of music but to suggest that in sub-cultural theory the hippies' articulate use of rock as a symbol of leisure, an expression of the opposition to the 'ethos of productivity', is taken to be an example of the use of music that is made by all youth sub-cultures. But the hippies really did have an ideology of leisure; their music was created to express a worked-out position. Their position can be directly contrasted to that of, say, the teds.

In his detailed empirical study of teddy boys Fyvel points out that if music is teenagers' 'most vivid link with contemporary culture', for teds it was the only area where they were 'at one' with society: 'tunes are the one subject where you can be sure of getting them to talk'. Fyvel suggests that 'his love for pop music appears to be the chink in the teddy boy's armour of non-participation'. If teds were against hard work and getting on:

Sweat and toil to learn music is one of the few exceptions. A boy willing to devote every day to practice in a band is not derided for his pains. Even in the toughest Ted circles, musical ambition is generally regarded as legitimate.

This echoes Mills's comments on the hippie musician negotiating between the hip and the straight, but the hippie was armed with an ideology, the teddy boy was not: rock'n'roll wasn't a symbol of the teddy boys' independence but of their continued dependence on the world of the teenage consumer.[31]

In my survey of Keighley it was clear that music was important as a symbolic expression of values only for those young people who were rejecting their given class cultures, whether middle-class pupils rejecting academic success or working-class pupils rejecting the street, and the 'hairies' equally rejected the values of commerce. In his study of working-class boys in London Willmott described 'another kind of rebel' than the traditional criminal deviant:

He was alone, playing records by Billie Holiday and Miles Davis. He says of his parents, 'They couldn't understand me in a hundred years. Like most ordinary East End people, their idea of living is to have a steady job and settle down with a nice little wife in a nice little house or flat, doing the same things every day of your life. They think the sorts of thing I do are mad.' What sort of things? 'Well, I might decide to take the day off and go up the park and sit and meditate. Or go round my friend's pad for an all-night session. A group of us drink whisky and smoke tea and talk about what's happiness and things like that.' He says that he and his friends regularly take Purple Hearts too: 'It may seem sinful to some people. But we're just young people who like to enjoy ourselves and forget the Bomb.' He reads Jack Kerouac, Norman Mailer, James Baldwin – 'That's the sort of thing I dig. I suppose I'm really searching.'

Willmott makes the point that such 'rebels' were rare in his sample, but their importance for rock (and rock's importance for them) must not be underestimated, nor can the use of music involved simply be explained as an expression of a middle-class sub-culture. Anyone who grew up in the 1960s knows the importance of such local 'hip' figures, not just in turning us on to blues and politics and poetry, but also in acting as the link between the culturally adventurous of both classes. From this group (particularly from its creatively successful version in art colleges) came the majority of British rock musicians.[32]

Ironically, it is also this group which, excluded from most

sociological accounts of adolescence, most clearly uses music as a source of autonomy and status. For most young people leisure is not enjoyed in self-conscious opposition to work but as an aspect of it, their work and leisure complement each other; only for hippies, hairies and equivalent groups does it make sense to read rock for values. Such groups are ideologically based and claim their music as meaningful; it is crucial to their position that they make music and don't just consume it in their 'free time'; a contempt for commerce and for commercial leisure is essential to their mode of rebellion and differentiates it sharply from the mainstream youth use of music, whatever deviant styles the latter may adopt. In Keighley's youth culture rock was important and meaningful *in itself* for only a few pupils; only for a rebel like Peter was it not just, as it was for most of his peers, leisure's garnish.

This contrast, between music as the focus of leisure and music as the accompaniment of leisure, can be made equally by looking at another kind of leisure 'deviant' – people who are deviant not in the way they value music, but in the way they consume it. Some such musical deviants are straightforward fanatics, fans gone to extremes for Elvis, the Beatles, country music, whatever. In this they are hardly different from fanatics of other artifacts, whether trains, the English Civil War or pre-Raphaelite paintings, and are not usually part of youth culture. Then there are the people who share their peers' tastes but take them to extremes, for whom membership of a commercially provided fan club is not enough, but whose life revolves around their idol to the extent of imitation (the Bowie boys who dyed bits of their hair green), sexual pursuit (groupies) or compulsive flaunting of their idolatory (the Roller girls).[33]

For such groups the object of attention is a star rather than a genre, but there are, equally, musical fanatics. Britain has a long tradition of jazz, blues, soul and other musical freaks – hence fanzines (and rock critics). Such groups are composed of scholars, interested in fact and document, functioning less as a group than as a network of communication, but such purists may meet to play and listen to their music (as did the Stones and other early sixties blues fans) in their own clubs, pubs and halls. Britain is scattered with jazz clubs and folk clubs, with rock'n'roll nights and country evenings. For their participants music is more than a casual accompaniment of leisure, it is leisure's purpose.[34]

The most interesting of such groups in youth culture is that revolving around Northern Soul and its life of all-night dancing to obscure black music. It has been estimated that this scene has 25,000 adherents (I had one in my Keighley sample), many of whose leisure time is concerned entirely with soul music:

I can't stand to be with anyone who doesn't like soul. . . .
My whole life centres around soul. . . .
I couldn't imagine going out with a girl who didn't like soul. . . .
I like Black films and I like the life-style that they depict.
Soul has given me so much that me and my girl have contemplated
adopting a black baby. . . .

The Northern Soul scene draws its members from the same sources
as the non-musical deviant youth groups. It has continuities with
both the mods (in its emphasis on dancing, its use of pills, its soul
cult) and the skinheads (in its self-conscious anti-progressive and pro-
working-class stance) but the differences reveal what a sub-culture
looks like when it's *really* focused on music![35]

In the last chapter I suggested that sociologists of youth, whether
approaching young people as consumers, adolescents or deviants,
end up with a sociology of choice. In looking at the explanations of
youth's use of music we can see some of the difficulties that result
from this focus on choice. While adolescence theorists, for example,
provide a theory of youth's leisure 'needs' they can't account for the
particular forms in which these needs are expressed and satisfied or
explain the undoubted pattern of different youth cultures. The sub-
culturalists do claim to understand such differences, but they explain
them by reference to values: leisure choices are seen as expressions
of leisure values, which can then be related to the vaguely defined
class position which produces such values. But this argument is not
helpful for an understanding of rock. The music is explained as a
symbol but not as an activity, and because leisure groups are frozen
into 'sub-cultures' most young people vanish from the analysis alto-
gether. The sub-culturalists may be able to make sense of the music
of groups engaged in a deliberate value rebellion (though the source
of such rebellion remains unexplained) but for most young people
music just doesn't have such importance as either symbol or activity,
as can be illustrated by comparison with those groups which really
are deviant in their musical consumption.

Most of the pupils in my survey saw their leisure not as a matter of
choice but of opportunity (the commonest response in all youth surveys to the question, 'What is there to do here in your free time?', is
'Nothing!'). Opportunity was defined in very narrow terms. One girl
explained to me where skinheads went at night: there were not many
places besides pubs and youth clubs, and the latter were closing as the
skins started fights and did damage. Anyway, they were boring and
nothing exciting ever did happen unless a fight started. In detail,
there was the Holycroft disco (7p admission); Churchill House disco
(25p, but stopped because of violence); Temperance Hall disco (25p);

Victoria Hall for an occasional dance (25p–50p); and Haworth, Oxenhope and some school youth clubs. Otherwise, two pubs, the Star and the Rodney, and the latter tended to fling kids out for being under age. This girl and her skinhead friends were well aware of the effects of labelling: 'just by being dressed mod style we get blamed without any evidence at all'.

I want to consider leisure opportunities in rather more general terms than this. If we are to understand youth use of music and the particular patterns of leisure involved, if we are to bring class into the analysis of youth culture, then we must look at leisure as a relationship between choice and constraint. In the next chapter I will discuss how the consumption of rock is affected by youth's relation to production.

4
Music and leisure

The young people went to dance; and I went to look at them, and I was afflicted with melancholy. And about eleven o'clock the party was over and I went home; and, as I went, I communed with myself darkly, and I said, 'These poor creatures don't even know how to play.'

The girls at this party were nearly all Lancashire factory girls; the young men were mostly factory and colliery workers. I had seen them at work in their greasy, malodorous, sickly mills and gloomy mines, and had not felt half so forcibly as I now felt, how hard, and dull, and starved, and unlovely their lives were.

There was hardly a pretty girl in the room; the best favoured were those who might have been, or ought to have been, pretty. There was not *one* girl in the room who could stand or walk with grace or freedom. They were all more or less round-shouldered. They had sickly, murky complexions and harsh loud voices. They were dressed awkwardly and with bad taste, and they looked anxious, dull and *tired.* There was some hilarity of a rather noisy kind, but there was an utter absence of 'happiness': no gaiety, no sparkle, no lightness.

The fact is these people had never been taught to be happy.

Yes; but besides that, they had never known what it is to be free. (Robert Blatchford in the *Labour Prophet*, 1894.)

Both TV channels now run weekly programmes in which popular records are played to teenagers and judged. While the music is performed, the cameras linger savagely over the faces of the audience. What a bottomless chasm of vacuity they reveal! The huge faces, bloated with cheap confectionery and smeared with chain-store make-up, the open, sagging mouths and glazed eyes, the hands mindlessly drumming in time to the music, the broken stiletto heels, the shoddy, stereotyped, 'with-it' clothes: here, apparently, is a collective portrait of a generation enslaved by a commercial machine. Leaving a TV studio recently, I stumbled into the exodus from one of these sessions. How pathetic and list-less they seemed: young girls, hardly any more than 16, dressed as adults and already lined up as fodder for exploitation. Their eyes came to life when one of their grotesque idols – scarcely older than they – made a brief appearance, before a man in a camel-hair coat hustled him into a car. Behind this image of 'youth', there **are**, evidently, some shrewd older folk at work.

(Paul Johnson in the *New Statesman*, 1964.)

The ideology of leisure in a capitalist society (the ideology reflected in the literature on youth) is that people work in order to be able to enjoy leisure. Leisure is their 'free' time and so the values and choices expressed in leisure are independent of work – they are the result of ideological conditions. There are a variety of sociological approaches to these conditions but they are all concerned to explain choices. When class and work are brought into the analysis, it is indirectly: class/work experience is seen to create a culture with values that are expressed in leisure, or the work/class experience is seen to leave unsatisfied essential social-psychological needs which are met, instead in the worker's free time. When youth is observed to be a distinct leisure group, the problem is to explain young people as consumers, to explain their particular use of their freedom; sociologists examine their distinct needs as adolescents, or their distinct values as members of sub-cultures. But as Blatchford and Johnson suggest, the 'freedom' involved in youth leisure is deceptive. If people work to enjoy leisure, they also enjoy leisure in order to be able to work and it is important to consider the effects on free time of the latter relationship.

Young workers

In a Marxist perspective, leisure has three purposes for capital: to refresh labour physically, so that it will be fit to work again the next day; to refresh labour ideologically, so that it will be willing to work again the next day; to provide a market for the consumption of commodities so that surplus value can be realised. In some respects the resulting constraints on leisure are direct. The size of the pay packet determines what resources people have for their free time in the first place; work prospects, career possibilities, limit the leisure 'risks' people are prepared to take; work discipline, the organisation of workers' time and of their physical and mental capacities on the job, limit what's physically possible in leisure. The most obvious expression of this work/leisure relationship is the weekend (see Table 5): Friday and Saturday nights are freer times just because there's no work to go to the next morning.

In general terms, though, the relationship between choice and constraint in leisure is complex and involves a number of contradictions. If nineteenth-century capitalists, at their crudest, sought to maximise

Table 5:
Percentage of weekly expenditure on entertainment by day of the week

Mon.	Tues.	Wed.	Thurs.	Fri.	Sat.	Sun.
12	11	11	11	19	28	8

Source: IPC: *Marketing Manual of the UK*, 1975, Table A.8.12.

surplus value by extending the working day and reducing the labour time necessary to produce the value the worker needed himself for sheer physical survival, the workers organised successfully to reduce the working day and to extend the notion of the 'necessities' of proletarian life. In both struggles they had support from 'enlightened' capital which, on the one hand, believed that happy workers would be more efficient and amenable than those selling their labour power under the 'dull compulsion of necessity', and, on the other hand, realised that labourers were also consumers – Marx contrasted the attitudes of capitalists to their own and to other employers' workers.

The overall result for capital is that control of leisure has been exercised indirectly. Leisure choices can't be determined, but they do have to be limited – the problem is to ensure that workers' leisure activities don't affect their discipline, skill or willingness at work. In part this has been achieved by formal rules and restrictions on leisure time (hence, for example, the First World War origins of the licensing laws), but as significant has been the positive promotion of forms of leisure, whether by ideological means such as the 'Rational Recreation' societies of the nineteenth century and the mass media today, or through the effects of state policies on housing, education and health. Active promotion of a particular leisure pattern has also, of course, been the concern of commodity salesmen, creating 'needs' for the goods capitalist enterprises produce, obscuring those for which commodities aren't available.

It is in this framework that youth should be seen as a distinct leisure group. Young people's distinction is not that they have much more free time than adults (see Table 6) but that their free time is more 'free'. Young people are free of the detailed restrictions of childhood institutions (family and school) and not yet bound by the adult institutions of family and work (adolescence theorists are right to focus on the problems of 'transition' even if their subsequent analysis is unhelpful). It is precisely for this reason that the young are subject to far more direct pressures on their leisure choices than anyone else – whether from state institutions like youth clubs, youth workers and juvenile courts, or from the commercial organisation of teenage ideology. But it is also true that young people have differing degrees of such freedom, depending on their place in the labour market.

Table 6:
Total hours worked per week (including overtime), April 1973

All males:	43·2	All females:	32·3
full-time manual over 21	46·7	full-time manual over 18	39·9
non-manual over 21	38·8	non-manual over 18	36·8
full-time youths under 21	42·3	full-time girls under 18	39·0

Source: Dept. of Employment, *New Earnings Survey,* 1973, Table 14.

The most 'free' are the unskilled young workers (who are, in consequence, the most trouble for the youth agencies). Their casual relationship to work, their absenteeism and horseplay, go with a casual self-indulgence in leisure. In some respects such young workers are useful to employers because of their very casualness. They may lack the obligations and steadiness of married men but they also lack the commitments, the conservatism and immobility. If most industrial jobs are only open to married men over 22, preferably with children and mortgages, there are some tasks which depend on casual, 'free' labour – the Army is the most obvious employer of young unskilled men. Young men are, indeed, expected to spend a few years before 'settling down', and young marriage is not encouraged – the problem is to ensure that such young people are ready and able to become respectable married men when their time does come. The young are kept constantly aware that their youth is temporary, a feeling of impermanence is ever-present in youth culture. The hedonism involved is a 'sowing of wild oats' and not something which can be enjoyed for long – consider, for example, the lack of housing facilities for the young unmarried.

The life of the young skilled, the apprentices, has much the same impermanence as that of the young unskilled but their hedonism is indulged with less abandon. Apprentices go out less, take fewer leisure risks. They are already committed to a career and can't afford an employer's displeasure; they have a clearer knowledge of their future and are preparing for it more systematically. But the leisure differences between skilled and unskilled youth are matters of degree rather than kind: for the apprentices, too, leisure is the opportunity to enjoy a temporary good time to the full, and in the long run the 'skilling' of the unskilled that I described in Chapter 2 will affect not the mainstream of teenage culture but only its most bizarre and delinquent excesses. The young understand the limits on their freedom. They know, for example, that most employers don't care what they do in their free time as long as it doesn't affect their discipline and regularity on the job. The casual criminal drunkenness and hooliganism that lead to fines and cautions are sharply distinguished from behaviour that leads to imprisonment, loss of job and gaps in the stamps – only the most casual workers will risk the latter. Similarly, teenage freedom is licensed within the obligations of family life; most young workers live at home until they marry and, as I have already suggested, indulge themselves in the context of a sufficient family income.

If youth leisure is a temporary moment of freedom, bound by the needs of present and future work, present and future families, the young unemployed are, ironically, much less free than their working peers because their future is so uncertain. They are idle without choice, unable to prepare for anything, in no position to indulge themselves. They are hemmed in not just by the continuously humiliating experience of job-hunting, but also by the insecurity of having no productive purpose at all. Dole-queue rock, punk aggression, may indeed express the feelings of these abandoned kids, but it does so not as the articulation of any group identity or consciousness but as a simple bleat of existence.

For most teenagers, however, skilled, unskilled, and even unemployed (the expectation of a job any day now dies hard), leisure means, as it did for Craig and his friends in Keighley, having a good time – physically, irresponsibly, spontaneously. It means drinking and laughing and doing nothing and sex and trying anything once before you have to do something for ever. For these young people music itself neither satisfies needs nor symbolises values, it is simply the noisy and buoyant context for all the other activities. These teenagers' needs are clear enough: they want music to dance to and not to think about (it has to stand up to disco stomping) but reject anything too mindless or patronising; their music has to recognise their market power as well as their energy, has to reflect their common concerns and identity. Seventies teenagers, like their comrades of the fifties and sixties, know, *pace* Johnson, that they're being exploited: the thrill is that all this commercial effort is being made just for them!

The exhilaration of a night out at a good disco is infectious, but we should not be completely deceived by it. My analysis of teenage leisure, like most of the descriptions of teenagers in the literature, is applicable to young male workers only. If they are the most free of young people, girls, their partners in the very same discos and clubs, are the least free.

Girls

Skinhead girls admire the way their boys treat them. They treat them as if they weren't there. They never include them in their conversation, you must do this yourself, and even introduce yourself to new friends.

They have no manners, are cheeky and disrespectful, but the girls respect them for being this way. It is all part of the understanding that goes with being a skinhead, and being a true one. (14-year-old girl, 1971.)[1]

I might marry sometime if I find a decent girl. I don't think I'll bother if she's a virgin as long as she hasn't knocked around too much. Girls who're shop-worn get old before their time. Girls think boys are just out for one thing, but if they make a boy respect them it's different. Unless I really like a girl I wouldn't waste time if she doesn't want to go to bed. I think most boys are the same – it's only natural. (18-year-old boy, 1964.)[2]

Angela McRobbie and Jenny Garber have pointed out that 'the absence of girls from the whole of the literature in this area [youth culture] is quite striking'. One explanation for this, revealed by the statistics, is that girls spend far more time than boys at home.[3]

There are three immediate reasons why girls stay home more. The first and most important is that parents exert their control over them – forbidding them to go out every night, limiting where they go, who with, for how long – control which is not exercised to anything like the same extent over boys and which leads to girls being more closely integrated into family life as teenagers (thus, for example, the oft-observed close relationship between working-class girls and their mothers). The second constraint follows from this: girls, unlike boys, have a role in the home; they have tasks to do – baby-sitting and child-minding; they are expected, even if in a comparatively light way, to help with cleaning and cooking; they are a part of the home organisation. The third constraint has a different immediate source but the same effect: girls spend longer than boys preparing to go out, with clothes and cosmetics and toiletries. It is at this point that girl culture becomes the culture of courtship; I'll return to this later.[4]

If girls are more confined to home, they are not completely bound by the family or excluded from youth culture (though they are less visible at youth culture's most dramatic and analysed moments). Rather, girl youth culture becomes a culture of the bedroom, the place where girls meet, listen to music and teach each other make-up skills, practice their dancing, compare sexual notes, criticise each other's clothes and gossip. Their reasons for being at home don't prevent the home being used as a youthful place – friends can share in tasks, girls are allowed out to friends' houses, even evenings with boy friends are acceptable if they end, not too late, together at home.

At girls' youngest and least free stage the result is teeny-boppers. Teeny-boppers are very young girls (10- to 13-year-olds). If the focus of teeny-bopper culture is usually a pop star (such teeny stars come and go in three-year cycles), the cultural symbol is less records than magazines – idol-related products like T-shirts and tea trays sell as well as the records anyway! At this age girls' youth cultural activities are heavily concentrated on what is immediately accessible in the home. TV is more significant than radio, the sight of the star more important than his sound. Teenage girl magazines (since they started with *Marilyn* in 1955) have always shown 'a dominant interest in pop stars and the pop scene', but their interest has been less in music than in gossip, clothes, possessions and pictures. The circulation of such magazines is heavily dependent on the potence of the *image* of the latest teenage idol.[5]

The boys use rock as their stockade on street corners and the dance floor; the girls' music comes out of the culture of the bedroom and the pin-up, of *Jackie* and gossiping in corners. A girl's identity is built on her idol – no poster, no friends. David Cassidy's records, for example, were less important than his pictures, than the constant contact his fans had through everything they read. Seeing him in person was not important for the power of the actual experience but for the status it conferred. In every group of Cassidy girls one or two could now swagger a little more proudly. Sure, the Cassidy hysteria was stirred and faked by the media for their own circulation ends, but this, too, was part of the game. How do you think it felt to be an Osmond girl and see bloody David Cassidy in the *Sun* every day?[6]

Girls grow out of the fantasy sexuality of teeny-bop as they begin to date and dance and go out more seriously, but the relationship between rock and the bedroom continues. Their public use of rock might be much the same as boys' (for background and dancing) but girls' home use remains different, with a continued emphasis on personalities. Girls' magazines feature rock stars rather than rock music and the lack of female interest in 'serious' rock is revealed clearly in the readership patterns of the music press, the audience patterns for radio and TV. Even within sixth-form and student culture girls have less interest in music than boys: they may potter about on guitars, but while the boys wax complex and hi-fi, it's the lyrics the girls get into, singer/songwriters and rock as angst – in my Keighley sample the girls in all groups were far more interested than the boys in rock words.[7]

Girl culture starts and finishes in the bedroom. As Alderton points out in her study of girls' magazines, all teenage romance stories end with the heroine getting married, which marks the end of girlhood, but one of the things that distinguishes girl from boy culture is its

The consumption of rock

continuity. The transition from *Jackie* to *Woman* via the girl magazines is virtually imperceptible, and the girl moves from the organisation of one household to another with a much less abrupt process of 'settling down' than her male peers (and this includes an easy transition to adult-appealing pop singers like Tom Jones). But in order to move from one bedroom to another, girls do have to find a husband – hence the significance of dancing and the culture of courtship. It has been claimed that more 16- to 24-year-old brides met their husbands at a dance than in any other way, and one of the more dramatic leisure statistics is the abruptness with which girls stop dancing on marriage (see Table 7). In Chapter 2 I suggested that marriage is a girl's career and the source of the constraints on her leisure. This argument can be pushed further: a girl's leisure *is* her work. It is leisure activities that are the setting for the start of her career, for the attraction of a man suitable for marriage.[8]

Table 7:
Percentage of leisure periods throughout year when dancing cited as chief pursuit

All in full-time education	15–18 Single	19–22 Single	Single	22–30 Married without children	Married with children	Whole population
Male 5	6	9	6	3	*	2
Female 11	15	15	18	1	*	2

Source: Sillitoe, Tables 9, 10.   (*less than 0·5%)

The process begins at home in the business of making oneself generally attractive – market researchers continually emphasise how much of girls' income goes on clothes and cosmetics – but once at the dance hall or disco the problem for the girls is to attract a particular man as a partner, and this problem limits female youth culture in a number of ways.[9]

The convention of courting is that the girl be 'passive' – she waits to be asked to dance and then becomes the boy's 'possession' – but it is really the girl who is actively seeking a partner. It is she rather than the boys who will be seen as a 'failure' if she hasn't attracted anyone by the end of the evening, and it is she who has to judge what the boy is worth, where to stop, how to let things develop (the boy, conventionally, is 'only after one thing').

This active/passive contradiction is matched by the individual/collective one. Girls go to dances in groups, prepare for them as friends, support and advise each other, dance together, help each other keep their self-respect and sense of fun. But the object of the exercise is to be picked up, as individuals – girls, in fact, are dependent on their friends to support them in the process of ceasing to be friends. One commonly observed compromise solution to this tension is the friendship pair:

> One guy trying to split two girls and therefore leaving one 'in the air' is unlikely to be successful – in most cases a girl will not abandon her friend.[10]

A third tension is between the public and private aspect of courting. Once a couple is paired off their activities, romantic or sexual, are essentially private, and yet crucial to a girl's marriage chances is her 'reputation', which rests on the public knowledge of her private behaviour (pregnancy, in this context, is the most obvious public sign of a private act). Hence even when a girl has got a partner there are constraints on her behaviour – another convention of the dance is the 'going home' negotiation:

> There is a noticeable reluctance among many of the girls to accept lifts home from boys and many will make their own way home (probably by taxi) rather than go with the boys they have met during the evening. Girls are unlikely to accept a lift unless they consider the boys 'trustworthy'. Some evidence of the existence of the 'trustworthiness' criterion employed by girls can be found in the fact that I have on occasion been asked by groups of girls to give them a lift as they had seen that I was alone in my car (and of course that I was absolutely trustworthy!). On these occasions they told me that they were not worried travelling with me because I was outnumbered (three to one) – but they still jokingly quibbled about who was getting out last.[11]

What does all this have to do with music? In some respects, not much – music is there, for the girls as for the boys, simply as background, to dance to, kiss to, make up to – but there are sexual differences. Most obviously, the girls do dance well (boys, notoriously, don't and don't care to) and buy and practise to dance records – such records become part of girl group life. Less obviously, but as significantly, music becomes a way of managing the sexual and emotional tensions implicit in a girl's role; rock is both an expression of them and a source of release: music and musical idols provide a focus for girls' hopes and fantasies as pop and film stars did for their mothers and grandmothers.

Once the girls start going steady their leisure changes drastically and most of these tensions are dissolved. As part of a permanent couple, of a couple looking forward to marriage, the girl can relax from the problems of pursuit and publicity and begin to adjust to her future as wife and mother. She begins to go out almost exclusively with her boy friend, and it's at this stage that the distinctions between 'respectable' and non-respectable girls become most obvious. Boys will take their steady girl friends out to respectable pubs and clubs, while going with their male mates to the rough ones – the reputations of the girls who even enter the latter suffer accordingly. It is also during this stage of courtship that the girl begins to break from her female peers, a separation symbolised by the pre-wedding-day hen party:

> I have never yet been into the City Centre Club on a Thursday without seeing at least one hen party and on occasion there have been as many as four. The high visibility of hen parties is produced by the traditional bride-to-be's hat. I do not know the origin of the practice, but it was also common in London. When a working girl is going to be married all the other girls at work make her a very large cardboard hat which is decorated with paper flowers, tinsel, tassels and often saucy jokes about the wedding night, etc. She may also have things like L-plates pinned on the back of her dress or coat.[12]

My argument has been that girls' leisure is not really free time, a break from work, at all, but is, rather, an integral part of their careers as domestic labourers: even the most romantic expressions of girl culture are tempered by realism (there is no equivalent, for example, to the blatant fantasies of young male *Penthouse* culture). But this is not to say that girls have no free time at all. There are times and places where the constraints lose their force – on holiday, in such temporary places as fairgrounds – where girls can risk reputations out of sight of community pressures and gossip. And this relates to a final point about music and girls' leisure. Female deviance is seen, by the media and public opinion, almost entirely in terms of sexual misbehaviour (male deviants are seen as deviant in terms of violence). 'Moral panics' about girls concern schoolgirl pregnancies and prostitution; the worries are about promiscuity, the pill, too-easy abortion and too-mechanical sex education, the media scandals have been the 'yellow teddy bears' and 'passion-flower hotels'. Girl deviants are threats not to order but to the family. And music has a role in this – it is a source of excitement and sensuality which keeps the possibilities of an unconventional female future alive (and which features heavily among the fears of the moralists).[13]

Students

I have been describing teenage girl culture at its least free. While the effects of the sexual division of labour are felt in all youth groups, I don't want to exaggerate the constraints on girls' leisure. My analysis rested on the premise that marriage is *the* female career and, to the extent that it is not, other leisure possibilities open up. Women may achieve independence through their work and earnings (there appears to be some movement in this direction even within teenage culture) or through the political and ideological conscious- ness developed by the struggles of the women's movement. Girls can be just as militant rebels against cultural expectations as the male rebels I described in the last chapter, and rock music can be import- ant to such rebels for its expression of feminist ideas. If the struggle against the male-dominated music industry is likely to be a long one, one of the features of the 1970s rock scene has been the emergence of feminist musicians and records.[14]

Thus, although female students are subject to many of the same pressures on their leisure as female workers, they are less likely to see marriage as their only career possibility and more likely to reject a life of domestic labour on ideological grounds. The sexual differences within student culture are less blatant than those within teenage culture: both sexes share the student version of the sixth-form culture that I described in Chapter 3.

The student market is now as vital a target for record sales as the teenage market used to be – this is reflected in record release policy, in the placing of advertisements, and so on. Indeed, the college circuit is now the most important setting for live rock music and most campuses have nightly discos as well. Student expenditure has been crucial for the development of shops like Virgin Records, magazines like *Melody Maker* and *Rolling Stone*, record companies like Island (I will be discussing this further in Chapter 6). Music is such an im- portant part of student life that most universities have followed Leeds' example in employing a sabbatical entertainments officer, and since the mid-sixties an increasing number of rock musicians have themselves had university education. Lindisfarne, to give one example, were helped in their early days by funds provided by Durham's student union.[15]

In many ways students use rock just like young workers, as an aid to relaxation. But if they are engaged in much the same sort of hedonism and fun, if they are just as heavy drinkers, as sweaty dancers, as sexually eager, students are also distinct from young workers in that the line between their work and their leisure is blurred.

Students have very few direct constraints on any of their time. They don't have much money and they have to study, but the resulting organisation of their days varies from individual to individual and is often difficult to classify: students spend much of their time desultorily reading and writing and thinking as friends drop in and the record player goes full blast – are these times of work or times of leisure?

Students' peculiar organisation of time has a number of consequences for their use of music. Firstly, although most students have a much more intensive collective life than most young workers – living together on campus rather than scattered between parental homes – they are also involved in a much more clearly transitory experience. Student life is bound by the three years of the degree course, and after it is over students are unlikely to live in the same place or even to have the same friends. Preserving their independence and individual identity is important not just for the immediate needs of study but also for the long-term expectations of a different life, and music, as we have already seen in sixth-form culture, can be the key symbol of an individual's tastes and style. It is not the only or even the most common basis for such identity – student groups, cults and friendships are based on a great variety of interests and activities – but when music does become important for a student group it becomes important as the *focus* of attention: rock takes on an ideological purpose that is rarely needed in working-class youth culture.

Students' leisure is further confused by the realisation that higher education is not just the grind of degree work, but involves a much wider process of 'civilisation'. Higher education gives access to culture as well as to knowledge, and 'free time' activities are, in fact, part of the wider learning experience. Leisure concerns art as well as entertainment and in so far as students learn the conventions of traditional high culture, rock may get dragged into the argument, to be given intellectual and aesthetic justification and not just casually enjoyed. Students' tastes become significant, as does their ability to argue their tastes; music is used as a source of value.[16]

In the last ten to fifteen years students' use of rock – whether for relaxation or as a form of art – has transformed not just the predominant sound of universities and colleges but also the music and marketing policies of the record industry. This brings me to my final point. In this section on the consumption of rock I have been arguing that if rock is music aimed at the youth market, that youth market contains different youth groups who use rock in different ways: class, sex and occupational differences have a determinate effect on the leisure choices that young people can make. But there is another source of constraint on youth music that I have mentioned but not analysed: the leisure industry has a determinate effect on the leisure choices that are *available*. Young people's leisure is not just limited by their relation to production as workers, it is also limited by their relation to production as consumers. To understand rock it is not enough to describe what young people do with musical products when they get them, we also have to describe how these musical products got there in the first place.

PART TWO

The production of rock

5

Making records

In this chapter I want to consider the process by which rock music is produced as a commodity. The commodity form of rock is the gramophone record and I will focus on the organisation of record production. Record making is economically, as well as technically, a complex process: music cannot be *just* a product, even in its rawest commodity form, and the artistic value of records has a complicating effect on their production and use. Paul Hirsch has suggested that because the use value of cultural products depends on their consumers' aesthetic preferences, the demand for specific cultural items is much less manageable than that for more straightforwardly utilitarian goods – cultural industries have to make available a far greater number of goods than are eventually successfully marketed. In 1976, for example, British record companies issued 3,152 singles, of which 229 made the Top Twenty, and nearly four thousand albums (including more than a thousand classical discs) of which about two hundred made the Top Thirty. The record industry rests on a comparatively small capital investment per item, but there is intensive competition between items, and sales depend on marketing mechanisms which record companies do not completely control. The consequence is a 'filtering process' that is essential if record companies are not to lose their profits through over-production.[1]

Musicians

To begin, then, with the artist. The show-biz myths of pop artists concern either genius (will-out-despite-being-hidden-in-rags/oppressed-by-philistines/raddled-with-drugs) or luck (he-just-happened-to-be-standing-on-the-pier-when-the-producer-drove-by), but 'creative input' is not just plucked from the sky. Skill and creativity are the result of training and practice, and the real show-biz ideology rests on the Protestant ethic of hard work and dedication – the select earn their star status with years of good work, the show-biz hero is the professional. Being a musician is not just a matter of spontaneous self-expression, but requires the right attitudes and values. In the words of Tony Hatch:

Whether you're a performer or writer, you're the designer, manufacturer and salesman of your own product. Just like a company
producing a new line in household goods, you must put time and
effort into the initial development. Furthermore you will have to
invest money in the promotion and presentation of your product.[2]

It has been estimated that there are fifty thousand rock groups in
Britain, of which less than a thousand have even a hope of getting a
recording contract, but even without recording such musicians are
vital economically to the music industry. Musical expression needs
musical means – on the one hand, musical instruments, on the other
hand, amplification equipment. The average rock group has spent
thousands of pounds before it is even ready to play, and the history
of rock is intimately linked to the history of rock instruments. At the
very beginning of the record-making process are second-hand instrument shops and hire-purchase agreements; recurring rock stories are
of the drummer in a group not for his skills but for his drum kit,
of the guitarist who had to be band leader because he had the only
amplifier. One effect of the technological development of rock – the
increased sophistication of sound systems, the use of synthesised
instruments – has been to up the cost of making the right sounds (let
alone the right music); by 1972, for example, Pink Floyd had spent
more than £40,000 just on their sound equipment.[3]
  Such investments enable musicians to play; once they reach the
next stage, playing publicly, new costs become necessary – a van to
move themselves and their equipment, a roadie to help with the
humping. It is at this stage that 'middlemen' appear, the people who
organise musicians' methods of public communication:

> How many bands do you know that handle themselves, record
> themselves, sell their own records, fix their gigs up? Even the little
> groups that have to scramble for gigs get two of their mates to
> roadie for them. There's no way that Alvin [Stardust] can make it
> on his own. He's got to have an accountant, for example. He
> doesn't have time to sit down and count up his money. His job is
> to sing and perform, nobody tells him how to do that because he's
> got years of experience behind him. If he was a fresh young kid
> he'd have to be taught how to do it. I taught Billy Fury, I helped
> Marty Wilde. Of course they're manipulated. . . .[4]

The music-business formula is that:

> Singers provide the art, managers manipulate it into a saleable
> commodity and record companies give it a vehicle to ride on.

The basic recipe for rock success is sufficient talent, efficient management, and an enterprising record company.[5]

The central ingredient in this recipe is the relationship between the record company and the artist: the company makes its equipment available to the artist to turn his music into a saleable mass commodity. The basic arrangement between musician and company can be simply described:

> The artiste signs directly with the record company for the purpose of making records. The record company pays all the recording costs and pays the artiste an appropriate royalty on the records sold.[6]

But the record company does not just act as the record publisher. The standard recording contract makes it clear that record companies, who are the legal owners of the finished product, expect to exercise the rights of their ownership, controlling what music is issued, how it is produced, when it is released. Companies decide what songs will be on a record, in what order, with what packaging; they are at liberty 'to determine arrangements, accompaniment, etc.'; they can organise an act's performing schedule, as an aspect of record promotion. Companies have the final power to decide whether a song or sound is of sufficient quality to meet the artist's contractual obligations – they are thus able to prevent him recording elsewhere.[7]

The standard contract begins: 'We hereby employ you to render personal services for us or in our behalf for the purpose of recording and making phonograph records'. But if recording artists are providing a service, they are not (like session musicians or the women who pack the discs) paid for it by the hour. They have a stake in the finished product, their payment derives from a proportion of the profit made on every record sold. On signing with a record company musicians get a lump-sum advance against their future royalties, and this advance and the costs of their records' production have to be met before further royalty payments are due. The risk for the record company is that a record may not sell well enough to cover its initial investment; the reality for many musicians is that the value of their contract is deceptive:

> When you take an advance on royalties of say £30,000 up front it looks very good on paper. They say the contract is for two albums a year for three years, so out of that money you have to pay to make six albums and it's hard to make an album for less than £5,000. As the group itself has to pay for recording and mastering,

etc., from a technical point of view all the money has been swallowed up.[8]

It is because of the potential financial conflicts of interest in a recording contract that the relationship between record company and musician is usually negotiated through intermediaries – on the company's behalf, the A&R man and his legal and financial team; on the musician's behalf, the manager and his advisors.

A&R Men

A&R stands for Artists and Repertoire: an A&R man is responsible for what music goes out on a company's label – for getting artists signed to the label, for keeping them there (or dismissing them) and for the records that are issued in their names. It is the A&R men who, like football managers, have to carry the can for failure, and their job, like football management, requires diverse skills.[9]

A large part of an A&R man's time is taken up with watching and listening to unknown acts, assessing their potential. But this is only one form of talent-spotting. Another is poaching, picking up an act when its contract with a rival company runs out. There are various reasons for doing this. Sometimes the hope is to revitalise a fading career; sometimes the move involves a complete change of musical direction; sometimes the new company simply offers an act a greater freedom to carry on doing what it it's doing, in the belief that it has yet to reach its maximum market – in these deals an A&R department is offering sympathy as well as money. At a more cynical level a company might simply outbid its rivals for a known successful act; the decision is based on a straight calculation – what is the act's earning power? What can we afford to offer? These signings are the equivalent of transfer deals in soccer – even with the most established stars, judgements have to be made about future playing potential.[10]

A&R men don't just judge acts, they've also got to be able to spot records, and this, again, in various contexts. Firstly, there are the tape deals offered by independent producers – are they worth it? Secondly, there are foreign, particularly American, catalogues to go through – is an American record, for which a licensing deal is available, likely to be a British success? Thirdly, there are the possibilities of an astute re-release from the back catalogue – there's less money lost if an oldie flops and the profits on a successful re-release are greater; going through back numbers is now part of the A&R routine.

All A&R decisions are basically financial and the calculations have to be precisely made. Companies don't just sign a group and leave them to get on with it, they have to weigh the necessary invest-ment against the possible returns. There are obvious questions to be asked. How ready is the act to record? How much rehearsing time does it need? What advance should it get for equipment? What re-cording costs are necessary? How much help should the company give with organising gigs, tours and publicity?

The answers are not absolute but depend on one simple considera-tion – how much is the act going to earn? And this is where the problems start. Not only may companies calculate this all wrong, but they can't avoid splitting their acts into potential divisions, and a future Division One act is going to get more investment than a possible Division Three-er. The latter musicians inevitably feel neglected, and this becomes one of the major causes of transfer deals – a Third Division act with one company hopes to be treated as First Division with another. It is in this context that competition between record companies is unequal – some have much more capital to risk than others.

Another calculation that A&R departments have to make in signing an act concerns the balance of their label. Some companies like to dabble a finger in every pie – if teeny-bop idols are selling they'll sign a teeny-bop idol; if it's drug-crazed hippies or new-wave punks then they'll have one of them; if discos are a market, they'll make disco music. The problem with this is that a label's identity may become so diffuse that it can attract neither musicians nor audience from the special scenes it's trying to cover. Some companies create their own special labels, as EMI established Harvest, their progressive label, in the late sixties; other companies have tried to change identity with huge, well publicised, signings (CBS's response to progressive rock). Still other companies deliberately develop a specific identity and only sign acts that match it. The independent progressive rock companies, Island and Charisma, are examples: their hope was to build up an audience that trusted the labels and listened sympathetically to any act on them.

Such calculations rest on an assessment of the market, on an under-standing of how records get sold: a record is rarely made without reference to who it's being made for. But ultimately the A&R man's chief responsibility is for the translation of the talent he's signed into a saleable product; traditionally, his most important role was as record producer. At EMI, for example, Cliff Richard in the early sixties was the responsibility of Norrie Paramor, the Beatles in the mid-sixties of George Martin; both men were part of an A&R team, both were expected to supervise recordings, to arrange, engineer and realise their acts' music. These days an A&R department's produc-tion role need not be so direct; the job is still to get the right sound but this means, more and more, getting the right outside producer, studio and engineer. Derek Green of A&M Records explained the eighteen-months gap between signing Andy Fairweather-Low and recording him, this way:

> The reason the first album took so long was because we were searching around for the right producer. We approached all the big names, but none of them could hear the potential in the music. They all said no. Then we finally got through to Elliott Mazer, Neil Young's producer. Although he liked some of the stuff, he wasn't too sure about it at first. We eventually persuaded him. . . .[11]

An artist is bound to a record company by a contract which demands so much 'product' per year; the A&R department has to ensure that the terms of the contract are met. But there's no way to force a musician to make music, and certainly no way to force an act to make good (or commercial) music. Enforcing a contract means keeping everyone happy; preventing freak-outs and piss-abouts, papering over group cracks, having the lads (or lasses) on the road when they should be on the road and in the studio when they should be in the studio; keeping the costs down and the spirits up.[12]

Managers

The relative power of the two sides in the record-company/musician relationship depends on the proven popularity of the artist and on the state of his contract; when the time comes for contract renewal a successful act can use the competition for its services to improve both its financial returns and its musical control. In such dealings musicians' interests are represented by their own managers:

> Strictly speaking, a manager is a personal manager who manages all affairs of the artiste he represents. This means advising on all aspects of the artiste's career, negotiating with agents, press, promotion and publicity, record companies and music publishers. His activities might also include travel arrangements and accompanying the artiste to engagements, assisting with facilities at a club, keeping a watchful eye over the artiste at TV shows or coping with an over-enthusiastic fan at a stage door.
>   In general, a manager does everything for his artiste except actually get up there and sing.

As Hatch suggests, 'a good manager should be an astute businessman, convincing salesman, and part-time psychologist.'[13]

If the A&R man's basic task is to ensure the profitability of his company's musical investments, the manager's goal is to get the best returns for his client. His detailed tasks will vary as his client's career develops – from the early stages of getting an act known, to the final stage of protecting a star from exploitation – but a manager's basic role is as a businessman. His job is to organise his client's finances, to negotiate the best deals with record companies. The earliest involvement of a manager with a musician is often, in fact, as a source of the capital which enables a group's members to buy their equipment, to support themselves while they rehearse. The group is as much an investment for the manager as for the record company. According to Tony Stratton-Smith, manager of Lindisfarne, Bell'n' Arc, Genesis and Van Der Graaf Generator:

> . . . all our bands are on a wage or retainer, whatever you want to call it. The reason for this is that in the early days their earnings are very uneven and sometimes they'll have a good week, sometimes they'll have a bad week, and I feel that a minimum amount of security anyway is necessary for a band to keep, to remain really objective about the important things, the important things being their performance and their writing, and as long as they can pay the rent and live and all this sort of thing every week they're more likely to work well. It's the old thing about contented cows giving the best milk. Therefore you've got to be prepared, on our method anyway, to run a band on a deficit for quite a long time.[14]

Managers may become involved in the creation of the product itself. Chas Chandler, manager of Slade:

> I look for material, work with the group, advising on songs they write, on the stage act, seeing them as often as possible on stage so that you can advise them as often as possible.[15]

Even if they are not so directly involved in the music making, many managers see their role as showmen: their task is to ensure the overall impact of their clients, to organise the 'image' that will best sell them. At a more personal level, managers have to be both elder brothers, keeping their musicians happy, and hustlers, protecting their boys from attack, from whatever source. The complexity of the managerial role makes it unsurprising that at least two managers – Albert Grossman and Peter Grant – have succeeded in upstaging their own acts (Bob Dylan and Led Zeppelin) for sheer on-screen dynamism in documentary films supposedly showcasing their clients.[16]
When conflicts do arise between manaegr and band there is often

confusion as to who really made the band what it is. *Melody Maker* once presented a nice parody of the process of act creation:

> Up in the boardroom of a record company the fat cigar brigade are scratching heads. Binn and Batman have come up with another surefire hit and they want somebody fresh to market it. They ponder a few names and finally decide on one with slight but clear sexual connotations – suggestively camp.
>
> Name settled, they work on the people who will be in this new band. They might be able to find a ready-made group to fit the bill but better to mould their own. There's a singer who has been around a few years.
>
> He's not great but he knows how to throw himself around a stage, has a hairy chest and can hit the high notes. Give him a new name and he'll do. Somebody knows a lead guitarist who can play a bit and looks good. They can advertise for the others.
>
> They'll work out a sensational stage act, rig them up in some flash gear, buy them the best equipment and arrange a string of appearances in some influential venues. Plunge a few thousand quid in launching them with advertising and posters and 'They'll be the biggest thing since sliced bread', chief fat cigar tells his underlings.
>
> Session musicians are employed to record the single, and being a Binn and Batman special the radio stations label it 'chart bound' and play it twenty-five times a day. Seeing the glossy photos in the bop mags the kids gather up their pennies and buy it.
>
> VOILA, stars are born – or manufactured.[17]

An increasingly important role in the British rock business in the 1970s has been played by independent manager/producers like Binn and Batman. They function, in creative terms, as mini record companies: the producer finds and contracts his own acts, records them at his own expense and brings the finished tape to a record company; the company presses it, releases it on one of its own labels and pays a royalty to the producer on every copy sold. If the record flops it's a cheap deal for a record company, which has been spared the production costs; if the record's a success, the company has to pay a higher royalty on every copy sold than if it had put the record together itself. Independent production was pioneered by the successful writer/producers of the late sixties – Mickie Most, Shel Talmy, Tony Hatch, Roger Cook and Roger Greenaway, Tony Macauley; there are now few successful A&R men who don't eventually work as independents.[18]

Publishers

Once the musician and his manager have made their contract with a record or production company, there is one more 'input' necessary: the music. Recorded rock needn't have lyrics, needn't be written down, may be improvised on the spot, but a recording is, legally, always a recording of a specific piece of music, a song, and song recording involves a further character, the song publisher. The music publisher was the central figure of the music industry before the development of recording and, although his role has changed, he remains important. Firstly, the publisher is a source of material. Freddie Bienstock:

> For years I would collect and submit all songs to [Elvis Presley] before a recording session, and he would not look at a song before I had seen it first, which didn't mean that I would pick them, I would just screen them for him, and then out of those that I had screened, he would make his own selections.[19]

The publisher, in this case, acts as the link between a song writer and a recording artist, on the one hand placing his clients' work with record companies, on the other hand advising recording acts on possible hit material. The latter job is often a matter of advice on well known and previously published material – a publisher's back catalogue is a permanent source of potentially re-recordable songs; the former job involves acting as the supporter and promoter of a writer in much the same way as a manager acts as the supporter and promoter of a performer. Publishers are writers' employers, either subsidising them until their songs are successful (as the publisher Dick James subsidised Elton John and Bernie Taupin), or using them to produce songs to a given formula. Carole King:

> Every day we squeezed into our respective cubby holes with just enough room for a piano, a bench and maybe a chair for the lyricist if you were lucky. You'd sit there and write and you could hear someone in the next cubby hole composing a song exactly like yours. The pressure in the Brill Building was really terrific – because Donny [Kirshner – a music publisher] would play one song-writer against another. He'd say: 'We need a new smash hit' – and we'd all go back and write a song and the next day we'd each audition for Bobby Vee's producer.[20]

In either case, in order to sell and place their songs, publishers have to make their own 'demo-discs' and are obliged to develop their own independent production companies.

The publisher's second role is as the administrator of a song's rights after it has been recorded and performed. Even when musicians are recording their own material and don't need a publisher to provide or place material, they do need someone to ensure that their rights in their own songs are protected, that they get the income due from their songs' sales and use. Publishers provide the necessary legal and administrative expertise and are involved in the promotion and marketing of their clients' material – not just records, but sheet music, live performances and cover versions.[21]

Producers

We have now got together the necessary inputs for record making – a musician's skill and art, a record company's capital, a song. The next stage in the process is the combination of these inputs into the product, the record, and the most creative role at this stage is played by the record producer. If A & R can be described in terms analogous to football management, record production is best described as analogous to film production. The first task of the record producer is as organiser and coordinator. It is his task to get the artist into the studio, to make sure the necessary session musicians and engineers are on hand, the right recording equipment set up. The task involves musical as well as administrative decisions. A producer has to plan a recording session in advance, decide how the potential material can be best arranged and embellished. As producer John Anthony put it:

> There's one right way to do an album and four hundred wrong ones. That's the point of having a producer. Groups don't know what their faults are.[22]

In making such decisions producers are obviously liable to clash with the recording musicians, and a producer has to be able to manage the tensions, has to keep his whole team happy in what can be an extremely tedious and fraught process. In the words of Bob Johnston, 'the whole thing of record producing to me is psychiatry really'; for Gus Dudgeon, 'the whole job of the producer is to make the artist as comfortable as possible'.[23]

It is in these administrative and managerial respects that a record producer's job is like that of a film producer, and he has a similar production team: an arranger, equivalent to the screen-play writer; an engineer, equivalent to the cameraman; numbers of technicians, from the lowly tape operators (this is the normal starting point for a career in record production) to the highly skilled and experienced session musicians.[24]

But in other respects the record producer's job is more creative, more like that of the film director: it is the producer who is responsible for getting the sound that is the essence of a record. To some extent he is dependent for this on technology; the possibilities of sound recording lie in the technical equipment available in a studio and in the skills of the studio engineer. The latter's job may be simply to 'get on tape what's going out in the studio' but his individual ear is important, even in this electronic process. As engineer Glyn Johns has pointed out:

> If one of the engineers in there and myself, if we both did a session with identically the same set-up, even, and the same musicians, the same piece of music, it'd sound totally different. It's the way that the engineer hears the piece of music. He injects a tremendous amount into the atmosphere, that's the other thing. Any record, to my way of thinking, has to have, has to give you a mental picture when you hear it. I think the engineer's job is to present a mental picture in sound that he thinks suits the number and the artist.[25]

As studios have developed in complexity, and as consumers have demanded increasingly sophisticated sounds to play on their hi-fis, the engineer has begun to share the producer's creative job. This is most obvious at the mixing stage (equivalent to the editing stage in film making): the results of recording sessions, these days recorded on 16 or 24 tracks of a tape recorder, can be mixed to bring up certain sounds and obliterate others, to alter tones, overdub harmonies, wipe off mistakes; sessions can be cut and edited without any reference to the musicians involved and the record which results may be as much the expression of the technical skills of the producer and his engineer as of the musical skills of the credited artists.[26]

The importance of their contribution to a record is such that producers may become more influential than the people they produce, as record companies look to them as the source of sales success; but in looking at the careers of producers we can distinguish two different approaches to the job. The importance of some producers rests on their ability to translate an artist's music into a recorded sound, on their ability to realise on record musical ideas that are fundamentally those of the musicians concerned. Production from this point of view is 'doing the best you can for the artists to get their music out'; in the words of producer Norman Smith, 'I am there simply to highlight a melody and create accompaniment.' The problem is that producers also have an obligation to the record companies that employ them. The object of recording is to realise music in a commercially successful form and, in Mickie Most's words, 'the trouble is most artists have a private view of themselves and most of the time it's wrong'.[27]

Partly as a consequence of this difficulty, a second approach to production has developed – the producer not as the realiser of a given sound but as its creator. In this case it is the musicians who express the producer's ideas and not vice versa. The results of this approach can be most clearly heard in teen-beat singles, a genre in which there is a tradition of producers perfecting a best-selling sound, to which every other aspect of the record – melody, lyric, performance – is made subordinate.[28]

Manufacture

Eventually, a final mix is approved by the record company for issue, but as a commodity the record is still not complete. It may take an exceptional event – the PVC shortage, the refusal of EMI's packers to touch the Sex Pistol's single – to publicise it, but there is always a post-studio stage of record production, as tapes are made into records, as the records themselves are packaged. This manufacturing process takes up about a fifth of the production costs of both singles and LPs, and cutting and pressing plants are the fixed capital of the record industry. Technical developments in manufacture have, as well, musical implications. When shellac was replaced by polyvinyl chloride as the raw material of records, for example, the result was not simply that the easily breakable and weighty 78 was replaced by plastic discs; the new cutting process meant that much more sophisticated and complex sounds could now be reproduced. This manufacturing change in the early fifties was the precondition for the development of rock in the mid-sixties.[29]

Rock's history has been similarly, if rather less significantly, bound up with changes in packaging, as companies have appeared who specialise in sleeve design. There is little evidence that cover design has any effect on the sales of records (often, in fact, covers seem to be aimed at attracting the retailer rather than the consumer) but successful musicians often seek to have control of their records' packaging built into their contracts. The sleeve design is used to complement the music, as another form of creative expression; the costs of such 'artistic' packaging can be substantial.[30]

Promotion

I have described record production in terms that are appropriate for any process of commodity production: records are the result of contributions from a variety of forms of labour. If the basic inputs are musicians' skills, record companies' capital, pieces of music, the value of the finished product depends on inputs from many other workers – producers and engineers, labourers in the pressing plants, sleeve designers and printers. Each contribution to record making rests on its own organisation of capital, and the result is a complex industry in which the overall capital investment is large, but in which the actual cost of each commodity can be comparatively small. Record companies seek to exploit their fixed capital to the full, to use studios twenty-four hours a day, to operate their pressing plants without slack, but this is where we come to the special nature of records as cultural commodities – demand for them is not easily controllable. So far I have only covered one element in the consequent 'filtering process' – the A & R department, through which the mass of potential recording musicians passes, to emerge as a trickle. Once through this net, a musician can be almost certain that a record will emerge – that was the purpose of his contract – but for his record company the point of record issue is the point where the problems of over-production begin. The 'filtering process' becomes most apparent in the strategies which companies are compelled to adopt to realise the exchange value of their products on the market:

Things started to move for Queen about a year ago when they recorded their first album for Trident, who have a distribution deal with EMI. An advance was paid to them to help with the immediate costs of putting them on the road. Review copies of the album – about 400 of them – were sent out to everyone who might conceivably have any influence on the record buying public, from discos to the national press. Copies were personally distributed to radio and TV producers and extensive advertising space was bought up in the trade papers.

'They're all good-looking guys and I did a round of the teeny papers and all the girls in the office swooned over them. Brian, the lead guitarist, had made his own guitar and a couple of the nationals picked up on that. It was good, gossipy stuff.' [John Bagnall, EMI promotions man.]

Queen's publicity machine was working from all angles because they were also getting extra promotion from Tony Brainsby's promotion office. . . . The intensity of it all paid off when they were invited to do a spot on *The Old Grey Whistle Test*. Radio Luxembourg latched upon the single 'Keep Yourself Alive' and played it regularly.

Their first local tour, supporting Mott the Hoople, got the full works. Local press was saturated with releases about this new band which was shortly coming to their town, elaborate displays were arranged at the front of the house on the night of the concert, local disc-jockeys were informed, and window displays made in about 200 local record shops.

'Trident and EMI committed themselves right from the start to this band, to make sure they had a PA which was better than other bands had and to make sure they had the right clothes. Some of their outfits cost £150 each,' said Bagnall.[31]

In the event, neither Queen's initial album nor their single made the charts but their subsequent success has justified the original campaign (which cost 'between £5,000 and £10,000') and this description of it makes clear the variety of tasks involved. Firstly, every record company has its own publicity office. Its task is to get publicity for the company's acts and releases and its focus is mainly on the press; from its pens come streams of prose, whether news of who's recording what and performing where or hype – hyperbolic accounts of the latest product. The specialist press – music papers like *Melody Maker*, girl magazines like *Fab 208* – are the main recipients of record-company blurbs, but attention is always given to the promotional possibilities of other publications. Publicists are salesmen, and one noticeable feature of the British music industry is that record companies' public faces tend to be female. The press office is one of the few areas in the music business in which women can have a career; 'feminine' qualities, sexiness or beauty, are apparently seen as valuable aids in the job of charming favours from the sources of publicity.[32]

The work of the company staff is complemented by that of independent publicists, employed by artists or their managers directly. Their approach can be more intense – they can concentrate on their client and don't have to cope with a new product every week – but their object is, equally, 'free' publicity, publicity not directly paid for (like the companies' advertisements), even if it is, indirectly, the result of the costly distribution of free records, drinks, parties and promotional trips.[33]

The object of promotion is to sell records. To achieve that end it is not enough just to get the consumer into the record shop; it is also necessary to ensure that the record shop is stocking the product you're seeking to sell. One of the key jobs in record promotion involves working with retailers – persuading them to stock new records, organising in-shop displays, ensuring that they exploit the demand generated by local publicity. In America, with its vast selling area, local promotion is often handled by independent salesmen, carrying the products of several different companies; in Britain the job is done by field promoters, record-company employees with regional assignments.[34]

Given the size and expense of their teams of publicists and promoters it is ironic that most record companies agree that 'the only form of promotion proven to be effective in increasing sales of gramophone records is airplay'.[35] Telling people to listen to a record isn't the same as making them hear it, and one complete spin on Radio 1 is worth any number of full-page ads in *NME* or critical raves from a reviewer. To sell a record, companies have got to get a sound to the public, and to do this they have to go through a 'gatekeeper', the disc-jockey; the record companies' problem is that the most effective form of record selling is not under their direct control. The DJ, whether on radio or in a discothèque, is independent not just legally (payola, the record companies' attempt to control airplay by direct payment, is illegal in the USA and banned by BBC and IBA regulations in Britain) but also because of the nature of his job – to please his public. He can't just service the record industry, because if he doesn't play what his audience wants to hear he'll be out of work himself. But neither can he ignore his commercial importance – like it or not, his position is one of control over what the public will hear and his effect is on sales; a DJ who never moved anyone to buy anything would be a failure even by his own standards. A disc-jockey must hope that the records he plays will sell, not because that will benefit him directly but because if his taste is thus confirmed his audience will continue to attend his disco or tune in to his show.[36]

Radio

Even when payola is legal, it has its limits. There have been radio stations on the British music scene on which companies could buy plays direct: this was one of the reasons for the importance of the pirate radio ships, and for a long time it determined the musical policy of Radio Luxembourg. From 1946 until 1968 it was possible for companies to buy plays on Lux (at about £15 per play in the 1960s) and even to buy quarter-hour segments, so that the station was often, in effect, simply broadcasting a series of record-company commercials. In 1968, however, the station started using only live DJs (rather than pre-recorded programmes) and insisted that bought plays be spread through the schedule. In 1970 programme control was made even tighter: plays could still be bought but they were now programmed according to the needs of the radio station itself. It had become clear that the two goals involved – to sell records on the one hand, to attract listeners on the other – were not necessarily identical; when the two clashed too obviously not even direct payment was sufficient to ensure that the station would organise airplay according to the industry's needs. The history of Radio Luxembourg in the last decade has been the history of a radio station reasserting its control of its programmes.[37]

The BBC, for whom pay-for-play has rarely been a problem, has developed a very similar control over its programmes on Radio 1. The basic constraint on the BBC is the size of its potential audience. There's hardly anyone in Britain who can't listen to the radio and as a public service the BBC is obliged to consider the needs and interests of all this population. Since 1967, Radio 1 has been confined to providing a pop service; but even that is aimed at a vast and varied market, and this affects what comes out in two ways. Firstly, the BBC is obsessed with audience size, shape and satisfaction; secondly, the corporation can't escape consciousness of its responsibilities – its programmes are the product of an elaborate and cautious bureaucracy, there must be no scandal or uncertainty or offence. Underlying Radio 1's use of records is an old slogan: Giving the Public What it Wants.

The public is divided into three parts – weekday daytime, weekday evening, and weekend – and the most important of these is the weekday daytime; the daily 'strip' shows (programmes broadcast at the same time and with the same format every day) are the core of the BBC's presentation of pop. Originally it was the responsibility of the producer of each show to put together an appropriate programme, but this system had to be dropped when it was discovered that some popular (i.e. best-selling) records were never being chosen. Sales are the best indication of what the pop public wants, and if Radio 1 was ignoring sales then clearly the BBC was not fulfilling its obligations; hence, the play-list.

Play-list broadcasting originated on commercial radio in the States: the station manager would draw up a list of records and all the DJs would be required to play only records on the list. In 1973, soon after Radio Luxembourg had switched to its play-list policy, the BBC began to organise Radio 1 in the same way. Each week a panel including the four producers of the daily shows meets to put together a play-list of records for them all. Presently the list contains forty singles plus a 'second page' of new releases, oldies and album tracks; on each hour of daytime Radio 1 you can hear about ten tracks from the play-list page one, and about eight from the play-list page two. The basis of the play-list is the chart of record sales; the usual rule is that every climber in the Top Fifty will be on the list, and that every record that has dropped out of the Top Twenty won't be; the charts yield thirty to thirty-five of the records on the play-list and the balance is made up with new releases, but even these are often chart 'certainties' – new records from big stars, follow-ups to big hits.[38]

The BBC is contemptuously certain that Radio 1 satisfies its listeners, but it can only be so certain because its argument is circular. A record on its play-list has a good chance of being a hit, a single not on it has hardly a hope. These results seem to confirm the producers' judgements, but they are equally a consequence of them. BBC people refer to a record which gets *Top of the Pops* TV exposure but doesn't make the Top Fifty as a 'dog record' – it must be exceptionally unappealing to gain nothing from the industry's best promotional spot; but it's just as unusual for a record to get full Radio 1 treatment and flop, and even more unusual for a record to get no BBC airplay and make it.

Radio 1 knows its importance for the record business and doesn't wear its responsibilities lightly. One reason for its elaborate organisation is to minimise the possibilities of payola, and while the BBC has good relations with record companies (they're all part of the showbiz family) the business's direct radio salesmen, the pluggers (whose job it is to persuade radio producers to programme their wares) don't get much direct joy. But though the BBC's honour is intact, its account of its role in pop – as a sort of honest broker, benevolently selecting from the mass of weekly releases just those records its audience wants to hear – is disingenuous. The BBC moulds as well as responds to public taste and record companies respond to as well as mould the play-list. Pluggers may not be able to persuade BBC producers to use air-play deliberately to benefit record companies, but they can persuade them that record companies are producing the records that are the means to the BBC's own ends. The plugger's task is to convince a producer that a record is right for his show, and if a record company can suss out a radio station's ideology of entertainment then it can service the station's demand for music so successfully that airplay for its products does become indirectly controllable. British pop stations, whatever their source of income, have remarkably similar ideologies and almost identical play-list policies. I will be discussing radio use of rock further in Chapter 7; my concern here is with rock's use of radio, and my point is that even if record companies have no direct control of the 'gatekeepers' of the airwaves, their guesses at the passwords can be, none the less, well informed and routinely accurate.[39]

Discos

Much the same argument can be applied to the second source of airplay, discothèques. Clubs with records as their *only* means of entertainment came to Britain (from France) in the early sixties; before then DJs and records had been used in ballrooms but not as alternatives to live music. Initially discos served two sorts of in-crowd – rock aristocrats, seeking exclusion, and soul freaks; but by the late sixties, as live rock became increasingly undanceable, expensive and in the wrong places (colleges and concert halls), discos took on general significance as places where a lot of record buyers were hearing a lot of records. Record companies were slow to realise the implications, but finally began to notice inexplicably high sales for records which they had long since ceased to promote. Today, all record companies have their lists of five hundred or more clubs and DJs, and a substantial part of promotional energy is directed at discothèques:

Hi. Just a very quick note to ask you all for your extra help with the Don Covay single. We just heard that it's No. 54 this week so the Beeb may well drop it off their play-list next week. So what happened with 'You Can Do Magic', 'Walking Miracle', The Stylistics, etc. can happen again if you just give this record an extra push for a week. Then we may well have a chance of getting this record out of the ruts of the 50s and into the coveted Top Twenty where it certainly deserves to be as reactions have been so fantastic. Thank you.[40]

Jonathan King has explained why discos are worth a special promotional effort:

Discothèques have two great advantages: one, exactly the sort of person you're selling a record to goes to a discothèque, and two, you get your record played at massive volume, which is how a lot of records ought to be heard. And a third thing is that that class and that type of person is the all-time spread-the-word person – they've got nothing else to talk about except football.[41]

Payola in discos is not illegal, and at first glance there doesn't seem to be any reason why a record company shouldn't play a disco DJ to play its records. But, as with Radio Luxembourg, a disco DJ is constrained by his own purposes: his job is not to sell records but to entertain a crowd. A DJ puts on a show and it's for his show that his records are selected. His audience wants to dance (and sometimes smooch), it wants to be surprised (by something new) and confirmed (by traditional favourites), it wants to remember the past (oldies) and bask in the present (current hits); a DJ must put on a balanced show and the balance must be in response to the needs of a particular dancing audience. In the end, a DJ couldn't afford to let his show be determined by a record company, he has to be able to respond to the immediate demands of his crowd.[42]

Live performance

So far I have discussed two forms of record promotion: the first, making a record known to the public, depends on the co-operation of the controllers of publicity, writers and editors of newspapers and magazines; the second, getting a record heard by the public, depends on the co-operation of the controllers of the airwaves, disc-jockeys and radio-station administrators. The third form of record promotion is live performance, and this depends on the co-operation of two more 'gatekeepers' – the agent and the promoter. The agent is contracted by an artist to get him gigs (for a percentage of the fee he can negotiate) and acts as the link between musicians and the theatres, ballrooms, clubs and colleges that are their regular employers; the promoter puts on his own shows, himself hiring the venues and the musicians (whom he gets, in turn, from an agent). The most important rock promoters, like Tony Smith, promote tours:

> I provide basically a tour that makes sense so that you don't go to Glasgow one night, play Southampton the next, and appear in Newcastle the next. Then with municipal halls you have to put down a guarantee which means £100 up front for each concert. You arrange the lighting and spotlights, the box-office facilities, staff required on the night, poster design and printing as well as the tickets. Advertising in the local Press. Sometimes there are travelling arrangements, finding out the best hotels. You must go out on tour as well to ease the group over any problems. All this averages out at about £500 a concert, which would include the rental of the hall.[43]

Add the cost of the musicians, subtract the total from the evening's gate and you have the promoter's profit. Clearly his risk lies in whether or not an act will draw a crowd, and in the past it was vital for a rock promoter to have acts with hit records – the record acted as promotion for the performance. In the 1960s Robert Stigwood, among others, organised huge packages of acts from the Top Twenty, whose positions on the bill changed as their records changed places in the charts; even today small promoters, such as colleges, are predominantly interested in acts which have indicated their drawing power by selling records. But increasingly the tour has become a form of record promotion, fitting into a record-company campaign in which record sales are the end rather than the beginning. Dave Laing has described the standard chain that nowadays links the public and the live rock artist:

> Beginning with the artist's manager, the chain includes the agent who gets him work, the promoter who sets up nationwide tours, the record company which usually underwrites live shows, the venue manager responsible for security and for providing the required stage and power facilities, local radio stations and record shops for publicity, and the press, whose reviews can sometimes affect the success of a concert tour.[44]

Live rock shows have become very expensive, as stage and sound effects have had to reflect the developed technology of the studio and as musicians have adopted increasingly sophisticated standards of showmanship – acts whose reputations rest on the complexity or drama of their records can't afford to disappoint fans with anything less complex and dramatic on stage. For the biggest rock groups it has become almost impossible to make a profit on ticket sales alone. The Rolling Stones' 1976 European tour, for example, cost about £2 million to present:

> The purpose is not so much to make money but for the Stones to do what they like doing best – playing to live audiences. In addition the tour should add 300,000 to 400,000 copies to the sale of their latest album.[45]

The effect of these developments is to turn the promoter from an entrepreneur, risking his capital against box-office profit, into an expert, laying on a service for a fee and leaving the record company to carry the costs from its promotional budget. The promoter is paid for his ability to put on a show and, like the record producer, is dependent on a team of specialists, from the humble roadie to the skilled carpenters, electricians, lighting men, stage designers and sound mixers. The stage crew for a rock tour is as elaborate and as expensive as that of a theatre company – the difference is that whereas the theatre is subsidised by the state, rock concerts are subsidised by record companies, convinced that money-losing tours pay off, eventually, in record sales.[46]

Retailers

The final filter through which records must pass on their way from record company to consumer is the record retailer. I have already suggested, in my reference to field promotion, that record companies have to ensure that their products are readily available and, in Britain, that means ensuring that they are available in shops. There is no significant mail-order purchase of records and the record clubs, which rarely sell rock LPs, account for less than 10% of the total album market. The basic sales outlet is the record shop, and record companies are directly in charge of their own retail distribution – they do not work through wholesalers.[47]

The fivefold expansion of record sales since the war has not affected the number of record retailers (there have been six to seven thousand outlets throughout) but their form: records are now a significant part of the stock of the multiple department stores – W. H. Smith has been the country's largest record seller since 1963 – and two events have been significant in this development. Firstly, there was the fifties emergence of cheap labels, distributed by rack-jobbers through non-specialist shops (a rack-jobber normally pays a shop to let him keep a rack of records on its premises – he and the shop share the proceeds of the sales but it is entirely his responsibility to keep the rack stocked). Gala began such distribution in 1958, and the major companies began their own cheap labels in 1959; by 1974 there were at least twenty budget labels accounting for about a quarter of unit record sales – their importance for department stores is reflected in the statistic that Woolworths has about 8% of full-priced record sales and more than 30% of budget sales.[48]

The second major retailing event was the abolition of resale price maintenance on records in 1969 which led, after some delay, to a High Street price-cutting war, popular albums proving a valuable loss leader for the multiples. In 1972, specialist record shops still accounted for about 75% of full-price record sales; by 1974 their market share was less than half. The effect of this sort of competition seems to be a new form of specialisation: record shops can no longer compete for the general rock or pop market as *record* specialists, but they can use their expertise and stock policy to specialise in particular *musical* genres, focusing on classical music, rock, soul or country. The result is a new sort of filter for record companies to get through – they are faced with a market frozen into a series of specific tastes.[49]

Consumption

By now, though, the consumer has got his or her record and there is only one more piece to fit into the music-business jigsaw – he or she has to have something on which to play it! The record industry is an aspect of the hi-fi and electrical-goods industry: the more people who have record players, the more who will buy records and vice versa. And there is a qualitative relationship here too: the development of progressive rock albums in the sixties was made possible by the marketing of cheap stereo record players, and the developing tastes of stereo owners have had a clear effect on rock styles and recording techniques.[50]

In the end, though, the important thing about the act of record consumption is that it starts the whole process all over again. People are inspired by their records to make music for themselves; record sales are correlated with the sales of musical instruments. From the mass of rock consumers emerge new rock musicians, impatient to be the first input into a new process of record making.[51]

6

Making money

The classical music publisher Ernst Roth once suggested that what distinguished pop publishers from himself was not the pursuit of profit as such but rather the problems involved in this pursuit: whereas his task was 'to make the public like what his composers produce', the pop publisher's task was to make his composers produce what the public like. This argument is borne out by a pop publisher:

> My job is to sell entertainment to the public . . . I am no different to the man who sells soap or insurance. I don't tell the public what to like, I give them what they want.[1]

The implication is that in the pop business music is made to meet demand; the process of record production that I have described, from 'creative input' to final consumption, should be turned the other way: what the public consumes determines what gets produced. From this perspective the most significant 'gatekeeper' is the consumer. In the words of record company boss Dick Leahy:

> The first essential factor, of course, is selection of product. I hope we know what records to reject. We don't go picking up product just for the sake of it – we always ask first 'who is going to buy it?' If we can't answer that question we don't release the record.[2]

An economic survey of the record industry in 1971 concluded that 'the only certain factor in marketing records is the uncertainty'. It has always been the object of record companies to defy the uncertainties of mass taste, to produce certain hits, but in the last analysis successful record selling depends on the knowledge of a market that is not easily manipulated. Rock is music aimed at a youth market and the youth market has a decisive effect on the popular music that everyone hears. Hirsch has calculated that 70% of all records purchased by Americans are intimately related to the selection process by which Top Forty hits are made, and what happens on the charts 'profoundly affects' all music heard via the American mass media, whether on radio or TV, or in performance. The same argument can be applied to Britain.[3]

Exploiting the market

The youth market didn't become of central importance to the music
business until the 1950s, well after most of the important technical
changes in musical communication – the gramophone (first marketed
in 1899), sound broadcasting (1919), electrical recording (1925),
talking films (1927), long-playing records (1948), magnetic tape
(1950). Subsequent developments have really been refinements –
stereo (1958) and quadrophonics (1969). The effects of video recording (1963) have yet to be felt – and the technological development
that turned out to be the most significant for the record business
made its effect negatively: during the 1950s TV took over from the
radio as the basic form of home entertainment, leaving radio to
specialise in its appeal. One of the most important 'special' markets
turned out to be the young and, with the simultaneous development of LPs, adults ceased to buy singles. The day-to-day
attentions of record companies became focused almost entirely on
teenagers.[4]

The old pop musicians were not slow to express their concern at
the results. Harry Roy:

When *we* sang a song we really meant it. We learned the business.
It took me years, when I was in my brother's band, just to learn
how to walk to the stand and take a bow. The kids of today
couldn't care less about people who are artists.[5]

But at the outset the exploitation of the new market seemed to
mean, at least in Britain, little more than a new content for an old
form, 'the standard pop song'. For youth appeal the song simply had
to emphasise teenage subjects in the lyrics and be sung by

a working-class boy of not more than eighteen, preferably with a
shock of hair, preferably without a trained voice or musical
knowledge, who will put it over as though he believed in it.[6]

The marketing and promotion men soon had a variety of teen-
appeal media to use – the magazines *Romeo*, *Mirabelle* and *Valentine*,
the TV programmes *6.5 Special* and *Oh Boy!*, the radio show *Saturday
Club*, were all launched between 1956 and 1958. But the actual process of 'assembly-line production in music' (which Francis Newton
has called 'one of the few really original and appalling achievements
of our century in the arts') seemed unaltered.[7]

The music business had been founded in the nineteenth century as
a writing and publishing business, and the traumatic effects on it of

broadcasting and recording had both been worked through in the 1920s and 1930s. In Britain the Gramophone Company, established in 1898, merged with the slightly later Columbia Gramophone Company to form Electrical and Musical Industries in 1931; by 1952, when the electrical firm Philips created a record company, EMI's only rival was Decca, and in 1959, after the rock'n'roll explosion, the domination of the market by EMI and Decca was still complete (see Tables 8 and 9). Rock'n'roll had been adapted to existing company practices and the A & R men had simply turned their skills to marketing teenage show-biz stars. The only immediate business effect of rock'n'roll was the increased share of the market won by American material. For the record companies this was not a serious problem – American products still reached the British consumer via the British record companies acting as licensees – but the 'invasion' was a threat to British writers and publishers. The Song Writers' Guild sourly noted that 'of course, if you plug American music there is bound to

Table 8:
Share of UK record market by company, 1959–75

	% 1959	% 1965	% 1970	% 1975 45s	 LPs
EMI	} 75	34	25	18	16
Decca		24	13	5	8
Philips (Phonogram after 1971)	8	8	4·5	8	6
Pye	8	8	4	7	4
CBS	—	8	12	12	9
World Record Club/Concert Hall/Readers Digest	3–4	7	6	—	—
Saga	—	2·5	—	—	—
Deutsche Grammophon	—	2	—	—	—
Music for Pleasure	—	2	} 7·25	—	6
Pickwick	—	—		—	7
Polydor	—	—	7·25	9	7
RCA	—	—	6	5	6
WEA	—	—	3	6	6
Island	—	—	—	4	—
A&M	—	—	—	3	3
UA	—	—	—	2	—
Bell (Arista after 1975)	—	—	—	8	—
Magnet	—	—	—	2	—
K Tel/Arcade	—	—	—	—	6

Note: Figures refer to units sold, not cash turnover and are very rough estimates.
Source: RB, 23, 1960; 98, 1966; 159, 1971; *BPI Year Book*, 1976.

Table 9:
UK Top Ten singles and UK major record companies, 1955–66

	% Top Ten produced by EMI and Decca	% Top Ten produced by EMI, Decca, Philips and Pye
1955	77·5	97·5
1956	79	100
1957	73·2	97·2
1958	87·7	98·6
1959	74·3	96
1960	75·3	92·9
1961	71·8	94·4
1962	76·2	98·8
1963	79·6	100
1964	76	98·1
1965	65·5	90
1966	57·6	86·8

Source: Gillett, 'Big Noise from Across the Water.'

be a demand for it', and demanded a quota on foreign songs and records played on the radio:

> Only so will it be possible to arrest the persistent foreign infiltra-tions which have for some years strongly and undesirably influ-enced every department of popular music in this country.[8]

The secretary of the Guild argued that Elvis's records were only bought because teenagers sought to follow fashion, not because they really liked them: 'if the BBC started plugging quality songs for a change I'm sure the kids would go for them.' As it was, DJs had too much power:

> if we have to have a high proportion of American hits in our popular music diet, then it would be refreshing if British artists were allowed to make their own individual interpretations of these imported tunes.[9]

For both record companies and music publishers, rock'n'roll was just another product, rock'n'rolling off the assembly-line of standard pop; there was no reason, except biased DJs and gullible kids, why the British industry could not produce it just as successfully as the Americans.

It was because of rock'n'roll's lack of impact on the record business that skiffle, much less important musically, was much more import-ant for the development of the British youth market (skiffle was, indeed, seen by contemporary commentators as a much more genuine form of youthful expression). It was skiffle that gave young British musicians the chance to develop their own ideas (which soon reverted to rock'n'roll or R&B) outside the framework of the industry; skiffle gave them the folk confidence to play without skill, with poorly amplified instruments and crude rhythms. The most immediately noticeable thing for the business about the Beatles, when they eventually arrived, was their (and their manager's) detachment from Tin Pan Alley – they wrote their own songs![10]

Historians of American popular music have constructed a model in which musical innovation always comes from outside the major record companies. Only local independents can provide an outlet for the expression of new ideas and interests, and only when such ideas have been shown to be nationally popular do the major companies use their financial advantages to take them over, to homogenise and formalise the music, to create a new 'safe' product, which remains dominant until a new innovation emerges from a new local base. Such innovations in an oligopolistic industry are made possible by technological changes which open gaps in existing market control, but in the long run the important link is between record-company competition and musical creativity – the more sources of capital, the more chance of musical progress.[11]

If this model is applicable to Britain, it is so only in lagged form. The Beatles may have written their own songs, but they were signed to EMI and recorded by George Martin, an EMI staff producer. The other British groups in the beat boom of 1963–4 were signed to the other major companies and the boom was, in fact, a boom for the big British companies (see Table 9). The immediate impact of the beat groups matched that of rock'n'roll – new teenage magazines, *Jackie, Rave, Fab 208*; a new TV programme, *Ready Steady Go*; only the radio response was genuinely innovative, with the first broadcast, in 1964, from Radio Caroline. *Retail Business*'s special issue on records the same year made two firm assertions: the volatility of the teenage market would continue – 'even the Beatles' expectation of life "at the top of the pops" should be measured in months, not years'; and stereo records, then commanding about 12% of the market, would continue to have limited sales: 'the future of stereo would seem to be limited by the fact that its technical advantages can only be fully realised in the case of classical music . . . there are important marketing considerations which make it unsuitable for the pops market.[12]

Two years later *Retail Business* noted the introduction of a cheap stereo pick-up and the continued rise of LP sales – 'this may be the most profitable section of the market'; in 1968, for the first time, as many LPS were sold as 45s (see Table 10); by 1969 stereo had completely taken over in record manufacture, even though only 14% of households as yet had stereo record players.[13]

This was the technological development, and pirate radio (open, via payola, to small companies just like US radio in the 1950s) was the promotional development, that at last made it possible for record companies to compete with the British majors. Competition came partly from American companies, establishing themselves independently in Britain – CBS had taken over Oriole and its distribution network in 1964, and by the end of the 1960s WEA and RCA were also making their mark (see Table 8) – but competition also came from new British independent companies (see Table 11).

The most important effect of the Beatles' success had been to

Table 10:

UK production of records, 1955–75

		Production		Sales at Mnfr's Selling Prices
	78s 000s	45s 000s	LPs 000s	Total £000
1955	46,347	4,587	8,989	9,139
1956	47,508	6,903	12,116	11,153
1957	51,359	13,161	13,765	14,092
1958	28,314	27,521	15,620	13,786
1959	8,126	43,230	15,404	13,616
1960	3,803	51,811	17,057	14,996
1961	2,181	54,757	19,388	16,019
1962	1,944	55,239	20,361	17,423
1963	1,846	61,342	22,267	21,767
1964	587	72,841	27,829	25,602
1965	475	61,809	31,462	25,453
1966	400	51,196	33,275	25,082
1967	308	51,576	37,949	27,929
1968	206	49,161	49,184	30,140
1969	173	46,618	59,565	32,353
1970	106	46,978	65,857	39,333
1971	5	48,184	72,335	43,485
1972	n.a.	52,910	84,493	65,895
1973	n.a.	60,737	100,750	91,957
1974	n.a.	68,339	105,601	115,566
1975	n.a.	75,735	101,982	140,973

Note: Figures before 1971 were compiled by the Board of Trade or Dept. of Trade and Industry; figures after 1971 by BPI.
Source: BPI Yearbook, 1976.

Table 11:

Share of UK Top Ten singles, 1965–75

	% Records produced in UK by				% Records produced in US licensed to			
	Major UK Co.	Indep. UK Co.	Subsid. US Co.	Total	UK label	Own label with UK Co.	Own subsid.	Total
1965	70	—	0·9	70·9	10·9	9·1	9·1	29·1
1966	61·3	3·8	0·9	66	12·3	16	5·7	34
1967	57·7	12·5	4·8	75	4·8	10·6	9·6	25
1968	44·3	11·3	12·4	68	6·2	11·3	14·4	31·9
1969	31	19	8	58	6	19	17	42
1970	21·6	20·7	9·9	52·2	4·5	24·3	18·9	47·7
1971	20	26·7	14·3	61	5·7	18·1	15·2	39
1972	14·7	28·4	15·6	58·7	5·5	16·5	19·3	41·3
1973	22·5	26·7	20	69·2	0·8	12·5	17·5	30·8
1974	14·2	29·9	26·8	70·9	4·7	16·5	7·9	29·1
1975	13·1	29·9	24·8	67·8	2·2	18·2	11·7	32·1

Source: Gillett, 'Big Noise from Across the Water.'

spread rock appeal from its traditional working-class teenage base.
The general appeal of the Beatles and Stones and other groups, the
development of cheap stereo record players, the opening of pirate
radio and the college and club circuit, meant the development of a
youthful music market with attitudes and an ideology that the major
record companies did not understand. This market became clearly
visible in 1967, with its self-generated enterprises, its 'progressive'
musicians, clubs and venues; by 1968, when the popularity and commercial viability of progressive rock was obvious and was beginning
to be exploited by a new breed of independent record producers and
management companies, the majors became concerned that there was
a source of profit that they were not tapping. In 1968 EMI launched a
new 'progressive' label (Harvest), which was followed in the next
couple of years by Philips' Vertigo, Pye's Dawn, Decca's Nova and
RCA's Neon. To a large extent these labels simply worked distribution
deals with the new independent producers – Harvest for Blackhill
Enterprises, Dawn for Red Bus – and none of them was particularly
successful; only Vertigo and Harvest still survive.[14]
    A parallel development was the creation by successful musicians
of their own labels. Apple was formed by the Beatles in 1968 'to open

the way to artistic fulfilment for writers, musicians, singers and paint-
ers who have hitherto been unable to find acceptance in the commercial world.' The Moody Blues followed a year later with the
similarly idealistic Threshold. Neither of these and none of the other
sixties artists' labels survived, however, as much more than outlets
for the stars themselves, and the independent labels that were successfully established in the late sixties – Island, Chrysalis, Charisma –
were, in fact, extensions of successful management or production
companies. Their independence was based on financial rather than
ideological considerations and their success on a response to a new
market rather than to a new music. David Betteridge, managing
director of Island:

> There was a new intelligent rock – I don't mean that in any cynical
> way – there was a college circuit being built and a new audience
> was emerging. And we were running in tandem, supplying their
> needs. We were the vehicle for them so it all just clicked together.[15]

Or, in the words of Rohan O'Rahilly, boss of Radio Caroline,
'Youth was busting out all over. There was a lot of money to be
made.[16]

The new labels reached the new market not just with new musical
content, but through new promotional forms – concentrating on LPS
rather than singles, emphasising sleeve design and sound quality,
using the college circuit rather than dance halls, plugging John
Peel's rather than Tony Blackburn's radio programmes. It was because of these innovations at the end of the record-making process –
innovations which directly related to the audience – that the late
sixties felt like a time of change in the music business; hippie ideology seemed to be making a genuine mark. Virgin's first record shop
opened in 1969, *The Old Grey Whistle Test* assumed its first form, as
Colour Me Pop, in 1968; every town and province had its local hip
promoters, its political bands, its hippie pubs, its outdoor festivals;
London saw a flowering of hip studios, light shows, poster artists and
underground papers; progressive music had its own institutions and
in America *Rolling Stone* proclaimed a 'new community' based on the
'new music'.[17]

In the end, though, the apparent opening up of the record industry
did not have the expected competitive and creative consequences.
Partly, of course, because the major companies soon learnt their own
way around the new market and used their superior capital resources
to sign, record, and promote the most successful progressive acts.
This was particularly the response of American companies, who
treated Britain less as a market than as a source of talent, especially

after the success of British rock acts, like Cream, in the huge American youth market.[18]

But such straightforward muscling-in concealed a more subtle reorganisation of the music industry. The independent companies of the late 1960s were established in the 1970s as a permanent feature of the business. Record producers, arrangers, management and promotion companies now flourish outside the control of the major A&R departments and serve them not as staff members but as independent professionals – hence the proliferation of tape and licensing deals, the almost standard use of independent producers by all companies. In Britain the success of this system was revealed by the rediscovery of the teenage and dancing market in 1972–4; singles suddenly started booming again (see Table 10) and a new form of promotion emerged, discos. It was the independent producers and companies who most efficiently exploited this market (one which was confined largely to Europe) (see Table 11), but the seventies' independents are not, as the independents were in the USA in the fifties and even, to a lesser extent, in the UK in the sixties, the means of any sort of 'folk' expression: they are simply more efficient, because more single-minded, conveyor belts for the rock product; their independence is based on purely financial considerations. In the same way, the seventies' artists' labels – ELP's Manticore (now folded), Elton John's Rocket, Led Zeppelin's Swan Song – are much more 'old-fashioned' companies than the utopian Apple, designed to give their owners more money, to be a potentially profitable form of investment.[19]

The profitability of rock

The profitability of the rock business reflects the fact that individual consumption is not the only fate of records as commodities; they are also used as the 'inputs' for other media. This is most obviously true for radio, which, in Hirsch's words, has a 'symbiotic relationship' with the record industry. In America radio was opened to commercial interests in 1918. By 1926 there were 694 stations and fifteen million sets; three-quarters of the material on the radio was music and most of the music was 'commercial jazz'. The relationship of radio and popular music has become even closer as a result of the development of recording techniques, and although the British situation has been given a special twist by the role of non-commercial radio the two media here cannot be understood apart from each other. I have already discussed the importance of radio for record promotion and I will further examine radio's use of rock in the next chapter.[20]

But even when media are not so closely joined, the record industry can provide a means to further profits. The intense competition between the *Mirror* and the *Sun* for teenage rock fans in 1975–6 revealed the sales benefits to the press of coverage of the record scene, and the cinema, television and advertisers have all sought to attract audiences by using popular records as soundtracks. A rock score is now normal for youth-aimed Hollywood films (and a soul score for black movies); television has very successfully created its own teeny-bopper record stars; and the association of *any* product with a popular record has been found by advertisers to help sales.[21]

Records can also be used directly as a means of entertainment. Discos use records as the bait to draw the customers whose entrance and drinks money provide clubs and dance halls with their profits, and these days there are few public places without permanent background music. The earliest use of records as background was on juke-boxes in pubs, bars and cafés, but records are now a constant accompaniment of all forms of consumption – the biggest clothes stores even have their own 'broadcasts' – and the importance of music while you work has resulted in the United Biscuit Company being the major supplier of experienced DJs to commercial radio. (The second biggest suppliers are the hospital radio networks – music while you die?) Records are even, indirectly, an input into 'live' music, into the basic entertainment provided by Britain's network of clubs, cabarets, colleges and hotels: there are thousands of unrecorded musicians whose livelihood depends on their ability to reproduce, week after week, recorded sounds. What the public wants is indicated for them, as for Radio 1, by current and past record sales.[22]

These uses of records are a vital source of income for the record industry, and the licensing and copyright arrangements involved draw attention to an important feature of cultural commodities: the special status of artistic labour. The normal principle of commodity production is that the owner of the means of production owns the commodity produced. Its value may reflect the labour that has gone into its production, but the labourers are paid directly for their labour time and have no legal claim on the product whatsoever; the capitalist can do what he likes with both it and any proceeds of its sale. For most of the workers concerned with making records and the capital equipment of the recording industry the same relationship holds: they are wage labourers, paid for their time, without any economic interest in the product on which they're working. But cultural products are also the products of artistic labour, and artistic services are rewarded with a cut of the final profits – royalties act as an incentive to musicians whose creative skills cannot easily be controlled by record companies.

To clarify this point with reference to recording we have to distinguish the work recorded from the record itself. The Copyright Act of 1956 established that

a musical work (and any associated lyrics) acquires copyright protection immediately it is committed to paper or fixed in some other material form, such as recording.

The copyright lasts until fifty years after the death of the author and entitles the copyright holder to payment every time the song is performed or broadcast, and to a royalty on every copy of the song sold, whether in sheet music or recorded form (which can include its use on a soundtrack, commercial, segment of muzak tape, etc.). The copyright holder is usually the song's publisher, who has his own contract with the song writer, and the rights available to him are administered differently according to whether they are mechanical or performing rights.[23]

Mechanical rights are the royalty rights on the use of a song as a recording. In Britain copyright owners are entitled to $6\frac{1}{4}\%$ of the recommended selling price of a record and the proceeds are split equally between the publishers of all the songs involved, so that, for example, the copyright holder of a B side gets the same return from sales as the owner of the A side which is actually being bought. The resulting income is split 50:50 between the publisher and the composer – this is built into the original publishing contract. There are numerous variations on this pattern (to cater for all the other uses of recorded songs) but the mechanical royalties resulting from record sales are the most important. They are collected and distributed by the Mechanical Copyright and Protection Society, established by music publishers in 1910 (and by the much smaller British Copyright Protection Society). The rate of $6\frac{1}{4}\%$ was established after a Board of Trade inquiry in 1928 (the original figure was 5%) and publishers are presently campaigning for a rise to 8% to bring Britain in line with the EEC. As it is the MCPS distributes about £3m. a year.[24]

But even this sum is small compared with that emerging from the second source of composer income, performance: 'whenever a song is performed in public or broadcast on radio or TV the writer and publisher must be paid'.

The Performing Rights Society was set up in 1914, a non-profit-making association of composers, authors and publishers, to administer these rights

by granting to those concerned with the public performance or broadcasting of music a comprehensive 'blanket' licence. Most of these licences are issued to the proprietors of the premises at which music is publicly performed or the promoters of public entertainments. Only in exceptional circumstances are licences issued to performers in person. The licence charges are fixed according to a series of tariffs most of which have been settled by negotiation with associations of music users or by order of the Performing Right Tribunal which was set up under the 1956 Copyright Act.[25]

The great variety of public music use leads to a great variety of licences and licence fees. The BBC licence costs more than £3m. a year (Radio 1 itself contributed about £1½m. to the PRS in 1975) and the Society gets a detailed list of every piece of music used; otherwise PRS licensees range from barbers' shops and dentists, paying £2–3 a year for the right to run a tape, to large companies like Muzak; pubs and restaurants bring in about £500,000 a year, juke-boxes about £300,000; dance and concert halls return 1–2% of their takings, and there are returns from factories and hospitals, fairgrounds and ice-cream vans. The basic principle of performance licensing is that the PRS is entitled to a percentage of the income that results from music use (and thus premises are licensed rather than, say, DJs). In 1975, the PRS collected over £17m. – nearly £6m. from radio and TV broadcasting, £4–5m. from other public performances and more than £6m. from affiliated societies abroad, for foreign performances of British copyrights.[26]

The distribution of this income is as complex as its collection. Performances are awarded 'points' according to their length, type and circumstance; where possible, licensees return precise lists of the music involved, otherwise it is assumed that unknown patterns follow the known ones. Any composer who has had a work published is eligible for PRS membership and royalties are normally distributed 50:50 between publisher and composer – the latter will not get less, whatever the terms of the contract. In 1975 the Society had over 8,000 members, of whom 82% received less than £250 and 3% more than £5,000; 17% of PRS revenue goes to foreign copyright holders. These figures apply to all musicians, not just those involved in pop or rock, and they are all bound together by a simple legal assumption:

> music is a kind of property belonging to the composer, so that by controlling certain uses of his music he may earn a living. Thus one of the provisions of the law – the Copyright Act, 1956 – is that when you buy a record or some sheet music you may use it to play the music at home, but it does not give you the right to perform the music publicly – unless the composer's permission has been obtained.[27]

Composer's ownership of their compositions was established originally in the 1911 Copyright Act, which clarified the rights of all authors. The subsequent development of recording raised a new issue: could the publishers of a sound claim the same rights as the publishers of a text? The situation was confused until the 1933 Carwardine Case, in which the judge commented:

> I see considerable objection to the view that persons might take, without doing anything more than buying a record, the advantages of all the skill and labour expended by makers of records for the purpose of public performance.

He ruled that records could not be used for public performance without their producers' permission, and in 1934 the British record companies established Phonographic Performance Ltd, to grant record licences and administer the resulting revenue. In 1952 the Copyright Committee Report argued that

> in our considered view there would be something at variance with ordinary ideas of justice and fair play if an entertainment promoter, for his own personal profit, were to be at liberty to make use of sound recordings without any control or payment whatsoever.

And the 1956 Copyright Act granted record producers explicit rights in their recordings; records cannot be copied, heard in public or broadcast without permission. These rights were agreed internationally by the Rome Convention of 1961, although the USA still refuses to recognise copyright on a sound. American law accepts that the purchaser of a record is its owner and can do what he likes with it; even the 1976 amendment of the American copyright laws, which gave companies protection against unauthorised copying or bootlegs, did not give them broadcasting or performance rights. American record producers have to be satisfied with the 2% of net revenue royalty which the National Committee for the Recording Arts negotiated with broadcasters in 1967.[28]

In Britain, however, the PPL operates much like the PRS, licensing broadcasters and premises for the public use of records and tapes and having a similar structure of fees. Radio 1, for example, pays £250,000 per year for its PPL licence. But records are different from songs, and whereas the PRS is only concerned to reap the rewards of its copyrights, the PPL is also involved in controlling records and, on occasion, restricting their use. In its own words:

> The primary business of the producers is to issue recordings for sale to the general public for private amusement in the home. The

public use of recordings can therefore only be authorised subject to the condition that such use will not be detrimental to the recording companies and others who contribute to the production of sound recordings. The interests of the recording artists and musicians are also involved when sound recordings are broadcast and publicly used and it is socially necessary to take these interests into account.

The PPL's needle-time agreements with the BBC and IBA control the hours of record use as well as the costs. Record companies have always had mixed feelings about radio, both fearing its effects on sales (will people buy for themselves the sounds they can hear so easily on the radio?) and welcoming them (will people buy for themselves a sound they haven't heard on radio?). One reflection of the ultimate concern for sales in the PPL's licensing policy is the exclusion of new releases from needle-time agreements – the only regulation is that the name of the company issuing a new record be broadcast.[29]

These days, however, the basic record-company conviction is that radio is more effective as promotion than as competition. The pressure for restrictions comes from a different source, the Musicians' Union, and this reflects another difference between a record and a song. A song has an easily identifiable author, whose creative rights can be clearly established; a record however, as a sound, has a number of different 'authors'. As far as record sales are concerned, the musicians involved are being joined in their claims to royalties by producers, and even engineers, working for an advance rather than a fee. As far as public performances are concerned, creative rights are defined differently. Legally, the record company is the sole owner of its products' copyrights, but the 1961 Rome Convention recommended that at least 25% of the proceeds of record use should go to the musicians involved, and the PPL actually distributes $32\frac{1}{2}\%$ of its annual revenue to them – 20% going to the musicians named on the records. When the PPL feeds its computers with the play-lists from its licensees the data comes out in two forms: firstly, the total number of seconds broadcast of the products of each record company; secondly, the total number of seconds broadcast of the products of each musician. But the PPL also pays $12\frac{1}{2}\%$ of its revenue to the Musicians' Union as the representative of the anonymous army of session musicians on whom the recording industry is dependent. In this last case (and in the MU's successful pressure on the PPL to maintain its needle-time restrictions) the principal is not that session musicians have any right in the specific records to which they have contributed, but that they have a general labour right, won by trade-union organisation, to share in the general proceeds of the industry to which they sell their labour power.[30]

Underlying the various public uses of records and the substantial payments involved is the assumption that records are an effective means to other ends – listening and viewing figures, gates, circulations, sales. But it is not just rock on record that is a means to further profits; so are rock stars. The attractive power of a star is most obvious in the phenomenon of a fan club – in 1973, for instance, the Osmonds' British fan club had 60,000 members and an annual turnover of £45,000 – and the biggest recording stars are able to exploit their success by licensing the use of their names or images:

> Retailers of soft goods last year sold more than $20,000,000 worth of Presley products. Such items as pre-teen and teen-sized jackets, skirts, T-shirts, jeans, hats, nylon scarves, charm bracelets, sneakers and nylon stretch bobby sox, all bearing the Presley insignia, are big sellers in the nation's stores.
>
> Chain, drug and novelty stores now feature lipsticks in autographed cases bearing color names for such Presley hit tunes as Hound Dog orange, Loving You fuchsia, and Heartbreak pink.[31]

The music business doesn't only turn music into commodities, as records, it also turns musicians into commodities, as stars. When, in 1964, two Chicago businessmen bought the pillow cases on which the Beatles had slept in a Kansas City hotel for $1,000, cut them into 160,000 one-inch squares and sold the squares for $1 each, the profits reflected the 'value' that the Beatles, as stars, brought to every object they touched. And not the least of the objects made valuable by star quality are records. Record companies seek to create stars not just because of the non-musical spin-offs made possible, but also because stars' record sales are guaranteed, almost regardless of content. The biggest stars can, in fact, provide by themselves the major part of a record company's profits. The Beatles remain the most dramatic example. In 1963–4 the turnover from Beatle music leapt from nothing to £6m.; by the middle of 1964 Beatle records were bringing in £500,000 a month and that year EMI's pre-tax music profits rose 80%. Over the next ten years the Beatles sold the equivalent of 545 million singles and even in 1973, long after the peaks of Beatlemania, it was estimated that the sales on two Beatle anthologies would account for 28·6% of EMI's pre-tax music profits, 16·7% of its total profits. When Allen Klein renegotiated the Beatles' contract with Capitol (EMI's American subsidiary) in 1969 he got their royalty rate raised to 25% (the average in the business is about 10%), confident in the knowledge that the group had, for years, accounted for 50% of Capitol's sales.[32]

Stars make record promotion easy and it is in the star system that the 'symbiotic' relationships of the different music-using media can be seen most clearly. The importance of stars for *all* sales means that papers will publicise them as much as they can, radio stations play their latest records as soon and as often as possible, magazines litter their pages with their pictures. Record sales rise without the record companies having to lift a finger – when the BBC decides that it would boost listening figures to have an 'Osmonds Week' on the radio, an Osmonds TV spot every evening, who needs payola? A star guarantees sales and makes life in the record business not just more profitable, but easier; 'what the public wants' becomes a known, fixed quantity. Best of all, the buzz associated with big stars rubs off on little stars and so on down the rock line. The Osmonds/Cassidy boom of 1973 lifted the sales of all the music papers, even those which never mentioned them, and the commonest music business cliché when sales are slow is that what is needed is a 'new Beatles':

> A centre of excitement, like a highly successful new supergroup or a new sound, is what is most needed to give the industry an uplift during the current lull in trade, according to prominent members of the business consulted this week.[33]

The benefits of bigness

I have already described the reorganisation of the music industry that followed the Beatles' revelations of how big a business rock could be – by the 1970s rock appeared to be produced by a diverse collection of independent companies and experts. But this division of professional labour has concealed the extent to which overall control of the record business has remained in the hands of a limited number of major companies – diversification has been followed by a process of reintegration.

Reintegration has been both horizontal and vertical. In the former case, companies have simply bought up their smaller rivals – as Warners (owned by the American Kinney Corporation) took over Atlantic and Elektra to form WEA; in the latter case, companies have expanded their interests until they controlled the whole process by which records reach the public, and it is in this latter respect that the majors still exercise a decisive power.[34]

The proliferation of label names and independent professionals conceals a much more oligopolistic situation. At the levels where capital investment is important the majors still have no rivals. In

Britain, EMI, Decca, Pye, Phonodisc, CBS and RCA manufacture and distribute most of the records that are issued (so that, for example, WEA records are manufactured by CBS, Island's by EMI). The 1973 vinyl shortage made it clear how difficult it would be for newcomers to start manufacturing. EMI, RCA and Pye have long-term contracts with ICI, Decca with BP; it would be difficult for anyone else even to get regular supplies of the raw materials necessary. WEA's plan to start their own distribution in 1977 involved an estimated $2,000,000 investment.[35]

For companies that don't have manufacturing and distribution facilities there are four types of deal available: in the loosest deal the company just has its products manufactured and stored in someone else's warehouse; in a second, tighter, relationship the company controls all the phases of its releases but uses a distributor to get its products physically to the shops (for which service the distributor gets a percentage of the income from sales); thirdly, there are licensing deals, in which the distributor is also responsible for the release schedule and promotion (this is usually the deal for American records licensed to British companies) – in this case it is the licensing company which receives a fixed percentage of the retail price in return for its regular supply of product; finally, there are labels which are directly owned and controlled by the distributing company, even if they have their own identity and staff.

Within this framework the control of distribution by the majors remains powerful. Even in the loosest deal, as simple manufacturer and distributor, a major like EMI takes up to 20% of the retail price of an 'independent' record, and at times when there are heavy demands on pressing and distributing facilities, the independents are clearly at risk. DJM, for example, felt obliged to develop its own distribution after Pye's success in the 1974–5 soul boom, and Island supplements EMI's service with its own van system. Even in the world of rack-jobbing and budget records, the major distributor, Record Merchandisers Ltd, is owned by a consortium of the majors (its only market rival is Pickwick, an American firm which commands about a third of the market, the same as EMI's Music for Pleasure label) and the most successful record club, World Records, is also owned by EMI. The TV 'demonstrators' like K-Tel, genuine outsiders in record promotion, are dependent for their material on tracks licensed from the majors, and the latter take their due share of the TV promoters' profits.

If, in the 1970s, the majors have retained their control of the fixed capital of record making – and have, indeed, profited from the greater production costs of LPs – they have also begun to swallow up other areas of the music business. The most dramatic example of the extension of record-company control came in 1969 when ATV (which had controlled Pye Records since 1966) took over the Beatles' publishing company, Northern Songs, for £10m., despite the Beatles' well-publicised attempts to prevent this. ATV had already lost one publishing take-over battle in 1968, when Philips bought Chappell, and in 1969 EMI joined the chase, buying Keith Prowse Music (for £$\frac{1}{2}$m.) and adding Affiliated Music (for £$3\frac{1}{2}$m.) in 1972. EMI hadn't had any publishing interests at all until 1958, when Ardmore and Beechwood was formed, and this sudden flurry of record-company interest in publishing at the end of the 1960s was a response to the huge profits that the rock boom had brought publishers, despite their displacement from the music's creative centre. By the mid-seventies all the major record companies were also major music publishers and many of the apparently independent publishers, with their fanciful names, were actually, like their equivalent record labels, part of a huge combine. The continuing importance of publishing, even in its traditional form, is reflected in the fact that EMI gets more than half of its considerable publishing income from its newly acquired back catalogue; the majors, through their control of such catalogues, are in a position to exploit nostalgia to the maximum.[36]

But even the interest of record companies in publishing doesn't bring out the extent of the majors' involvement in every facet of musical entertainment. I have mentioned Pye's take-over by ATV and I can also point to the interlocking relationship of Phonogram, owned by the Dutch company Philips Electrical, and Polydor, an offshoot of Deutsche Grammophon, which is in turn a subsidiary of the huge German electrical corporation, Siemens – Phonogram and Polydor co-operate on manufacture and distribution through their joint ownership of Phonodisc. Or there are the recent travels of Transatlantic, an independent record company and profitable music publisher (which does its own distribution), first of all to Granada and then to Marshall Cavendish in moves by both companies to rationalise their publishing empires. Or, tangentially, there is IPC's stake in Radio Luxembourg. But the most dramatic example in Britain of interlocking entertainment interests is EMI, the world's biggest record company.[37]

EMI's extraordinary growth is best dated from 1954, when it was being outsold by Decca and Joseph Lockwood was appointed managing director. His first act of rationalisation was to sell off EMI's radio and gramophone manufacturing interests to Thorn, but since then the EMI story has been one of expansion not slimming down. The most dramatic take-over was in 1969, when EMI acquired the Associated British Picture Corporation and hence a controlling interest in Thames Television, but my concern here is not so much to describe EMI's far-flung empire (through one of its 33 overseas companies, for example, EMI has a 98% share of the record market in India) but to point to the implications of its empire for the particular process of record-making. What was interesting, in this respect, about EMI's take-over of ABPC was that it thereby got control of a chain of cinemas and theatres that is one of the major circuits for promotional rock tours (and which neatly complements the EMI-owned chain of Baileys Clubs).

Following our way through the complicated web of EMI's interests we find not just a publishing empire but also The House of Music, one of the leading distributors of musical instruments; not just Capitol Records, EMI's American record company, but also Audio Device, American recording equipment manufacturers; not just the chain of HMV record and tape shops (stocking, of course, Emitape) but also a highly successful record shopfitting service, regularly employed by HMV's High Street competitors. Behind the famous names of the organisations that EMI now controls – the Grade Organisation, Tito Burns, Harold Davison, Keith Prowse – is a network of talent and artist agencies, concert-promotion companies, ticket outlets. The mutually advantageous relationships between all these different aspects of the music business have been essential to EMI's growth as an entertainment empire. As Sir Joseph Lockwood commented laconically in 1969, on EMI's acquisition of another manufacturer of radio and record playing equipment: 'the indirect benefits to our record business are obvious'.[38]

A similar picture could be drawn of ATV, which owns not just Pye Records and Northern Music, but its own chain of theatres and halls, Britain's biggest supplier of muzak and various other music enterprises. The big American record companies are just as far-ranging in their musical investments. There the building of entertainment corporations began in the 1920s and 1930s as radio manufacturers and radio stations merged and took over theatres and theatrical agencies, as the developing film companies took over music publishers (to guarantee their cut from and control of film musical hits and themes) and established their own record companies and radio networks, and as the two groups merged to form today's gigantic concerns like CBS, RCA (owners of NBC) and WEA, whose interests cover all the mass media.[39]

The object of record companies is profits, and the size of their profits results, in accounting terms, from the difference between their costs and revenues; but record companies, particularly in the last decade, have found that greater costs can lead to greater revenue and should not necessarily be cut back. Their profit strategies have rested less on attempts to cut costs than on attempts to absorb them – hence the logic of vertical integration: if a company can control every aspect of record-making, then many of its costs will return as income; the object is not just to control production and distribution, but to make the instruments the musicians play, the equipment the producers need, the record players the consumers use.

Faced with these developments, it is not surprising that independent musical entrepreneurs have felt their own need to expand and diversify. It is noticeable that Britain's longest lasting independent record company, Saga (founded in 1954), owns not only its own studios and distribution facilities, but also does its own manufacturing and controls its own supply of raw material. More recent companies have had to diversify their interests similarly to survive. Music publishers, for example, have had to become independent producers, setting up their own studios and packaging their songs as demo discs, and because of the consequent focus on songwriter/singers they have also become involved in management and promotion. It is then a short step for a large independent publisher, like Dick James Music, to become a record company, like DJM. Independent record companies, meanwhile, have expanded in the opposite direction, establishing their own publishing companies and studios (like Island and Rak) or taking them over (Chrysalis have taken over both Wessex Studios and, for about £1m., George Martin's AIR). We can find examples of such diversification from every possible music-business base: promotion (Robert Stigwood is now RSO Records), recording studios (Trident were the original discoverers, managers, producers and packagers of Queen), agency (Bron is now the publishing, management and record company, Bronze), retail (Virgin Records started as a mail-order firm, and now controls a chain of record shops and a record company complete with studios, publishing and agency), and distribution (B&C, before its bankruptcy, had expanded from distributing Charisma and Trojan records into recording its own).[40]

One result of such diversification, as Hirsch has observed in America, is the remarkable mobility of personnel in the record industry not just between companies, but between roles. A&R men reach their position from every possible music-biz background – they have been pluggers, promotion and advertising men, engineers, critics, musicians, DJs; managers emerge from agencies and studios, from bands and A&R offices. If people fail in a new role they move back to an old one; if they succeed they move on in the hope that their 'magic' will rub off elsewhere.[41]

Another result is that it is difficult to measure the 'profitability' of the record industry – profits are generated at so many levels. The final results on a company's balance sheet reflect a very complicated balancing act. In the most general terms, we can say that the steady and occasionally spectacular expansion of the record industry over the last twenty years has fed a huge amount of money into the industry (see Table 10) and that record companies have benefited accordingly. In 1953–4 EMI employed 28,300 people, had sales of £32·1m. and pre-tax profits of £1·1m.; when Sir Joseph Lockwood ceased to be managing director, at the end of the year 1968–9, the company had 41,900 employees, sales of £176·3m. and pre-tax profits of £17·6m., the leisure sector (records, tapes and entertainment) accounting for 67% of the sales and 71% of profits. By 1975–6, as EMI continued to expand as an electronics giant, music sales accounted for only 51% of EMI's sales and 42% of its profits, but in money terms these percentages represented £344·7m. sales and £27·3m. pre-tax profits.[42]

Such figures conceal the variety of ways in which EMI makes money. An alternative way of assessing the profits of record making is to look at the costs involved. Firstly, there are a variety of fixed costs – studio and session fees, manufacturing, packaging and distribution charges; there is a minimum below which such costs can't fall, but as a percentage of total costs they fall dramatically as the number of units sold rises. Secondly, there are a variety of royalty costs – a percentage of the retail price of each record goes to the recording artist (10%+), to the song writer and publisher (6¼%), and possibly to the producer (2–3%), and there is also a cut on every sale to the retailer (33%) and to the VATman (8%) (see Table 12). Record-company profit is realised when the returns from sales after deduction of the royalties are greater than the fixed costs, and the problem of determining this breakeven point is that the 'fixed' costs, especially of recording, vary so greatly (though it is worth noting that such costs are usually met by the artists rather than by the record company – the breakeven point has to be met before the artist gets his royalty).

In 1958, Newton estimated the breakeven point on a jazz album as varying from 3,000 sales for a small company's cheap recording, to 7,000 sales for a larger company's more elaborate disc; in 1960, *Retail Business* suggested that 20,000 was the breakeven sales point for a pop album. By the 1970s the breakeven point for the major's biggest rock acts sometimes reached 100,000 – a rise which mostly reflected studio costs – though the average for rock albums is probably still around 20,000. Singles' breakeven points are less (about 15,000), though again variable – many singles are also album tracks, being used as promotional devices. The average single costs about £2,000 to make, the average album £15–20,000; costs of promotion and advertising start from about £2,000 a record. The essential point about all these fixed costs is that once they are covered, once the breakeven point is passed, then record company accumulation of profit is very rapid.[43]

The question is how many records achieve their breakeven sales, and this is not an easy question to answer because of the time factor involved – rock albums, in particular, may build up their sales over a long period of release and re-release. Nevertheless, one way of making the calculation is to measure the proportion of hits to releases. Records in the Top Thirty certainly pass their breakeven point, most non-hits do not – the number one record in Britain's singles and albums charts usually sells more than 200,000 copies, records at the lower ends of the charts sell 20,000 copies. In the British business the hits: releases ratio is 6–8 % for singles and 7–8 % for rock albums.[44]

Table 12:

Cost breakdown for records and tape

	% Full-price rock LP (£3·00)	Budget LP (£1·25)	Rock single (£0·65)	Cassette (£3·25)
Value Added Tax	8	8	8	8
Dealer margin	33	33	33	30
Distribution	11	11	12	11
Artist royalty	13	6	13	12
Copyright royalty	6	6	6	6
Sleeve (box +liner)	4	6	—	2
Disc and pressing	9	18	10	13
Marketing	6	3	9	7
Recording (studios)	3	1	3	3
Record co. overheads	4	6	4	5
Record co. profit	3	2	2	3

Note: Costs are too variable for this to be more than a 'rough indication' provided by British Phonographic Industry to its record company members.
Source: BPI Year Book, 1976.

The relevance of these figures is confirmed by *Retail Business*, which argued in a 1971 survey of the recording industry that:

> there is no market share in the conventional sense, since there is no homogeneous product. Survivals and profits are based on the manufacture of hits obtained related to the number of records issued.[45]

From this perspective, the ratio of hits to releases seems remarkably small, and this not only shows how hard it is for record companies to control their market, but also reflects the risks on which the record industry is based. This is another reason why it is difficult for independent record companies to compete with the majors – to achieve the necessary cash flow, they have to have a much higher hit-to-release ratio (which is why the independents tend to be so much more single-minded in their pursuit of hits from *every* release). The majors not only benefit from their manufacture of other people's hits, but their capital resources also provide them with their own safety nets. In the first place, the size and range of their back catalogue give them a continuing source of income whatever is happening to their new releases – the budget and TV compilation albums command, between them, about half the LP market, and if the big money is in rock best-sellers, a steady income comes from the 'middle market':

Pop stuff costs so much to produce and is a huge financial gamble. In the end the middle market is the strongest area because it provides the bread and butter, and pays the rent, lighting and heating bills.[46]

Secondly, the majors can take a much longer-term view of their investments – they can not only use singles as promotion for albums, but also use the first album as promotion for the second. The pattern of rock success that has emerged clearly in the USA in the last few years has meant record-company losses on albums and tours for anything up to three years until a record achieves a sales breakthrough – a breakthrough which often leads to the artists' back catalogues selling too, so that in the long term these initial records aren't, in fact, failures. Only the majors have the capital to carry many such long shots.[47]

If the cost of staying in the rock market is rising, so is the cost of entering it, as the demands made by each professional in the system – artist, producer, studio, etc. – rise. The majors can meet these demands and have, indeed, helped to escalate them by upping the competition. When CBS drastically increased its advances to musicians in the early 1970s, it also increased the number of sales necessary for breakeven and so the amount it was necessary to spend on promotion. The independents find the overall costs of success always rising. In 1972, Tony Stratton-Smith, boss of Charisma, reckoned £100,000 as the minimum initial investment for a viable independent record company. John Peel, who started Dandelion Records with £2,000 capital, found that the crucial problem of his lack of finance was that although he was as good a talent-spotter as anyone, he couldn't afford the advances necessary to attract future stars and was unable to promote them sufficiently even if they did sign. And the advances necessary these days don't just reflect artists' greed or delusions of grandeur: they rest on a realistic assessment of the costs of the equipment, transport and studio time necessary for rock recording. Even the smallest and least self-hyped group can reasonably demand a minimum £20,000 advance (while still depending on live performance fees to cover its £300 per week running costs) and six-figure advances to unknown acts with 'potential' are becoming routine.[48]

Two points emerge from this inflationary situation. Firstly, in the business as a whole, a large amount of money is always changing hands internally, regardless of the success of the final product – studios get most of their returns from records that never sell a copy; secondly, the returns on a successful act are hugely different from those on an 'ordinary' act – this is the reality of a mass medium and of the profits that come flowing in once a product starts selling hundreds of thousands of copies. It is the prospect of these returns that sets costs rising everywhere on the way to them – successful groups notoriously spend vast sums of money in the studio, and the often startling rises in royalty rates at contract re-signing times reveal what huge profits record companies were previously getting from their best-sellers.[49]

The dependence of record-company profits on artistic productivity and creativity can lead to bizarre conflicts of interest, as companies seek legal and financial control of supposedly spontaneous genius. This was one of the factors in the ATV/Northern Songs battle – at least part of the bid was for Lennon/McCartney's artistic potential. When Paul McCartney subsequently asserted that his wife had become his co-author, and was therefore entitled to half his new songs' copyright (a half in which Northern Songs would have no share, as she was not signed to them), ATV counter-asserted that she had 'never written music before her marriage' and therefore could not have made any significant contribution. The law was brought in to make an aesthetic judgement (did the song reveal Linda's contribution or was it all Paul's own work?) on which depended a substantial income. Such disputes are not uncommon in the music business and it is not surprising, given the amounts of money at stake, that the superstars are surrounded by 'interests' seeking all sorts of cuts from their success.[50]

This is not to say that the superstars don't have a share in their own fortune – in 1974 it was estimated that at least a hundred UK rock stars were earning in excess of £100,000 a year. The Moody Blues got around £450,000 for every album they produced, £100,000 from publishing royalties, and £1m. from touring; the group's total yearly income was £2m. ELP, meanwhile, earned five million dollars. Such earnings depended on the massness of the groups' market; such incomes (and they covered a variety of necessary expenses) were based on two-million album sales, on concerts grossing $30,000 nightly. One aspect of 'massness' is that Britain has become increasingly insignificant as a market for rock – it accounts for only about 8% of the world's annual record sales as against the USA's 50%, it is unable to provide concert venues large enough to cover current touring costs, and it is even losing its primary place in the European rock market. Another result has been that 'lawyers, along with accountants, have been among the chief incidental beneficiaries of the boom in pop music'.[51]

Superstars' income is the result of a large number of relatively small purchases (records, concert tickets); the income of the rock musicians who don't make it (the majority) is extremely small – they are getting the returns from a small number of the same small purchases, and their fixed costs, if nothing like as high as those of the superstars, cannot fall below the minimum necessary costs of equipment and studio time. Indeed, this minimum is rising as the public becomes used to the 'higher' sound standards set by groups which can afford the best facilities, as rock becomes more capital intensive. Few rock musicians without record contracts make more than £20–30 per week, and many, even with them, use their income to pay off debts and improve equipment and never sell enough records to go beyond that. The irony of this situation is that because of the nature of cultural production the industry depends, as we have seen, on marketing far more products than it will sell – poor musicians are as necessary to the system as rich ones. But if the record companies can more than cover their losses from their wins, the unsuccessful acts involved cannot. It is no comfort to the members of the Unknown Band, struggling along on £20 per week, that Yes earn £1m. per year each (even if their record company is, meanwhile, writing off their small, unrecouped advance to Unknown Band against another Yes two-million seller). The 'exploitation' in this situation is not of the successful musicians, but of the unsuccessful one.[52]

7

Radio

I put out inane chatter – that's my job. Rubbish, that's what it's all about. (Tony Blackburn.)

. . . nobody would play it ['Leap Up And Down And Wave Your Knickers In The Air'] because it was a ghastly record, but one person picked up on it – Bryant Marriott, who was producing Jimmy Young's show at the time – and he played it and I rang him up and said thanks and added, 'It's awful, isn't it?' and he said, 'Yes, it's awful, but so is the whole audience for the Jimmy Young Show and this will appeal to them totally because it's their music.' (Jonathan King)[1]

In Chapter 5 I described the relationship between the record business and radio from the record companies' point of view – airplay is their most important form of promotion. In this chapter I want to examine the relationship from the radio companies' point of view – records are their most important form of entertainment. The BBC, for example, relies on records for its programming of Radios 1, 2 and 3, and Radio 1 has been Britain's biggest consumer of rock records since it was established in 1967 to fill the entertainment gap left by the outlawed pirate stations. To understand Radio 1's use of music, it is not enough to refer to the BBC's own history; we must also look at the form of commercial radio to which Radio 1 was a direct response. The early history of that form lies in America.

American Radio

If, as I have already suggested, American radio was dependent on music and records for its programmes from the start, the origins of rock radio are found in the 1950s when, as I have also suggested, TV took over as the basic medium of home entertainment. Radio stations, in order to attract the disappearing advertisers, began to research their audiences in detail and to aim their programmes at the specific markets they discovered. It was soon found that teenagers were less TV-bound than their parents and, especially with the spread of portable radios, far more regular, if casual, radio listeners. In the mid-fifties a style of broadcasting evolved in America that was aimed exclusively at the teenage audience. Day-long record shows, based on a limited number of records played extensively for a brief period (four to six weeks), were split into four-hour segments by teams of DJs who developed their own individual quirks and styles. DJs' importance for record promotion had been recognised by the industry since the 1940s, but their power now increased rapidly; there were fewer and fewer syndicated and networked shows, and programming relied more and more on the simple permutation of locally produced record shows. Radio stations and record companies were now aiming at exactly the same narrow market – teenagers – and airplay took on a greater significance for record sales than ever before. Radio and DJ hit parades were used to calculate ASCAP and BMI copyright returns; radio play-lists determined record shops' stocks, record companies' promotional campaigns.

This new radio power was largely in the hands of the DJs. A 1941 FCC regulation designed to increase competitiveness had resulted in a large number of small independent stations heavily dependent on records for cheap programmes (record companies had begun to distribute records to radio stations free) and heavily dependent on their DJs for putting these record programmes together. This was the setting for payola, paying the DJs for plays, whether directly or through a variety of indirect arrangements (for example, employing a DJ as a 'release consultant' for a fee he advised on what records should be released, and, having given this advice, proved its validity by playing the record!). Payola was not just the most effective form of promotion (it guaranteed airplay) but also the cheapest (and so gave the independent rock'n'roll labels the opportunity to compete with the majors):

> Payola is the greatest thing in the world because it means that you don't have to spend time with some schmuck you don't like, eat dinner and all that, you pay him off and tell him to fuck himself. Instead of having an army of promotion men spending your money, fucking your broads, living off your expense account, you give it all to one guy and save yourself a million dollars.[2]

American payola was outlawed by a Federal Bribery Act in 1960, after an extensive, muckraking Senate investigation (which was at least partly designed to show that rock'n'roll was corrupting youth) and the result for radio was a tightening up and standardisation of the music format. Programme directors were put in to supervise the DJs, who became increasingly anonymous; play-lists were determined by administrative rules; direct payments were replaced by the elaborate conventions of plugging. The big companies regained their promotional advantage and Top Forty radio emerged: tight programming according to a fixed formula – hit/station-jingle/hit/news/oldie/hit/station-jingle/hit, all punctuated by the recurrent commercials. In 1965 KHJ of Los Angeles refined the formula even further to make 'Boss Radio': a weighted play-list from the Top Thirty (the higher the chart place the more often the play) plus three 'hit bounds', a pile of oldies and virtually no DJ chat; even the musical content was regulated – one ballad an hour, one soul record, one singer/songwriter, and so on. The subsequent development of American Top Forty radio has merely been an 'improvement' on this KHJ formula – some stations have reduced their play-lists to as few as eighteen titles.

Given their competitive situation (most Americans can tune into at least two Top Forty stations) the programme directors' major concern is not switching off but switching over; their advertising rates and revenues depend on comparative listening figures. Behind the development of the tight play-list lies the audience-research finding that American teenagers switch stations the moment they hear a record they don't like. In their attempts to reduce the risk of playing an unpopular record, Top Forty stations have made their programming policies dependent on records that have either proved their popularity already by local and country-wide sales and airplay, or have shown strong evidence of potential popularity by being included in the play-lists of 'barometer' stations and professional tipsheets and by showing up as 'regional breakouts' on sales returns.

The logic of Top Forty radio is that a station can attract listeners by playing the records that, on the evidence of sales, they currently most like. These records are then played over and over again – the argument is that Top Forty listeners are irregular, always switching off or over, impatient to hear their favourite tunes. Even when Top Forty programmes are kept on for long periods they are used as background music – the listeners' attention is assumed to wander even when they're not pushing buttons. Top Forty radio rests on one of the central paradoxes of the record industry: radio programming policy is determined by record popularity as measured by sales, by the number of people buying a record so that they can, presumably, play it at their own convenience. Why, then, do they also want to hear it so often on the radio? Record companies have never really understood this feature of record use and the result, as I suggested in the last chapter, is an ambiguous attitude towards radio – in the 1960s, for example, British record companies became convinced that the declining sales of singles was the result of their 'over-exposure' on the pirate radio stations – but there is little evidence for such fears, and the basic principle of Top Forty radio continues to be that the greatest number of listeners can be attracted by playing the currently best-selling records as often as possible.[3]

Another aspect of the rationalisation of American music radio in the 1960s was the increasingly sophisticated use of 'demographics' by broadcasters and their advertisers – stations' markets were broken down by researchers according to the day of the week and the time of the day, according to the most precisely measurable buying habits. The process by which radio had become a mass medium was reversed: stations which had, in the 1930s, sought to put together huge heterogeneous audiences, now concentrated on exploring the differences between small, homogeneous ones. One market gap became increasingly evident to researchers: if Top Forty radio catered for 9- to 18-year-olds, and if MOR radio catered for 35- to 49-year-olds, who was tapping the consumer potential of 18- to 34-year olds? This age-group was still tuning in to the Top Forty stations on which it had grown up (particularly as the stations' more inane teen-appeal gimmicks were cut out) and advertisers could still reach it that way, but its listening was becoming increasingly desultory – Top Forty programmes contained less and less of the music it wanted to hear, the LP boom and the development of stereo seemed to be passing music-radio by.

In 1966 the Federal Communications Commission ruled that where a broadcasting company controlled both AM and FM wavelengths, it must programme them differently. The freed FM bands, with their possibility of high sound quality, were ideal for the broadcasting of the new rock music and the immediate result of the FCC ruling was the emergence of so-called 'Underground Radio' and its programmes of album tracks, laid-back DJs, and long stretches of uninterrupted music. In terms of initial licensing costs, FM radio was cheaper than AM and could run on fewer commercial breaks.

FM radio, however 'underground' in its initial exploration of the demands of the 18- to 34-year-old audience, was very quickly standardised and soon became as vital a form of record promotion as Top Forty radio – the rise of Warner Brothers as a rock label is commonly seen as having been totally dependent on the simultaneous rise of FM radio stations. Nowadays, indeed, FM stations take as many pains as AM stations to keep the ears of their specific 'demographic', to avoid the risks of unpopularity. In the words of the historian of American broadcasting:

Radio, which had been at the start of the broadcasting empire, had gone back to its beginnings, relying mainly on gramophone records. But most stations now aimed at unity of mood, to hold specific audience groups. . . . The specialised, fragmented nature of radio programming made it easy for the average listener to get push-button confirmation of his tastes and prejudices. Once he had 'his' station, he was in 'his' world.[4]

Radio Luxembourg

Until the 1960s, the only source of radio promotion for British advertisers was Radio Luxembourg, and its history is similar to that of American commercial radio stations.

British firms had begun sponsoring airtime on European radio programmes in the 1920s; by 1931, Radio Normandie (among other French stations) was broadcasting Sunday night programmes of 'hit' records punctuated by English advertisements, and the BBC was regretting the popularity of these shows in the 'blatant American manner'. The English language service of Radio Luxembourg went on the air in 1933 and its mixture of variety and light music, its use of 'the cheapest of all programmes to produce, gramophone records', soon commanded a large enough audience to attract British programme sponsors, aiming at the 'lower middle and lower class market' which tuned in to Luxembourg's evening and weekend English language shows. The station was soon claiming about 10% of the British weekday radio audience and 50% of the Sunday one (figures broadly confirmed by the BBC) and it quickly eclipsed its Continental rivals. Radio Luxembourg was particularly popular on Sundays because its style of entertainment was not tempered, as was the BBC's, by a concern for the Sabbath.[5]

Luxembourg's programming policies were much the same as those of its American contemporaries: sponsored programmes were aimed at a mass market and featured Britain's most popular live variety acts and musicians. But most of the music played was on record and the station was soon heavily involved with record companies and their promotional strategies. The war (during which Radio Luxembourg was controlled by the Germans) was only a break in this relationship. Luxembourg returned to the British entertainment business in 1945 (in the evenings only now) with programmes which consisted almost entirely of records and were sponsored almost entirely by record companies. A 'Top Twenty' show, started in 1948, proved to be the station's most popular programme and the range of music played became increasingly narrow. The 1950s development of TV, particularly commercial TV, hit both listening figures and advertising revenue hard (especially as Luxembourg was an evening station) but, as in America, the development of the teenage record market and teenage commercial radio proceeded together, and by the late 1950s

Luxembourg was programming records to attract teenage listeners almost exclusively.

There were two features, however, which distinguished Radio Luxembourg from its American equivalents. Firstly, record companies could and did pay for plays (and, indeed, sponsored almost all the music heard on the station). This wasn't payola in any shady sense, but openly formed the basis of Luxembourg's programming – pre-taped quarter-hour segments featuring the music of a particular label. Secondly (and this is what made such bizarre programming possible), Radio Luxembourg had no competitors. When listeners heard a record which they didn't like (which they did constantly, as record companies competed with each other to get the most plays for their newest release) they had nothing to which to switch over. It was not until competition did arrive that the station developed a true Top Forty format.

These days the pirate radio stations are remembered nostalgically, as part of the youth explosion of the sixties, an aspect of cultural independence and freedom that marked the emergence of British rock. But in most respects the pirates simply represented American commercial radio interests – represented them not just ideologically, in terms of their programme ideas and styles, but also represented them directly, in terms of capital investment:

> The music-and-news station, backed everywhere by American advertisers, was a world-wide phenomenon; disc-jockeys calling themselves The Good Guys erupted even on 'pirate' stations operating from ships around the British Isles – almost all financed by American capital. Along Madison Avenue in New York girls in pirate costume drummed up business for this novel form of international freebooting; which for a time earned small fortunes.[6]

The pirates flourished briefly (1964–7) and their significance lay in their effects on the broadcasters who survived them – the BBC on the one hand, Radio Luxembourg on the other. I have already described the latter's changes of policy: pre-recorded sponsored shows were replaced by live DJs and spread paid-plays in 1968; a play-list was introduced in 1970. Radio Luxembourg's format became identical to that of American Top Forty radio – these days only 'a very small proportion' of plays are directly paid for – and this development was accompanied by the decision to cater much more carefully for the 'Target Market Audience' of 10- to 34-year-olds – both programmers and advertisers aim to respond with precision to the demands of British youth. Radio Luxembourg was, for example, one of the chief promoters and exploiters of the 1972–5 teeny-bop boom, while simultaneously developing its own FM shows – album tracks and 'intelligent' DJs – for its older, post-midnight audience (the station's sound quality is not really good enough for extensive FM-type programming, but it gets better as the evening gets later).

By 1973, Luxembourg was claiming eight million listeners from the 10- to 15-year-old age-group and thirteen million listeners aged 15 plus; the station's annual turnover was £1m. and it had diversified into publishing and record production. With the demise of the pirates, Luxembourg was once again without competition as a commercial station, and it has not been much affected by independent local radio stations which, by the evenings, have, like the BBC, used up most of their needle-time (Luxembourg has no such restrictions on its use of records – it is not bound by PPL regulations). The station's problem is, once more, not people switching over but people switching off or not listening at all – Luxembourg did experience discothèques as a threat (and now runs its own touring show) and remains concerned to keep as high a proportion as it can of its target audience. The playlist is programmed according to an assessment of this audience's tastes based on the BMRB charts and Luxembourg's own information from retailers (and it should perhaps be pointed out that probably half its audience, even for the English language programmes, is non-British, living on the Continent or in Ireland).

Whatever its peculiarities as a commercial radio station, Luxembourg's programming policies remain those developed by American music stations. The aim is to provide the programmes appropriate for the casual radio use of the British youth market. In the earlier part of the evening the focus is on the 10- to 18-year-olds, and the Top Forty format is adopted accordingly; by the late evening attention has switched to the 18- to 34-year-olds, and programmes are in the FM style. For Radio Luxembourg's owners the object is advertising revenue: as long as their programmes attract a big enough audience to interest the admen, then the station is fulfilling its purpose – what its listeners do with the music they hear is an irrelevant question. If the competition of the pirates meant major changes in Luxembourg's programme policies, it only served to confirm its broadcasting ideology. In this respect, the effect of the pirates on the BBC was more interesting because the BBC had a different tradition of music use.[7]

Radio 1

In the 1920s and 1930s, the BBC devoted between 30% and 40% of its programme time to light music, and its use of records slowly rose, particularly after the success of Radio Luxembourg – records occupied about 10% of programme time by 1938 (the first British DJ had broadcast for the BBC in July, 1927). The importance of BBC airplay for show-biz success was soon apparent, as were the related problems of the corporation's involvement in plugging and promotion. But before the war the BBC used records far less than its commercial contemporaries and this policy was not just a matter of resources, taste or ethics (Reith once declared that there would 'never be jazz on Sundays'). The policy reflected above all a different attitude to the purpose of broadcasting. When the Radio Manufacturers' Association eventually complained that the BBC broadcast too much culture and not enough popular entertainment (the Association called for 'bright, tonic music') they were making an accurate point. Under Reith, the BBC refused to separate education and entertainment, refused to differentiate between high- and lowbrow listeners or programmes. The BBC's object was to enlarge horizons and create audiences; its object was, indeed, the exact opposite of that of the modern commercial broadcaster, whose aim is to confirm and satisfy his audiences' given divisions and tastes.[8]

Even after the war, when the BBC made distinctions between the Home, Light and Third programmes, an underlying educational purpose remained. If, at one level, the Light Programme resembled prewar commercial radio, with its mixture of variety, comedy, light music and records, the BBC continued to acknowledge the need

> to improve the taste of the least critical groups of listeners by the introduction into the broadcasts to which they listen of a certain amount of material of a better quality than they would normally choose.

The BBC was still praised for 'the skilful blending of the Light Programme to include cultural items such as excerpts from operas and brief concerts of classical music'.[9]

This residue of Reithian ideology was slowly eroded in the 1950s – firstly, by the development of television, which reduced the significance of radio whether as a source of entertainment or education, and secondly by the development of commercial television, which made the BBC's concern for audience size so powerful that it infected radio too. In 1960 the Musicians' Union suggested that the danger of commercial radio was that it impelled broadcasters to seek the widest possible audience, to ignore minority tastes, but by then the BBC was responding to these pressures even without commercial-radio competition. Within the corporation the status of light entertainment fell, as giving the public what it wanted became more important than giving it what it might want. Light entertainment was designed to cater for the masses, drawing them to the news, talks and drama which became the exclusive areas for enlightenment. The result was precisely the differentiation of education and entertainment, high- and lowbrow attitudes, serious and light programmes, that Reith had once resisted. The reorganisation in 1967 of BBC broadcasting into Radios 1, 2, 3 and 4, although obviously a response to the pirates' revelations of the size of the demand for pop radio, was also a confirmation of existing BBC attitudes towards its radio audience.[10]

It is with this background in mind that we can begin to understand the problems of Radio 1, the BBC's version of pop-music radio. I've already discussed its programme policy in some detail and I don't need to emphasise further the similarity of its chart-based play-list to those of commercial Top Forty stations. Radio 1 shares with Top Forty radio the assumption that its music is being used as background, a context for doing other things, that people are constantly turning on and off throughout the day, rarely listening for longer than half an hour at a time; the need is for a regular pattern of sounds so that listeners can predict what they will hear; the result is the same form of radio, a limited number of three- or four-minute singles, played repetitively, hour after hour.

But Radio 1 is not exactly the same as a commercial Top Forty station. The PPL needle-time regulations mean that the station cannot be exclusively record-based (though with the astute use of 'live' tapes – musicians recreating their records in the BBC studios – this is barely noticeable), nor can it be as cheap as American commercial radio (which plays its records free). Given the BBC's sparse resources this, perforce, limits the Radio 1 service. And, obviously, Radio 1 does not have commercial breaks. In fact, its programmes are the result of a peculiar attempt to combine two quite different conventions of radio – the BBC tradition of public service on the one hand, the American commercial tradition on the other.[11]

The point of commercial radio is profit and the source of profit is the difference between programme costs and advertising revenue. Record-based music-radio developed in America because it contributed to the profit formula on both sides – it was cheap, and it could attract an audience large enough to interest advertisers at good rates. The audience itself is not the end for commercial radio, it is the means to the end of advertising revenue, and although the BBC has adopted the content of commercial music radio – DJs spinning a limited number of singles – it has done so without being subject to the constraints which, in fact, determine the commercial approach. American music stations, whether Top Forty or FM rock, must attract the audiences that their potential advertisers want to reach –

which means not the biggest possible audiences, but the biggest possible percentages of particular audiences: Top Forty radio is aimed at teenagers, FM radio at 18- to 34-year-olds; advertisers buy air-time accordingly. But this is not the policy of the BBC:

> You see there is really a wide spectrum of interesting forms of popular music. The out-and-out teenage cult public tend to think they represent the whole of their generation. They don't, thank goodness.[12]

The object of Radio 1 *is* to appeal to the biggest possible audience (listening figures are calculated as a percentage of the total number of available receivers) and the BBC would regard it as irresponsible to its licensees to focus an entertainment channel on a specific minority (Radio 3 is not, in this context, regarded as entertaining). Radio 1 makes concessions to more specialised tastes in its limited evening and weekend programmes, but the daily strip shows are aimed explicitly at a mass audience – the only use of 'demographics' is to trace the changing composition of this mass audience through the different times of the day: 'The first premise we start with is we are here to entertain the largest number of people. We are not here to make hits or sell records.[13]

The second problem for an American radio station, given its competition, is to ensure that its audience, once attracted, stays with it. As I have already described, once a station is down to its minimum of legally and commercially necessary talk it can only be particular records that turn listeners off – on comes a bad record and punch goes the button. This was the reason for the ever-narrowing chart-based play-list – people are less likely to dislike one of the Top Forty than they are one of the Top Hundred:

> It stands to reason: if you're playing the thirty-fifth worst record in town, and somebody else is playing the eighty-seventh worst record in town, you're better off than they are.[14]

Radio 1 has a similarly tight chart-based play-list but justifies it with a different argument: if American stations use sales as a guide to what to exclude from their programmes, the BBC uses them as a guide to inclusions. The charts are the only available measure of popular taste and while the American aim is to ensure that no one in the youth market hears a record they don't like, the BBC's aim is to ensure that everyone in the mass market hears a record they do like: 'During the period they listen they expect to hear their own favourite records, the current hit material.'[15]

The type of music that Radio 1 favours is also determined by a third factor, the role of the station's DJs. As one Radio 1 boss has commented: 'we set up Radio 1 originally as a personality station.' The art of commercial radio programming is to integrate records and commercial breaks so that the words slide in and out of the music – smoothly enough to keep the listeners cool but firmly enough for the product name to stick. The advertisements are the focus of commercial radio, not the DJs, and American DJs are (despite the obvious exceptions) anonymous – at the end of a Top Forty day it's not their names you should remember but those of the products they've plugged. For Radio 1, with its audience as the end in itself, the DJs are not just equal to the music as a source of entertainment but even, as in the case of David Hamilton and Tony Blackburn, more important. Although Radio 1 is based on the notion that people listen in short bursts while doing other things, Hamilton and Blackburn assume that they have an audience that is listening explicitly to them – the records they play become an extension of their own personalities. And despite Radio 1's general appeal to a mass audience, Hamilton and Blackburn also assume that their listeners are mostly women and housewives.[16]

The musical result is an emphasis on easy-listening records – riskless, punchless, familiar – which don't interfere with the bland and breezy charm of the DJs. In theory, Radio 1 is a rockin' station, a contrast to Radio 2's middle-of-the-road, but in practice David Hamilton straddled the two stations without showing it and, anyway, the point is not that Radio 1 confines its records to the easy-listening genre per se, but rather that it selects from within the rock genre the easiest-to-listen-to sounds. And so we hear comfortable rock, soul, disco or singer/songwriters. Just as the Muzak Corporation, for its own reasons, edits all the highs and lows and tensions out of its melodies, so too does the BBC favour records which don't have the power to startle a Blackburn-charmed audience.

This policy applies only to the daily strip shows – Radio 1's other programmes are aimed at much more specifically musical markets. In the evenings and at weekends, when the audience for radio is smaller and more homogeneous (see Tables 13 and 14), the BBC does seek to satisfy minority tastes, including those of both teenagers and the youth/student audience. But the distinction between 'culture' and 'entertainment' remains. The justification for cultural broadcasts is not their audience size but their aesthetic value – Radio 3 has a minuscule audience but broadcasts 'good' music; the justification for entertainment programmes is the size of their audiences – aesthetic criteria are not considered in the BBC's Radio 1 policies:

Time	Weekdays					Saturdays					Sundays				
	7–9 a.m.	9–12	12–2 p.m.	2–4.30	4.30–5.45	11–12	9–10 a.m.	10–12	12–1.30 p.m.	2.30–5	9–10 a.m.	10–1 p.m.	1–2	3–5	6–7
Aged 5–14	7·5	1·8	1·0	0·7	0·3	0·0	8·9	1·8	0·4	0·3	6·7	1·2	3·0	0·3	14·9
15–19	14·4	14·8	10·7	10·3	4·4	0·2	15·9	11·8	6·0	4·5	10·4	12·0	13·9	4·1	33·1
20–29	11·8	13·8	7·9	8·6	2·9	0·5	15·8	10·0	5·9	3·9	11·1	10·5	12·7	3·5	22·4
30–49	6·1	8·1	4·1	6·0	1·5	0·1	13·4	4·3	2·5	1·9	10·2	5·6	6·9	1·6	13·1
50+	2·1	2·8	1·4	3·4	0·5	0·1	8·1	1·6	0·9	0·7	5·4	1·7	2·1	0·4	4·0
Women—employed*	11·2	9·1	5·4	6·5	2·0	0·1	14·0	7·5	3·7	2·3	9·6	8·6	9·5	2·3	18·7
Women—unemployed	4·4	8·8	4·1	6·1	0·9	0·0	13·4	4·1	2·2	1·4	9·8	5·3	6·0	1·1	9·2
Adults (15+) Upper middle class	4·7	3·2	2·1	2·6	0·5	0·2	8·7	2·3	0·7	0·8	5·0	2·2	2·9	0·9	7·6
Lower middle class	6·7	5·6	2·8	4·4	1·2	0·2	11·4	4·2	2·2	1·9	8·5	4·7	5·4	1·5	12·3
Working class	6·5	7·5	4·4	5·5	1·6	0·1	11·6	4·8	2·7	1·8	8·3	5·1	6·7	1·5	14·4
All persons over 5 yrs old	6·5	6·7	3·8	5·0	1·4	0·1	11·4	4·5	2·4	1·8	8·2	4·8	6·1	1·5	13·4

* includes part-time employed.

Source: BBC Audience Research Department.

Notes:
1. Summer figures tend to be lower, except for the 15- to 19-year-old group.
2. The daily strip shows have an audience of 2 to 3 million, as do the general Saturday and Sunday morning shows; the evening and specialist week-end shows have much smaller audiences—well under 1 million. The most popular Radio 1 show is still the *Top Twenty* on Sunday afternoons, with nearly 7 million listeners; *Junior Choice*, on Saturday and Sunday mornings, has about 5 million listeners.
3. IBA research suggests that the total radio audience is divided among available services in the following proportions: Radio 1, 37%; Radio 2, 23%; Radio 3, 4%; Radio 4, 15%; ILR 14%; Radio Luxembourg, 1%; BBC Local Radio, 6%.

Table 14:
Index of average audience composition, Radio 1, autumn 1976

Time	Weekdays						Saturdays				Sundays					Television	
	7–9 a.m.	9–12	12–2 p.m.	2–4.30	4.30–5.45	11–12	9–10 a.m.	10–12	12–1.30 p.m.	2.30–5	9–10 a.m.	10–1 p.m.	1–2	3–5	6–7	Top of the Pops	Old Grey Whistle Test
Aged 5–14	115	26	25	13	18	0	78	39	17	18	82	25	48	17	111	161	5
15–19	222	221	281	206	312	132	140	266	246	258	127	249	227	276	248	180	270
20–29	181	205	206	172	201	354	139	223	240	220	136	217	209	241	168	138	246
30–49	93	121	108	119	105	72	116	95	103	110	125	115	114	108	97	84	110
50+	32	42	37	68	38	45	71	36	37	41	66	35	34	27	30	47	29
Male	87	83	90	92	112	181	84	86	100	114	86	79	89	102	94	90	134
Female—all	113	116	109	108	88	24	115	113	100	87	113	119	110	98	106	110	67
—housewives	68	131	109	121	67	7											
Middle-class	99	78	70	84	79	148	97	88	84	97	97	90	83	96	88	96	110
Working-class	101	112	116	109	111	74	102	107	110	102	101	106	109	102	107	102	94

Source: BBC Audience Research Department.

Note: This table is a method of comparing the composition of the Radio 1 audience with the composition of the listening population as a whole. If a group is represented in a programme audience in the proportion to be expected from its position within the listening population, then it is indexed as 100. Numbers greater than 100 indicate group's 'over-representation' in a programme's particular audience; numbers less that 100 indicate 'under-representation' (the formula is $x = \dfrac{\text{proportion in programme audience}}{\text{proportion in listening population}} \times 100$).

The index numbers thus make no reference to the particular size of audience involved.

'We are playing every worthwhile new record the week it comes out.' 'Your definition of worthwhile is a record that will have the greatest appeal?' 'The widest appeal, yes . . . we try to create a list of records which we believe will be the most entertaining to the largest number of people.'[17]

It is because of this emphasis on mass entertainment that Radio 1's daytime programmes are central to the BBC's use of music: these programmes have the biggest and most heterogeneous audiences. Even people who don't listen to them are aware of their style and approach, hear them as an ever-present background to other people's lives. It is Radio 1 DJs who become media 'personalities', the Radio 1 play-list that most clearly affects record sales. But if it is easy to observe the effects of Radio 1 as a mass medium, it is less easy to understand its purpose. The BBC constantly reasserts that it is not in the business to sell records (or, for that matter, to enrich DJs), that the purpose of Radio 1 is simply to entertain as many people as possible. But if for a commercial station a large audience is the direct source of the profits which are the real object of the exercise, for the BBC a large audience is its own justification and so 'entertainment' comes to be defined as anything to which this large audience will listen.

The BBC's approach is tempered by other notions of 'service' – the provision of information, comfort to the lonely, links between distant friends – but Radio 1 is dominated by a contemptuous assessment of both the audience's need to be passively pleased and the music that satisfies this need:

> But heavy or progressive music, I don't believe there is anything at all to be gained from playing it on mainstream radio . . . we have every reason to believe it will not please the wider audience.[18]

It is extremely difficult to discover the reasons for this belief. Radio 1 producers slip quickly into cliché – 'we can't really play that to housewives' – and justify their musical choices by reference to the charts. But this justification is unsatisfactory on two counts. Firstly, 'housewives' are not resonsible for the record sales the charts measure – I have already described how women's participation in youth culture stops abruptly on marriage – and, secondly, Radio 1's programmes have a determinant influence on those charts anyway. 'It is not our fault if the general public tends to keep buying sloppy ballads', asserted ex-boss of Radios 1 and 2, Robin Scott. But it is, if the BBC tend to keep playing them.[19]

Radio 1 provides a peculiar form of broadcasting: its format and musical content are derived from Top Forty radio, rests on assumptions about the youth market and reflects that market's record-buying behaviour, but its attitudes to its audience derive from a much vaguer concept of 'entertainment', rest on much less explicit assumptions about the needs of 'the general public'. Nostalgia is one solution to the resulting problems – in recent years Radio 1 has devoted an increasing part of its daily air time to old rock records, to the youth music of an audience that is no longer young.

Commercial radio

One of the nicer ironies of British radio is that the BBC ideology of entertainment has been given its clearest expression by commercial broadcasters. From their origins Britain's independent local radio stations have resembled Radios 1 and 2 more than they have American stations – they operate under similar needle-time agreements (only 50% of programming or up to nine hours a day can be provided by records, and 14% of advertising revenue goes to the PRS, the PPL and the Musicians Union) and are obliged by the Independent Broadcasting Authority to provide a 'general service' to *all* the members of their local communities; not surprisingly, many of the station directors involved are, anyway, ex-BBC men.

Commercial radio was legalised by the 1972 Sound Broadcasting Act, and since LBC and Capital went on the air in October 1973 nineteen stations have gone into operation. The government's intention was to provide 'a very worthwhile service to the community' and the potential of ILR was explicitly contrasted to Radio 1's 'pop and prattle', but the result has been, for all the stations except the all-talk LBC, a solid diet of BBC-style entertainment programmes, their musical content falling somewhere on the Radio 1/Radio 2 border-line.[20]

The IBA's Annual Report for 1975–6 notes that pop music is the basis for 'most stations programming'. All of them use their needle-time allowance to the full and the 'average' station devotes 46% of its airtime to music, mostly on record. Stations share the BBC pattern of a daytime Top Forty play-list and evening and weekend specialist shows, and the play-lists involved are much the same, whether compiled by programme directors, producers' panels or the DJs themselves and whatever specific notice is taken of local tastes and sales. The similarities of ILR and Radio 1 are reflected in the findings of audience researchers – the listening profiles for the two services are much the same and regular ILR listeners use Radio 1 as their major alternative.[21]

Commercial stations, however, unlike the BBC, have had to provide us with public accounts of their programming ideology. Each station had to submit its 'programme plans' when bidding for the limited number of broadcasting licences. Capital, for example, promised to play only the 'best music', to avoid both the 'extremes' and chart material, which it heard as 'unoriginal and manufactured in a conveyor belt process'; it also promised to select its music according to the needs of each segment of the day's 'target audience' and to key its programmes to the 'average human tempo'. All stations were agreed that their daytime object was 'the maximum general audience' – if their planned programmes would consist of neither 'wallpaper' nor an 'endless repetition of the Top Fifty', they would provide the 'appropriate musical fare for that section of the public most likely to be listening at any given time'; they would, that is, attract an audience 'acceptable to our advertisers'. There was almost unanimous agreement about what this audience would need: 'lively tunes' to get them up in the morning; quiet music, 'the housewife's friend', during the day; up tempo again at tea-time, cheerful but relaxing music for dad and the kids home from work and school. In a vain attempt to distinguish themselves from each other, the stations emphasised that their services would be local – *their* consumer tips and swap shops and phone-ins would link a community. In an even more vain attempt to conceal their programming's almost exclusive dependence on record companies, the stations emphasised the proposed importance of their DJs ('presenters' was the preferred word). They would be 'very real people', who would give their stations 'character'. For British commercial radio stations the DJs are more important than the adverts – another reflection of the BBC ideology of entertainment.[22]

ILR practice has, for the most part, confirmed the implications of the programme plans. British commercial radio has meant a network of localised versions of BBC mass entertainment – the stations come across the airwaves with a cautious mixture of Radio 1 and Radio 2, though with commercials too. The needs of their advertisers have obliged commercial broadcasters to investigate the nature of their daytime audience even more carefully than the BBC has investigated its listeners.

The IBA itself claims that ILR already reaches 40–60% of the population, who listen for an average of 10–12½ hours per week, and stresses that the composition of the ILR audience matches that of the population as a whole – no station draws more than a third of its audience from the 15 to 24 age group. But JICRAR research also reveals that while 'light music' is the most liked type of music, it is so 'particularly among listeners to whom music in general is relatively unimportant'; those for whom music is important prefer 'pop' or 'classical'. And more detailed research does suggest that ILR has a particular appeal to 'younger adults', and that 'younger listeners felt more clearly than older ones that the station played music they liked'. 42% of Capital's regular listeners in 1975 were aged between 15 and 24, and more than 66% were under 34 – it was the young who most appreciated Capital's music programming. Both Capital and Clyde draw a young audience early in the morning, late in the evening, and at weekends.[23]

These findings match those of the BBC about Radio 1's listeners (see Tables 13 and 14) and the figures have a number of implications – the broadcasters' obsession with housewives, for example, seems a little misplaced. But I want to conclude with some points about radio and rock.

In America, rock and radio developed together because Top Forty programming was aimed precisely at the youth market – teenagers could use their stations just as they used their records, as an ever-present background to their leisure activities, as the sound of their young identity, as a way of distinguishing their places from those of adults. In England, American-style commercial radio – Luxembourg, the pirates – has been used in just the same way. But Radio 1 and the ILR stations do not provide such a service to the young. There have always been specific *programmes* for them – from *Saturday Club* to Rosko, from *Pick of the Pops* to John Peel, Alan Freeman, and their commercial FM-style equivalents – but even they can't be used completely casually; the audience has to remember to tune in on time, listening becomes a specific decision.

Meanwhile, the permanent background music that Radio 1 does provide serves as a background for adult as well as youthful activities; it is used in factories and shops, on building sites and motorways. The paradox is that because young people are the only Radio 1 listeners who care much about what they hear, who care enough to buy the records for themselves, it is mostly their music that every one else hears in the background – as long as it is not *too* heavy or progressive or raucous. What Radio 1 and the ILR stations do is use this music in a context that drains it of its significance as youth music and transforms it into an all-purpose muzak. The BBC is not concerned with rock as a cultural form; its interest is confined to the music's inoffensive ability to soothe, cheer and comfort a mass audience. And such is the power of Radio 1 that its ideology of rock is widely shared. Many people agree with Tony Blackburn, but generalise from the Radio 1 use of rock to the music as a whole: 'Rubbish, that's what it's all about.'

8

The music press

One of the most extraordinary things about rock (especially given the Marshall McLuhan theory of media) is the amount of words it generates. Britain currently supports four consumer weeklies devoted to the subject (as well as 3 weekly trade papers servicing the industry), numerous teeny girl comics semi-devoted to it, and an endless series of short-lived 'fanzines' and 'serious' rock music monthlies. Rock gets its share of coverage too in the non-specialist press. A new album or concert tour by a 'significant' rock musician (Rod Stewart, for example) gets more, and more varied, print coverage than any other form of popular cultural product. It'll be assigned space in the national dailies, from the *Times* to the *Sun*, in the serious weeklies and the glossy monthlies, in men's and women's magazines, in *Penthouse* and *She*. In this chapter I want to consider the place of these words in the rock process. I will concentrate on the music press, both because it is the most important print medium for the record industry, and because in it we can find the clearest expressions of the current range of attitudes to rock.

Before the Beatles

The oldest pop music paper in Britain, *Melody Maker*, started in 1926 as a trade paper for the growing number of dance- and jazz-band musicians (it continues to serve this function in its small ads) and, for a long time, provided the only informed and regular coverage of the popular music scene – it was soon used as a consumer's paper too. *New Musical Express* (1952), *Record Mirror* (1953) and *Disc* (1958) were founded explicitly to cater for the new explosion of music consumers in the 1950s – their focus was almost immediately on teen-age record-buyers. *Sounds* (1970) and the short-lived *National Rock Star* (1976) were designed to plug perceived gaps in the existing press coverage of the rock market in the 1970s. Whatever the origins of the various papers (they tend to be founded by ex-employees of the others) their current situation reflects the oligopolistic control of British media. IPC owns *Melody Maker* (acquired through Odhams) and *NME* (acquired via Newnes in 1964); Morgan-Grampian, in the form of Spotlight Publications, owns *Sounds*, *Record Mirror* (bought from the American publishers Billboard in 1974 and merged with the teeny-bop magazine *Poswop*), *Disc* (bought in 1975 from IPC and now also incorporated into *Record Mirror*), and the trade paper *Music Week* (bought from Billboard in 1977).[1]

In the 1950s the music press was uncomplicatedly a facet of the music industry and its growth reflected the increasing importance of records and record sales (as against songs and publishers) in that industry. Even the *Melody Maker*, which continued to provide a specialist service for musicians and jazz fans, became centrally concerned with record publicity, and the music papers' importance was considerable at a time when Luxembourg was the only other available form of record promotion. The papers' function was symbolised by their charts: in 1952 *NME* established the first regular and reasonably accurate chart of British sales of singles, and soon each paper compiled its own hit parade, using its own secret list of retailers' returns. In the days before Radio 1 these charts had a noticeable effect on stocking and promotional policies. In general terms, and even if their final ends were different (circulation figures *vs* record sales), the papers and the record companies saw themselves as having exactly the same interests. Music press 'news' was news of the latest recording stars, the latest entrants to the charts; all such stars were equally important and their importance lasted precisely as long as their chart success. The papers' lists of concert dates and record releases were made up of communiqués from record-company press offices, and the papers' 'investigations' and 'features' went little further than a quick interview (organised by the growing band of publicists) with the latest star. Such stories were designed merely to fill out a record-company 'bio' with some human interest and personality detail: what is your favourite food?

As Dave Laing has pointed out, the fifties music papers functioned like the film fans' magazines of the 1930s. They served their purpose competently enough, keeping pop fans informed of who was doing what and where. But as fan mags there were things that the papers did not do. They provided no perspective, historical or otherwise, on the music they covered; they had no developed critical positions or standards (what was popular equalled, by and large, what was good); they showed no curiosity in where records came from or where they went. The music papers presented the industry's own public view of itself and were written, accordingly, in a breathy, adman's prose. Their success was entirely dependent on how interested their readers were in the stars they covered: if the *NME* took over from the *MM* as the most popular music paper in the 1950s (see Table 15) it was because it provided better news of the current chart stars.

Table 15:
Circulation figures of the music press

	1955	1956	1957	1958	1959	1960	1961	1962	1963	1964 *	1965
Melody Maker	107,378	105,188	112,205	99,104	81,187	77,864	77,812	80,269	86,742	90,501	78,468
New Musical Express	93,127	88,839	105,575	122,267	110,384	122,272	170,322	244,912	294,700	289,359	250,911
Disc			**						92,595	100,121	68,029

	1966	1967	1968	1969	1970	1971	1972	1973	1974	1975	1976
Melody Maker	81,000	93,953	100,000 **	106,812	145,006	173,451	209,191	207,740	188,073	160,035	158,274
New Musical Express	213,399	265,652	247,380	207,497	173,175	136,092	173,580	201,482	189,607	179,023	183,566
Record Mirror		66,036					49,863		*** 52,599	110,782	
Disc		93,646	79,457		79,557	66,795	86,488	97,455	82,357	(110,782)	
Sounds							154,205	146,707	107,239	82,572	88,952
Fab 208				161,626	151,344	143,523	279,413	248,586	177,641	136,588	117,444

Source: Audit Bureau of Circulations: *Half Yearly Circulation Reviews* (average net sales at recognised trade terms – July to December figures).

Notes: * In January–June 1964 NME circulation peaked at 306,881; MM at 95,544; *Disc* at 107,872.
  ** Figures for January–June.
  *** Now incorporating *Popswop*.

We give the kids what they want. We write about their current idols. And we're not so much a jazz paper, like the *MM*, as a pop paper. A lot of our competitors write about stars who have dropped out of the charts, why they've lost their popularity etc. And they write about up-and-coming singers who are going to be the stars of tomorrow. It's the stars of today the kids want to know about, not the stars of tomorrow.[2]

The music papers' unprecedented circulation heights in early 1964 were just another aspect of the phenomenal appeal of the Beatles and of British Beat and didn't immediately change the nature of the papers' music coverage; they continued to assume, like the record companies, that their basic market was working-class teenagers with a limited, immediate interest in the latest pops. The Beatles' success, from this perspective, was a matter of quantity rather than quality and its immediate print effect was more, rather than different, as such old-fashioned fan mags as the *Beatles Monthly* reached temporary mass circulation. The TV show *Juke Box Jury* continued to encapsulate the music papers' own view of rock – a mixture of showbiz condescension to the youngsters' tastes and an assumption, apparently shared by the youngsters themselves, that music criticism was the same thing as the assessment of chart potential. The Beatles just revealed the most chart potential that there'd ever been.[3]

But as the Beatles phenomenon went on and on these assumptions were challenged on two fronts. Firstly, it became clear that the Beatles' and other British groups' market was not just working-class teenagers; secondly, arguments began to emerge that did not relate the Beatles' value simply to their sales. There had always been non-teenagers interested in rock and even non-teenagers concerned to show that some rock records were more valuable than others according to non-commercial criteria. But such writers' interest had been in teenage culture as a social fact; they were outsiders, and their critical judgement usually involved 'rescuing' particular performers or records from their teenage context and placing them in some tradition of 'proper' music. Some of these efforts seem decidedly odd in retrospect – the amount of attention intellectuals paid to Helen Shapiro, for example – but it is not surprising that the Beatles were particularly interesting to these writers, and William Mann's famous musicological analysis of them in *The Times* in 1963 differed from previous 'serious' analyses of teenage music only in its use of the critical vocabulary of classical music rather than that of jazz or the music hall.[4]

If the Beatles were important in establishing the idea that rock could, in certain circumstances, be art, so that rock coverage has now become a normal part of the arts pages of the quality press, this was far less important for the music papers' attitudes than the development of a new sort of music market. In the late 1960s the emergence of this market was reflected in progressive rock, in album sales and in new musical institutions, and the music papers' traditional approach to rock was increasingly exposed as inadequate. The new rock audience had attitudes to music that were not expressed in the pages of the music weeklies; readers were turning to their own self-generated papers for the articulation of their musical ideology; the music papers found themselves with a new competitor – the underground press.

The underground press

In order to understand the relationship between the underground press and rock it is necessary to understand the development of music writing in America where, because of the lack of equivalents of the British weeklies, the contribution of the underground to rock journalism is much clearer. In the 1950s and early 1960s the USA had no music papers between the trade press, on the one hand, and the teeny-bop mags on the other, and America's rock press emerged from two other sources.

Firstly, there was the underground press proper. This had its origins in *Village Voice* (1955), but its real foundations were laid by the *LA Free Press* and *Berkeley Barb* in 1964, papers which were not concerned with music as such but with life-style, with 'dope, sex and revolution', with, in the words of the White Panthers' subsequent slogan, 'revolutionary motherfucker armed love'. Music was valued in as far as it could be connected with these interests and it soon became important as the most fertile source of underground income, whether the money came from record-company advertisements or musicians' benefits. Rock turned out to be the basic form of underground culture, but in becoming so it was imbued with an ideology that was at marked variance with previous notions of pop. Rock was valued for its politics, its freedom, its sexuality, its relationship to cultural struggles. The music that was most despised and mistrusted by the underground press was precisely the commercial, successful, teenage pop that had been essential to the development of the British music press. Rock was defined as the music that articulated the values of a new community of youth, it was opposed to the traditional values of show-biz; and as the appeal of the underground spread from its original bohemian roots so did this notion of rock. In 1967 the Underground Press Syndicate was formed. By 1969 it was claiming 125 member papers in continuous publication and 200 other papers in 'erratic' appearance. Two of the regular members were British – *Oz* and *IT*.[5]

I don't intend to trace the history of the underground press, and I don't want to exaggerate the extent of its readership; my point is that underground papers were important as the source of what became the dominant ideology of rock. This ideology was confirmed and developed by a second American event, the creation of new, specialist music magazines: *Crawdaddy* began publication in 1966 and was followed over the next few years by *Cheetah, Fusion, Mojo-Navigator* and *Creem*. These magazines varied greatly in their format, style, success and concerns, but they had in common the serious treatment of rock as a cultural form, and they made, from their side, the same connections between rock and life-style as the underground papers made from theirs.

The most important of the new music papers was *Rolling Stone*, a San Francisco fortnightly the first edition of which appeared on 9 November 1967. Its founder, Jann Wenner, 'wanted the publication to focus on rock music, but it was also to cover everything else in the youth culture', and the magazine's intentions were made clear in the first issue:

> You're probably wondering what we are trying to do. It's hard to say: sort of a magazine and sort of a newspaper. . . . We have begun a new publication reflecting what we see are the changes in rock and roll and the changes related to rock and roll. Because the trade papers have become so inaccurate and irrelevant, and because the fan magazines are an anachronism, fashioned in the mould of myth and nonsense, we hope that we have something here for the artists and the industry, and every person who 'believes in the magic that can set you free'. *Rolling Stone* is not just about music, but also about the things and attitudes that the music embraces.[6]

For the first four years of its existence *Rolling Stone* experienced tensions and conflicts over the successful achievement of its proclaimed role. The paper found a disjunction between the available ideology of rock – an ideology drawn from the concerns of the underground – and the demands of rock promotion, demands coming from a record business that was beginning to understand the new market and was exploring the ways to reach it. The contradictions involved were symbolised by CBS's famous advertisements – 'The Revolutionaries Are On Columbia' and 'The Man Can't Bust Our Music' – and in 1969 the tensions of the situation had an English expression: Jann Wenner opened an English office to publish *Rolling*

Stone in 'a regional edition', but his English editors followed too closely the practices and policies of the underground and were dismissed (they founded a new English underground paper, *Frendz*).

In America, meanwhile, *Stone* slowly established itself as by far the most popular of the new publications by developing a tradition of in-depth reports on youth cultural events, but the excellence of its coverage of, for example, the Woodstock and Altamont festivals, rather than resolving the tensions inherent in its role, increased them. As the paper which most clearly understood the new youth culture, *Rolling Stone* had the hopes of both the record industry and the rock ideologues focused on it. By 1971, after numerous crises and staff changes, it had become clear that it was record-company hopes that would be satisfied; *Rolling Stone* became integrated into the American rock business.[7]

Chet Flippo argues that Wenner's own approach was consistent from the start:

> exhaustive coverage of the superstars, inside information on the performers and the music industry, and competent, often excellent, reportage of anything of interest to young people.[8]

What this meant in practice was, in the words of one of the staff who left, 'a tastefully executed fan magazine'. The music was treated seriously, readers were not teeny-boppers, but *Rolling Stone* did not, in the end, represent any fundamental break from the traditional show-biz conception of stars, selling and consumption. The paper had its own version of news, gossip and interviews with the stars, had its own sort of cynical treatment of the latest singing sensation, but its dependence on the concerns of the music industry was soon as obvious as that of the British music press. If, in its early years, this was tempered with different notions of investigation and community, these notions became less evident in the 1970s as staff were sacked for 'negative' reviews, for failing to have 'the proper attitude toward the artists', for writing 'an unflattering review of Bob Dylan'.

Rolling Stone's ideological dependence on the music business reflected its material situation. It was supported through the various financial difficulties of its early years by record companies. WEA loaned the paper $100,000, CBS helped with distribution and administration, record companies supplied virtually all of *Stone*'s considerable advertising revenue from its beginning. They believed that 'the paper was good for music' and agreed with Clive Davis of CBS – if *Stone* 'blasted us occasionally' it was simply 'to protect itself against charges of "selling out"' from its 'allegedly anti-establishment readership'.[9]

In August 1973 *Rolling Stone* changed format and became, formally, 'a general interest magazine, covering modern American culture, politics and arts, with a special interest in music', but by now *Stone*'s readership – 20 to 30 years old, mostly male, white, affluent, interested in rock even as they settled down and lost their youthful fanaticism – was precisely the same market in which the record companies were interested. *Stone*'s move away from music made no difference to its advertising revenue or to its importance to the record industry: 'Within this business all anybody cares about is an article in the *Stone*. It has more impact than any other magazine.'[10]

Much the same description of progressive integration into the rock business could be made of America's other music magazines, whatever their origins, and an appreciation of this process can help us to understand the apparent differences between the English and American rock press. While *Rolling Stone* was becoming, from nowhere, the dominant paper in the American music business, nothing much seemed to happen in Britain at all. The British music press in 1976 was much the same as it had been in 1966 – the same weeklies with their massive circulations, the same lack of 'alternative' magazines. Numerous such magazines had been launched since *ZigZag* showed the way in 1970 – *Cream, Let It Rock, Street Life* – but only *ZigZag* has survived and none of these magazines achieved a circulation comparable to that of the weeklies. *Rolling Stone* itself has never had much sales success in Britain. The point is that the 'alternative' approach to music that it represents has been developed here not in alternative publications, but within the pages of the traditional weeklies themselves.

After the Beatles

I have already noted how little the Beatles phenomenon affected the attitudes of the music press; even more surprising is how little these attitudes were affected by the initial expressions of rock ideology. In 1968, by when the *MM* was already running a feature entitled 'Where Have All The Hippies Gone?', the basis of *MM*'s music coverage was still the excitement and news generated by action in the singles charts – Esther and Abi Ofarim! Don Partridge! Singles got more review space than albums, the criticisms of which were brief, unattributed and eclectic – from Love to Jack Jones in half a page; serious analysis was confined to folk and jazz. In the 1968 Readers' Poll, Scott Walker was voted best male singer (pipping Tom Jones) and Herb Alpert was the third best musician in the world (pipped by Eric Clapton and Jimi Hendrix). John Peel, however, won the best DJ spot, rising from sixth the year before, and from October the paper started listing the

Top Twenty albums – previously they'd only bothered with the Top
Ten. By the time of the poll a year later the paper had taken on four
new young staff members and the poll results were sufficiently striking to elicit this editorial comment:

> The poll results generally were proof of the tastes of the vast
> majority of young people in Britain today – they want pop that is
> progressive played by musicians who are honest. And they don't
> want old-style show-biz type pop.[11]

The *Melody Maker*'s belated recognition of these demands was
soon reflected in both the content and the sales of the paper (see
Table 15). Album reviews became longer and were signed, the British
and American Top Thirty album charts were printed; in 1970 a
'College Column' was started and the space for specialist jazz coverage was cut to give room for longer and more serious rock features;
the 'Melody Maker Interview' was introduced, on the *Rolling Stone*
model of the 'in-depth' questions appropriate for real musicians. The
1970 poll results revealed the extent of *MM* readers' submersion in
progressive rock taste – the winners were Led Zeppelin and ELP, Joni
Mitchell and Leonard Cohen, CSNY and the Who, Hot Rats and
'Bridge Over Troubled Waters'. In 1971 the paper's circulation finally
overtook that of the *NME* and the editor commented:

> The scene we report, reflect and interpret is now accepted as a
> great deal more serious and creative than previously catered for by
> a 'bubblegum philosophy' of popular music. It's a subject that re-
> quires careful, sympathetic analysis. And the *Melody Maker* is the
> thinking fan's paper.[12]

The thinking fan was not obsessed by the latest chart entry, but
was interested in the history of the music (at least occasionally) and
concerned to read about the bands that might make it in the future
(in 'Horizon'); the thinking fan expected to learn, in 'Band Bread-
down', not the colour of the guitarist's eyes, but the make of his
amplifier. Album and concert reviews were now the *MM*'s basic
service to its readers; singles were confined to Christ Welch's column
of zany meandering.

In 1968, the *NME* had shown even less understanding of the rock
ideology than *Melody Maker*. Its readership was still almost 250,000
and its poll results showed a decade's continuity of taste – British
beat had been an addition to *NME*'s concerns rather than a sign of
change (see Table 16). The paper's singles-based, teenage pop formula
remained intact; the only concession to progress was that young staff

Table 16:
Winners of the NME Readers' Poll, 1959-68

Category	1959	1960	1961	1962	1963	1964	1965	1966	1967	1968
World										
male singer	Elvis Presley	Elvis Presley	Elvis Presley	Elvis Presley	Cliff Richard	Elvis Presley	Elvis Presley	Elvis Presley	Elvis Presley	Elvis Presley
Female singer	Connie Francis	Connie Francis	Connie Francis	Brenda Lee	Brenda Lee	Brenda Lee	Dusty Springfield	Dusty Springfield	Dusty Springfield	Lulu
Vocal group	Everlys	Everlys	Everlys	Everlys	Beatles	Beatles	Beatles	Beatles	Beatles	Beatles
Personality	Elvis Presley	Elvis Presley	Elvis Presley	Elvis Presley	Elvis Presley	Elvis Presley	Elvis Presley	Elvis Presley	Elvis Presley	Elvis Presley
Britain										
Male singer	Cliff Richard	Cliff Richard	Cliff Richard	Cliff Richard	Cliff Richard	Cliff Richard	Cliff Richard	Cliff Richard	Tom Jones	Tom Jones
Female singer	Shirley Bassey	Shirley Bassey	Helen Shapiro	Helen Shapiro	Kathy Kirby	Dusty Springfield	Dusty Springfield	Dusty Springfield	Lulu	Lulu
New singer	Craig Douglas	Emile Ford	John Leyton	Frank Ifield	Gerry Marsden		Donovan	Steve Winwood	Englebert Humperdink	Mary Hopkin
Small group	Lonnie Donegan	Shadows	Shadows	Shadows	Shadows	Beatles	Beatles	Beatles	Beatles	Beatles
DJ	Pete Murray	David Jacobs	David Jacobs	David Jacobs	David Jacobs	Jimmy Saville	Jimmy Saville	Jimmy Saville	Jimmy Saville	Jimmy Saville
Personality	Frankie Vaughan	Lonnie Donegan	Adam Faith	Joe Brown	Joe Brown	Cliff Richard	John Lennon	Cliff Richard	Cliff Richard	Cliff Richard
Instrumental group						Shadows	Shadows	Shadows	Shadows	Shadows
R & B group						Rolling Stones	Rolling Stones	Spencer Davis group	Rolling Stones	Rolling Stones
New group						Rolling Stones	Seekers	Spencer Davis group	Bee Gees	Love Affair

Source: NME, 7 December, 1968.

member Nick Logan was occasionally sent off to cover 'underground acts'. But in 1970 *Sounds* was founded by a breakaway group from the *MM*; a market gap had been spotted – there was a potential audience at the younger end of *MM*'s readership. These teenagers, 10 to 16 years old, were progressive fans, contemptuous of *NME*'s pop assumptions, but also uninterested in *MM*'s comprehensive coverage of folk, jazz and the rest. They wanted more gossip and pix – *Sounds* included pull-out colour posters in its service. Between 1969 and 1972 *NME* lost over 100,000 readers; it was overtaken by the *MM* and had *Sounds* nibbling away at its teenage appeal. Finally Andy Gray, who'd been editor for fifteen years, was replaced by Alan Smith, who was given the job of attracting readers from the new rock audience. The paper was restaffed, and its new team was deliberately recruited from underground and specialist rock magazines. The first such arrivals – Charles Shaar Murray, Nick Kent, Ian MacDonald – had written for *Oz*, *Frendz* and *Creem*.

Their immediate effect was on *NME*'s style rather than on its content; their writing was hip and knowledgeable, their cynicism about the rock business was out front, they clearly loved their music. By 1973 the effects of these new attitudes on the paper were obvious even to its most casual readers. On the one hand, the *NME* had developed a calculated eccentricity in its layout, sub-heads and picture captions – the paper mocked itself in a zany way derived from the underground and from the American magazine, *Creem*; on the other hand, music coverage was beginning to stretch beyond the latest chart sensations, to reflect a critical vision of rock that was derived from the rock magazines. Historical and retrospective pieces appeared; *NME*'s coverage was extended systematically to specialist areas – jazz, soul and reggae; the staff were given the space for 'think pieces', arguments and opinions not necessarily hung on any star or record. The writers developed their own personalities and flaunted their individual critical criteria. The old underground notion that rock was only one part of youth culture was expressed in the extension of coverage to non-musical arts – film, science fiction and comics. By 1975, *NME*'s combination of the rock approach and an entertaining style had put it back at the top of the pile, above the now rather staid and stodgy *Melody Maker*. *Sound*'s challenge had been seen off, and by 1976 *Sounds* was, in turn, echoing the compliment and imitating the *NME* approach – there may be only two music press publishers, IPC and Morgan-Grampian, but competition for readership among their various papers remains intense.

In marketing terms what the *NME* had achieved was a movement 'up market'. What this really reflected was the marketing fact that by the 1970s there was a clear split in the rock audience between the

'teeny-boppers' – singles-buying, chart-concerned, female, pop-idol-
isers – and the 'progressives' – album-buying, hip, male, music
freaks. The implications of this split for the music press were made
clear by the teeny-bop boom of 1971–3, when the market was flooded
with magazines containing nothing much but pictures of David
Cassidy and the Osmonds. *NME, Sounds* and *MM* derived their own
circulation rewards from the occasional Osmonds feature and
Cassidy cover, but their styles and attitudes were by now too obviously detached and cynical about the hysteria to be of much appeal
to the teeny-bop market. *Disc* and *Record Mirror* were still aimed at
that market, but if the immediate result of the boom – increased circulation – was obviously beneficial, the long-term effect of the sudden
competition from the instant poster-based pop mags was not. When
the bottom fell out of the teeny-bop market, it fell out of the market
for the traditional pop paper too, and whereas the newcomers could
switch their cameras from the Osmonds to the *Planet of the Apes* to
the Bay City Rollers to *Starsky and Hutch* without a jolt – music was
incidental to their marketing approach – the teeny-bop music papers
couldn't without ceasing to be music papers.[13]

The 1974–5 merger and rationalisation of *Record Mirror, Popswop*
and *Disc* was an attempt to retain a market place for one such music
paper against the competition of such successful semi-music magazines as *Fab 208*. In 1976 a new editor was appointed (from *Sounds*)
and began to move the *Record Mirror* a little up-market, partly to
ease the risky dependence on pin-ups and partly to reach that same
market gap perceived by IPC and the unsuccessful *National Rock Star*.
In the 1960s the music papers had been able to straddle the teeny-
bop/progressive markets and *Record Mirror* was trying to do it again.
In its 1976 form *Record Mirror* resembled a sixties pop paper: colour
cover pic and pull-out colour poster of a Top-Twenty star, page of
charts, news pages cobbled together from the week's press handouts,
star interviews with current good sellers, a page of singles reviews,
a guide to gigs, a soul page, readers' letters, gossip, astrology and
jokes.

The up-market music press does have a very different feel, even if
the basic form – news, interviews, reviews – is the same. The tone is
different, different musics and musicians are covered. In *Sounds,
NME* and the *MM* the reviewing emphasis is on albums and concerts
(several pages of lengthy analyses) rather than singles (a one-page,
usually flippant, column), and both reviews and features reflect the
papers' apparent freedom from chart tastes – concert reviews, for
example, cover a fair proportion of unrecorded bands and the music
papers now see it as part of their function to assist A&R men in
assessing new groups' potential. If these papers' major features in any

week tend to be the same – reflecting a visit to town or to a publicists' office of some major star – there is a much wider variety of who and what will be covered otherwise. *NME* and *Sounds*, at least, make no attempt to include features on acts just because of their success. Interviews are less sycophantic than in *Record Mirror*, enthusiasm for an act or record is more personal. The late sixties' rock ideology is still apparent – indeed, two eminent underground figures are now ensconced in the music press: Caroline Coon, of Release, writes for *Sounds*, Mick Farren of the Deviants for the *New Musical Express*, and there is a continuing undercurrent of the old commerce *vs* art stance – very successful acts get suspicious treatment, rave reviews are reserved for unknowns and cults. The papers' treatment of music varies in detail, but not in substance. *Sounds* and *NME* are Americanophile, with a tendency to what Flippo calls the 'anti-culturalist' response, valuing music for its effects on and relationship with an audience rather than for its creators' intentions or skills; the *MM* represents the progressive, 'culturalist' approach – music's value lies in the technique and complexity of the 'text' itself.

The music press and the music business

The music papers' general approaches to rock are based on careful research into their potential markets (see Table 17) and such market

Table 17:

Readership profile of the music press, July 1975–June 1976

	Sex		Age		Class					
%	Men	Women	15–24	25–34	A	B	C1	C2	D	E
NME	66	34	70	14	2	8	23	35	24	3
MM	66	34	68	14	3	10	29	34	22	3
Sounds	67	33	78	8	1	10	29	33	23	4
Fab 208	16	84	70	6	—	7	24	34	29	6

Source: JICNRS: *National Readership Survey, 1976.*

research also reveals the importance of their readers for the record industry: *MM/NME* readers are the section of the population most likely to own record playing equipment, most likely to buy records, particularly albums, most likely to influence what the rest of the rock market buys. The marketing men's image of the typical reader is of a provincial 18-year-old male, a student or white-collar worker, with a group of mates whom he likes to impress at work or in the pub with the knowledge of the rock world that he has gleaned from his music paper. He may be mocked about his obsessions, but his assertions about what's happening and where it's at are taken seriously – it is his record collection that is scanned when friends are wondering what to buy, it is his advice that determines the concerts people attend.[14]

The seventies rock market may be different from the fifties teenage market, but the relationship of music papers and record companies in the exploitation of these markets is much the same – the changes of style and content through which the music papers have gone conceal the basic continuity of approach. News and interviews are still integrated with publicity and promotion, and if concert tours have replaced the charts as the starting point of press attention that is only because of the new record-company strategy of LP selling. Promotion has become a long-term process and so, while the papers no longer cover exactly the same people every week, they still hang most of their reports on some record-company initiative – a new album or tour, a change of labels, a new image. Interviews, if more cynical, are still superficial (an essence of the form) and carefully planned and monitored by a wary press officer; the papers still adopt the scatter-gun approach – cover as many disparate people as possible in the hope that there'll be somebody of interest to everybody, and if the parameters of seventies rock coverage are different from those of fifties and sixties rock, when sales were the only sign of importance, they are also less clear – sales success is now combined with vague notions of rock as art.

The music papers are not newspapers. Events get reported, occasionally acutely and critically, but there is no place for investigation – a special feature on some aspect of the business just means a quick round of interviews – and no place for continuity. The task, each week, is to make that week's stars seem exciting and important. Once someone's been done he'll be put back in the files, to be brought out and dusted off again at the beginning of his next tour, or on the release of his next album, when the same questions from the same people will get the same answers. The music papers remain dependent on press offices for their stories, and whatever the integrity of the writers involved they are still essentially record-promoters rather than detached reporters. In 1976–7, for example, each paper had its own punk spokesman (or spokeswoman) and each paper drew its punk clichés, assumptions and put-downs from the music's record-company publicists. The latter, in turn, depended for their general promotional arguments on the ideology of punk developed by the music papers. In the end the punks' journalist champions were more single-minded in their commitment than the record companies' own PR departments (which always have to keep half an ear open for tomorrow's sensation). At least one journalist (Jonh Ingham of *Sounds*, an ex-press officer at EMI and Island) left his job to manage a punk band for himself.

The reasons for the subordination of the music papers to the record business lie in the nature and value of the products at issue. It was in the interests of the music papers to help hype punk rock because if it did become popular, partly thanks to their efforts, they would benefit from the new readers turning to them as sources of news, enthusiasm and knowledge – the papers' and the record companies' interests in rock sales are identical. The music papers' editorial discussions are attended by the papers' own marketing men and the decisions on whom to write about depend on judgements of readers' tastes. The charts are no longer the only source of answers to the questions – who is popular? who would draw readers? – but the questions remain important. In short, the reasons why the press and the companies are so tight (and this applies just as much to *Rolling Stone*) is not because of the press dependence on record-company advertising, but because their images of the world are much the same.

In the end, the rock writer's job is controlled by record companies. His news is provided by them, his interviews, his access; music writers' lives involve a constant consumption of company-provided resources – free records, free trips to concerts, lunches, drinks, receptions, parties, weekends in Jamaica; virtually everything the writer does is laid on for him. In America the result is hundreds of freelance writers, poorly paid by their eventual publishers, but well off from all the perks they can get out of the business (in 1973 the National Association of Rock Writers had two hundred members in attendance at the record-company-provided weekend in Memphis). In Britain, where most rock writers are employees of the music weeklies, the result is an extremely cheap (and profitable) form of magazine production. In both countries there is continuous job mobility between rock journalism and rock publicity – record-company press departments recruit from the music papers, music papers employ ex-publicists. In America it is not even unusual for writers to do both jobs simultaneously – reviewing with one pen records that they are hyping with another.[15]

The most interesting position in the press/industry tie-up is occupied by the review. In the old pop press, reviews were little more than news of release plus a prediction of success. Reviewers didn't expect to influence readers' opinions and probably didn't influence them. But in the world of rock, where an album choice can be important for an individual's identity and status, the review is a reader's central interest – it is the reviews which arouse most of the readers' responses on the music papers' letters pages. A rock album or concert review is read equally carefully by record companies. Reviews rarely have an obvious direct effect on sales, popular acts have rarely been harmed by poor notices, unpopular acts rarely pushed to success by press praise alone, but they do influence promotion strategies:

> reviews can make or break you. A slagging of the opening concert of a tour affects ticket sales in other parts of the country where people still regard a review as gospel. And when a record company releases a single, they rush out to read the reviews. If they're good they'll go with it. If not, they often won't promote it.[16]

Record companies care little about what's written about their acts in a feature – it's the publicity and pix that count there – but a review can be significant, and part of its significance lies, paradoxically, in the reviewers' independence of record-company concerns. It is their independence that gives good reviews their authenticity and makes bad reviews useful warnings – if the *NME* guy doesn't like it, the public may not either. From this perspective, the review is another part of the record industry's filtering process.

For all their cosiness together, then, it is in record companies' interests to keep one part of the rock writer's role at a distance. This also gives writers the space to establish their authenticity for their readers; it is in their reviews that writers reveal their personal standards, their freedom from commercial pressures, their individuality. In the up-market press, album and concert reviews have replaced the charts as the central reader service and the writers in those papers see rock criticism, as opposed to rock puffery, as the essence of their job. But what is involved in such criticism remains confused, as writers seek simultaneously to provide a consumer guide, to comment on a culture, to explore personal tastes.[17]

Such confusion reflects the history of the music press. In his study of American rock writing Chet Flippo argues that because in the late sixties rock was an integral part of a genuine youth culture writing about it automatically involved writing about a variety of other issues. In the seventies the culture dissolved and the writers' role was reduced to servicing one or other of two consumer markets. On the one hand there was the sixties generation, older now, interested in rock only as a form of entertainment akin to *Playboy*, a movie, television; it was this generation at which *Rolling Stone* had always been aimed, and as it grew with it into a general-interest magazine, its music coverage became little more than a hip consumer guide. On the other hand, there was a new rock'n'roll generation, using its music and idols just like the teenagers of old, also wanting a consumer guide, but wanting it in the form of an old-fashioned, if a little more sophisticated, fan mag – hence *Circus* and *Creem*.[18]

A similar argument could be applied to the British rock press. The details are different – Britain has not developed so obviously a generation of 30-year-old rock consumers, *NME* is closer to *Creem* than to *Rolling Stone* – but the basic distinctions are the same: on the one hand *Record Mirror* or *Fab 208*, teenage fan mags that have hardly changed their concerns for twenty years; on the other, *Melody Maker* and the rest, providing a hip guide to the consumption of the thinking fan. But there are difficulties in lumping all the music papers together as consumer guides, differing only in the different consumers involved. These different consumers *use* rock differently; the notion of what it is to be a 'consumer guide' needs more attention.

The essence of rock fan mags, whether the British music papers as a whole in the fifties, or *Record Mirror* and *Fab 208* today, is that they *respond* to teenage tastes. Their consumer service is the provision of information, gossip and pictures of the stars whom their readers have already chosen. Their function is not to explain, assess or criticise their readers' preferences, it is not even to influence them, rather it is to reflect them – hence the importance of the charts in determining these papers' policies.

There is an aspect of this sort of 'service' in all rock papers – the *Melody Maker* and *Rolling Stone* too. They also provide information about and pictures of the musicians whom their readers are known to like; they too provide a confirmation of taste, a feeling of hip community. In this respect the music press specialises to serve particular markets just like American radio, and in this respect Flippo is right to equate all rock papers as consumer guides. But the consumers of the up-market rock press make other demands of their magazines. They don't just want to know what they do like, they also want to know what they might like and, even, what they ought to like.

The distinctions in music-paper publishing reflect marketing distinctions between the tastes of 'progressive' and 'teeny-bop' audiences, but these distinctions rest, in turn, on the youth-cultural differences that I described in Chapter 3. There I made the point that such differences are not just a matter of taste – they also reflect differences in music use. In particular, I distinguished the use of rock as background music from the use of rock as a source of meaning and individual choice. For the latter consumers, from whom come the vast majority of the up-market papers' readers, a consumer guide is a guide to rock's value. Reviewers are expected to judge records and performances, and their judgements are expected to be based on clear criteria of what makes a record good or bad. The *NME* is expected to display critical standards that would be irrelevant in the *Record Mirror*.

The difference between the two types of consumer guide can be shown clearly by reference to fanzines like *ZigZag*. The essence of the fanzine is not its amateur, non-commercial form but its uncritical content. The function of the fanzine is the enthusiastic communication of information and gossip about its chosen stars – in this it exactly resembles a fan mag like *Record Mirror* and it differs from the latter only in providing its services for a small coterie of cultists rather than for a mass readership, though even this isn't a necessary feature of a fanzine.[19]

In the 1973/4 disco/soul boom, *Blues and Soul*, a long established monthly for black-music fans, suddenly found its market being competed for – first by an IPC glossy monthly, *Black Music*, and then by a weekly tabloid, *Black Echoes*. *Black Music* soon claimed a circulation of 50,000 and became important for the record companies' promotion of black music, particularly reggae. It wasn't doing anything different from what *Blues and Soul* had always done but was appealing to the temporary mass black market with IPC verve and glamour and coloured pictures. In the long run, however, *Blues and Soul* was more likely to survive; it was less dependent on professionalism and advertisements, more the product of a genuine musical concern. *Blues and Soul* is owned by a record company, Contempo, and *ZigZag* was owned, for a while, by Charisma, but fanzines are, in fact, marginal to the record business – their readership is confined to people who are fanatical about their music already; fanzines don't have record companies' or music papers' interests in mass tastes.

There is a nice irony in this situation. The fanzines are irrelevant to the music business because they lack critical content, the weeklies are important because of the potential nastiness of their reviews. *MM*, *NME* and *Sounds* are the first line of the record business's opinion-leaders; their writers have the responsibility of making the first public responses to new records, musicians and genres. Obviously such responses are affected by the pressures coming from publicists and press officers, but, as I have already argued, it is in the record companies' interests that reviews should be independent, and for the critical criteria involved in the music papers' treatments of records and concerts we have to look outside the business. We have to look at the cultural ideas introduced into the rock press from the underground, at the musical and historical perspectives of the specialist rock magazines, at the concepts of rock on the arts pages of the national press; we have to examine the meaning of rock not as product, but as music and as ideology. This will be my concern in the next section.

PART THREE

The ideology of rock

9
Rock musicians

People have some crazy idea that *star status* is a wonderful life of sleeping late in the morning and dining off caviar and champagne. Apart from never having tasted the first and not liking the second, I can tell you star status is hard work – hard work in the most glamorous and exciting profession in the world but nevertheless hard work. (Cliff Richard, 1960.)

All that business was awful, it was a fuckin' humiliation. One has to completely humiliate oneself to be what the Beatles were, and that's what I resent. I didn't know, I didn't foresee. It happened bit by bit, gradually, until this complete craziness is surrounding you, and you're doing exactly what you don't want to do with people you can't stand – the people you hated when you were ten. (John Lennon, 1971.[1])

In his book on jazz, Francis Newton suggests that the jazz musician is 'nearer to the ordinary randomly chosen citizen than most other artists . . . jazz has been able to draw upon a wider reservoir of potential artists than any other art in our century'.[2]

Rock musicians are almost exclusively young, but otherwise Newton's comment is just as true for them. In the 1950s rock'n'roll musicians were assumed to be working-class teenagers. The archetype was Tommy Steele – born and brought up in the East End, leaving school at 15, escaping a life of tedium in the local factories by joining the merchant navy, discovering and imitating American music, his subsequent career a matter of luck as much as talent, of manipulation as much as art, of image as much as music. For years rock musicians were presented as the boys-next-door, making music for a working-class audience which identified with them, which shared their background, culture and values. During the beat boom of the mid-sixties Paul McCartney's O-levels, Mick Jagger's time at the LSE, were still matters for news comment.

But by the late sixties such backgrounds for rock musicians were becoming commonplace. The new stars had degrees, came from bourgeois homes in suburbs and the country, made cultured references to literature and art. It became hard to pin down any obvious relationship between class background and musical style, between rock and class consciousness. Within rock ideology the fifties show-biz values of sincerity and decency and professionalism merged with the sixties hip values of rebellion and sex and no respect. These days the sharpest distinctions between rock musicians are not those of background or ideology, but those of success and situation. 'Being a rock musician' covers the huge range of experience from that of a superstar, moving leisurely and luxuriously between studio and stadium, cocooned by an entourage of servants and sycophants, to that of a local group, moving desperately and sporadically between social security and squalid gig, sustained only by dreams.

It is not easy to generalise about the role and ideology of rock musicians, and the task is made harder by the thousands of words that are turned out in the music papers' weekly diet of interviews. The more we find out about musicians' individual biographies, tastes and hopes, the less easy it is to uncover any shared beliefs or values. Music press and show-biz myths have themselves fed musicians with the clichés they feed the public. Even the career of the rock musician is an ideological construct, as the years of 'dues-paying', the time of starvation, are rewarded with the years of 'making it', the time of stardom. Everybody gets what they deserve. In order to get at the problems and tensions that underlie this cosy notion we have to go beyond the clichés and consider rock musicians in two contexts – their relationship with the rock industry, their relationship with the rock audience.[3]

Musicians and the business

Popular musicians make their living by selling their services to record companies and promoters, and to understand their lives we have to begin with these economic relationships. Two sorts of service are involved. Firstly, there are musicians who are only musicians; their craft is their music, and they sell only their musical skills. Thus session musicians offer their services to producers and record companies, to radio and television, to film-score makers and advertisers, to anyone who is making a musical product. Secondly, there are musicians who are also entertainers. Through a promoter or record company, they sell their music to the public, as entertainment. In the pop-music industry there is, in fact, no sharp dividing line between music and other forms of entertainment; in clubs, cabarets and TV shows many entertainers move effortlessly between pop, comedy and sentiment. The musical values involved are subordinated to more general notions of what it is to entertain a crowd.[4]

The essence of this system is that the purchaser of the service determines its content. On the one hand the record-producer or jingle-maker asks for an A flat or a boogie rhythm, on the other hand entertainers prove their professionalism by giving the people 'what they want'. Most popular musicians are involved in both processes at once. They sell their services to an agent who is seeking to satisfy a public demand – the musicians thus have some flexibility in interpreting the expectations of their direct employers. It was in this context that the Musicians Union grew in the 1920s and 1930s as the organisation representing the interests of the musicians employed in dance bands and orchestras.[5]

Today the Musicians Union has more than 30,000 members, of whom well over half are part-time. The MU's aim is to control the conditions in which its members sell their services. It negotiates the minimum rates of pay that must be paid to any musician used in recording sessions, in clubs and holiday camps, in orchestras and theatres, on radio and television; it provides legal and contractual support. Over the years the Union has fought bravely to maintain employment opportunities, and, like all craft unions, it has been especially concerned to establish a closed shop. Thus, for example, it has done its best to confine British music jobs to British musicians:

> You can't have a flow of musicians coming in and occupying concert halls and restaurants and the rest, where our members expect to be employed.[6]

But if the MU has been able to establish an exchange deal with the American Federation of Musicians (US musicians can only come here if there are an equal number of British musicians going there), they have been less successful in their fight to keep jobs for live musicians in the wake of the rise of records as a means of popular entertainment. Radio needle-time deals have been won, but the replacement of live bands by discos in the last ten years has proceeded steadily and irresistibly.[7]

The policies and principles of the MU rest on two assumptions. The first is that the majority of its members are 'standard' musicians selling 'standard' services. All artistic unions have the problem of providing a collective organisation for sellers of individual and individually priced talents, and their chief concern has to be for their routine workers rather than for successful stars, but in the MU's case this policy has led to difficulties, difficulties that are particularly clear in its attitudes to foreign musicians. If the principle is that no foreign musician should be employed to do what a British musician could do equally well, the difficulty is to define the musical skills that are so reproducible. The union does have a category of 'concert musician', whose skills are accepted as unique, but this category has always been more readily applied to classical than to jazz or popular musicians. In the latter fields the union's policy remains:

> the position is ridiculous to say that there was only one man in the world who could do what you wanted. We would say you would have to find a British [musician] who could do what you want.[8]

The second MU assumption is that its members are primarily live performers. The union has always seen the development of recording as a threat to musicians' employment, and it has been slow to develop mechanisms to protect musicians from exploitation by record companies in the way that they are protected from exploitation by promoters and agents – the union's main dealings with record companies have been as representative of session musicians rather than of contracted artists.

For both these reasons the MU has always been out of touch with the particular needs of rock musicians – an explicit organiser for rock was not appointed until 1977 – and we can't use the union directly as a source of rock musicians' ideology. Nonetheless, rock musicians are craftsmen and they live by selling a service the content of which is constrained by those to whom it is sold; their ideology has to be related to their lives as professionals, even if there are great varieties in the 'professionalism' involved.

Some rock musicians are, quite straightforwardly, all-purpose players for whom rock is just another job. In his study of Hollywood session musicians in the 1960s Faulkner shows the extent to which they were used to make rock records and, even more graphically, the extent to which they despised the job: 'You feel like a prostitute doing those types of dates.'[9]

There is a second type of rock musician, one who sells himself to a manager or producer who uses his talents to realise a predetermined image or sound or music. This rock role was most common in the early days of rock – Cliff Richard provides a useful account of how his music was put together by his manager Tito Burns, his record producer Norrie Paramor, and his TV producer Jack Good: 'Jack felt he owned me. He felt he had discovered me and I almost began to believe he had but that isn't quite true. Actually Norrie Paramor had done that. . . '.[10]

Rock musicians are still used this way – groups are put together to satisfy a teeny-bop or other fad; anonymous players are bought, their personality and all, to meet a perceived demand – and even when the musicians are more directly responsible for how they please their public they have to take account of that public's demands. The youth market is as constraining as any other.

In his classic account of professional dance musicians, Howard Becker suggested that their ideology was determined by the contradiction between their self-image as artists, their music constrained only by the discipline of art and the needs of self-expression, and their reality as service sellers, their music constrained by the demands of the purchasers. Becker suggested that this contradiction led to a contempt for the audience, who, the musicians felt, didn't understand their music, and to the self-elevation of the musicians, as artists, to a social superiority symbolised by freedom from the usual social constraints:

> The musician thus sees himself as a creative artist who should be free from outside control, a person different from and better than those outsiders he calls squares who understand neither his music nor his way of life and yet because of whom he must perform in a manner contrary to his professional ideals.[12]

Becker describes how musicians isolate and segregate themselves from their audiences, developing a language and life-style that indicate their difference from the common listener (the 'punter' in rock terminology), but how at the same time they have to compromise their stance in order to solve the conflict between their art idealism and commercial reality. In the long run such musicians develop an ideology that rationalises their compromise. Commercial work is seen to offer its own craft challenges and satisfactions; musicians take pride in their ability as craftsmen, their ability to solve musical problems, to do a difficult job well; musical pleasure doesn't only come from unfettered self-expression. In the words of a British musician:

> In the case of someone playing at a jazz club, a hotel, a function, etc., the more creative power a musician has, working there (the sort of power which comes mainly from experience), the more he will be able to compromise a little, while still remaining *truly himself*.[12]

Rock musicians experience similar tensions between their artistic ideals and the commercial pressures, but in some respects their solutions have been different from those of their fellow-professionals. One reason for this is the special status of rock as youth music – rock musicians are less clearly contemptuous of their audience because part of their self-image lies in the belief that they express the values of youth in general (and not just of themselves in particular). I will return to this point in the next section. But another source of rock ideology lies in the history of rock musicians as professionals. In Becker's argument the musicians' problem lies in the adjustment to commercial status by players who started their careers as self-perceived artists. In rock the process has gone the other way – rock musicians have developed their artistic claims from commercial origins; paradoxically, artistic integrity has become, in itself, the basis for commercial success.

The traditional source of talent in British show-biz is not artistic self-expression but the ability to entertain; there is not, as for Becker's musicians, a conflict between skill and public demand. Rather, skill is defined as the ability to meet public demand. It is possible that, in private, show-biz stars gather to laugh at the low tastes of their audiences, but I doubt it; basic to the entertainer's self-image is a belief in the people – it is, after all, their tastes that alone justify his activities. Entertainers, unlike jazz musicians, don't have independent criteria of their worth.

The early values of British rock'n'roll were forged in this context. There was a new public – teenagers – and a new taste – rock'n'roll – but the value of the new musicians still rested on their ability to meet a demand. In Tommy Steele's words:

> Someone was looking for someone to be the exponent of rock and roll, and I was there. Show business is really 90 per cent luck and 10 per cent being able to handle it when its gets offered to you. The teenagers around at that time suddenly found that they had control of a certain part of the leisure market. Now, no one knows better than the leisure people; there were kids with pocket money, with their first year's wages, and they suddenly found, all of a sudden, that they could dictate policy. Just like that. They could dictate something. And they dictated music. And they turned round and said: 'This is going to be what we want, and what we want is our own age-group, singing our songs, in our way. In order to show you that's what we want, if you can present us with it we'll buy it if we like it.' And so I was an experiment.[13]

Tommy Steele, Cliff Richard and Britain's other original rock stars experienced no tensions between their skills and their audience, between their music and their success; art and commerce were integrated. Popularity was the measure of their talent as entertainers, and if there were elements of rebellion in rock'n'roll they were directed not against the structure in which the musicians worked, but against the adult generation to whom it was not, anyway, intended to appeal.

The situation was no different for the Beatles and the Stones and other British beat groups in the early sixties. What was at issue was not art *vs* commerce, but young taste *vs* old taste. The Rolling Stones, claimed their 1964 biography:

> have been Rebels with a Cause . . . the Cause of rhythm'n'blues music. They have drifted into the position of being shot at by half the population. They have been derided by politicians in Parliament, laughed at by road-sweepers, jeered at by mothers, despised by fathers. . . . They were determined to express themselves freely, through their music. And they decided unanimously that they were going to make no concessions to the demands of commercialism that they, frankly, openly, despised.

But, on the other hand, as this routine show-biz bio goes on to point out, they were

> . . . loved by the teenagers. For the teenagers have realised the courage of the Stones. The courage to kick hard against the solid, staid conventions and live life the way they feel it – and without causing harm or trouble to anybody else.
>
> They've gone out to produce sheer excitement for the fans and they've succeeded despite the criticisms.[14]

All that was involved in the Stones' 'rebellion' was the substitution of one measure of commercial success by another. Even the ability of these early sixties rock musicians to write their own material was not felt to introduce new artistic criteria. Pete Townshend of the Who remembers going to the recording studio to cut the group's second single:

> They said: 'We think you are a great R & B band, but the Beatles have set a trend of groups writing their own material. All the Liverpudlian groups write their own material, the Stones write their own material. You just really got to do it.' So away we walked, and everybody looked round and said 'Who's going to write?' And me being at art school, being able to say long words like 'perspicacity', which I heard on a Spike Milligan album, I was elected to do the job. About eight to ten weeks later, the song I had written, 'Can't Explain', was number 8 in the charts. So it all seemed automatic and easy to me.[15]

The notion of rock star as artist was slow to develop. A straw in the wind was Eric Clapton leaving the Yardbirds in 1965 because 'they are going too commercial':

I don't know if Eric wanted success then, certainly not that kind of success where it meant standing on stage repeating the same old hit songs – pop top twenty songs – note for note every time, that you hadn't written, that you didn't like.[16]

More straws were the commercial success of Bob Dylan and the values of honesty and sincerity that were introduced to rock by folk musicians. John Lennon remembers writing songs for the *Help* album in 1965:

I started thinking about my own emotions – I don't know when exactly it started, like 'I'm A Loser' or 'Hide Your Love Away' or those kind of things – instead of projecting myself into a situation I would just try to express what I felt about myself which I'd done in my books. I think it was Dylan helped me realise that – not by any discussion or anything but just by hearing his work – I had a sort of professional songwriter's attitude to writing pop songs; we would turn out a certain style of song for a single and we would do a certain style of thing for this and the other thing. I was already a stylised songwriter on the first album. But to express myself I would write *Spaniard In The Works* or *In His Own Write*, the personal stories which were expressive of my personal emotions. I'd have a separate song-writing John Lennon who wrote songs for the sort of meat market and I didn't consider them – the lyrics or anything – to have any depth at all. They were just a joke. Then I started being me about the songs, not writing them objectively but subjectively.[17]

By the middle sixties, then, rock musicians were developing an ideology which distinguished rock as art from rock as entertainment. On the one hand rock began to be used as a complex musical form which could not be constrained by the pop tradition of singles, package tours and reproduced hits; on the other hand rock began to be used as a means of self-expression which could not be constrained by the needs and demands of the marketplace. By 1967 there was an ideology of rock which was explicitly anti-commercial, even when commercialism meant pleasing an audience of youth. Arthur Brown, one of Britain's first hippie rock stars, remembers:

At the time [1967] I wanted to be successful and a star, but at the same time I used to go around and see all the people and think what their life is is a heap of shit. There were pressures like how would you like to do two sorts of things, one was the underground, the other was shave off your mustache, have a nose job, cap your tooth, and one night you can go out as a ballad singer doing Tom

Jones stuff and the next night you wear a false mustache and beard and do underground. There was all that shit and we used to do ten nights out of eleven and some of those we'd be doing two gigs a night. If you're just dealing with rock'n'roll, bopping energy, it's alright but ours was much stronger and that's one of the reasons why I packed it in. I made certain stipulations and none of them were met, but at the same time if you're told you've been booked out for the next twelve nights you can't say no. So you do it but say I don't want it to happen again and it happens again, and finally you just say fuck it, I don't want to go this way, I don't want to go in this direction. And they say fuck you, if you don't want to go in that direction we'll make sure you don't go in any other direction.[18]

Rock musicians had begun to experience contradictions between their own artistic urges and the demands of the industry and their fans for commodities, and rock musicians in this period, like jazz musicians before them, began to separate themselves, ideologically, from the circumstances in which their music was made.[19]

Such a separation was made possible by two developments in rock. The first was the increasing importance of recording. Previously, the studio had been the creative focus mostly for businessmen making teenage commodities. For most rock musicians, music came from live performance – records were simply a means of reproducing this music on a mass scale. The creative power and integrity of beat groups like the Beatles and Stones were founded on their origins as club musicians, developing a rock form that was determined not by show-biz conventions but by the immediate demands of dedicated dancers. But as recording studios and devices got more sophisticated, as musicians had the time and money to indulge themselves, as the industry began to care about albums as a medium, musicians got a chance to experiment with their music away from the immediate relationship with an audience, away from the constant beat of dancing feet. Such constraints were now felt indirectly, via record-company assessments of the market, and as long as musicians could prove the record companies wrong – by cutting records that sold – so long could they simultaneously indulge their artistic urges and despise crude commercial concerns. Problems only arose when the market didn't dig rock-as-art, and this was where the second development in rock became relevant – the musicians' artistic pretensions were supported by a new rock audience which shared this ideology of rock, which wanted to 'appreciate' music rather than to consume pop, which had the same contempt for show-biz values, for rock-as-entertainment, for singles, package tours, and the rest.

In the late 1960s rock musicians' ideology of artistic freedom and self-expression was integrated into a general youth ideology of freedom and self-expression – 'doing your own thing' became the operative phrase. The professional rock musician was in a unique (and temporary) situation in which art and commerce seemed complementary, not contradictory. Rock musicians had a self-importance that matched that of Becker's jazzmen. They presented themselves as creators, freed from commercial constraints in their innovations and experiments. The possibilities of rock were determined only by the skills and disciplines and personal values and ideas of its creators. But at the same time this elevation of rock to art did not seem to distance rock musicians from their audience in the way that it did jazzmen. If rock musicians were no longer in the show-business of satisfying the youth market, they were still the spokesmen and representatives of a youth culture, a culture that was not confined to the world of the hip musicians themselves. Rock musicians' ideology, their particular solutions to the problems of professional music making, had to be understood by reference to their peculiar relationship with their audience.

Musicians and the audience

Rock is often analysed as a contemporary folk music – a music made for young people by young people and therefore 'emerging' from young people's culture. This argument is applied to rock in general and to particular styles – the Who's relationship with the Mods, the Sex Pistols' with Punks – and I will return to these arguments in Chapter 11. Here I want to consider only one aspect of the argument – the cultural basis of rock musicians.

I have already suggested that it is difficult to pin rock musicians down to a specific class origin. To be a rock musician is to be detached from a class background – if rock is a way out of the working-class, a path to riches, it is also a way out of the middle-class, a path to bohemian freedoms. One of the most obvious sociological characteristics of British rock musicians, particularly of those who emerged in the classic 1960s period, is an art-school background (John Lennon, Keith Richard, Ray Davies, Pete Townshend, Eric Clapton, Jimmy Page, David Bowie – this list of the most famous only hints at the extent to which art school is a normal part of the rock career). In the British education system art schools allow for a particular sort of mobility – they are places where working-class kids can go who reject a working-class future without having the ability or desire to tread the meritocratic path (this was more true in the 1960s, when art schools had less clear academic entry requirements, than now), and they are places where middle-class kids can go who reject a middle-class future without seeing themselves as failures. Or, in Keith Richards' words: 'I mean in England, if you're lucky you get into art school. It's somewhere they put you if they can't put you anywhere else.'[20]

Art was the basis for such kids' luck, even if music replaced painting as the art involved, and the importance of the art school in the rock career suggests two general points about musicians as a class. The first is that just as the art-school route to fulfilment is an individualistic one, so is the pursuit of fame and fortune in rock. Paying dues may be a collective affair, making it is not, and even the most well-paid of session men, long adjusted to their lack of individual status, define their situation as failure. To have a career as a musician is to have a quality of self-obsession, an intensity of ambition, that can survive whatever crassness the businessmen put it through.[21]

The second point is that just as art schools offer a career that is 'different' – from the routines of both proletarian and bourgeois work – so musicians make a 'different' living, practice a 'different' profession. Cliff Richard has noted:

> You see we live at the wrong hours of the day. Seldom do we get home before half past eleven and you tell me a hotel that's going to give you a hot meal at that hour of night. Not many.
> After we've eaten we're too wide awake to think of bed, and the boys and I sit up till all hours talking away about all sorts of things. . . . You see all of us live, breathe and eat beat music. We love it. Believe me, although the life is strenuous we never get tired of performing. It's not a way of earning money alone – it's our way of life.[22]

Cliff is describing the experience (usually rather less innocuous) of all popular entertainers. Their work is everyone else's leisure, their way of life is everyone else's relaxation, escape and indulgence. To be a popular entertainer is to be involved, willy-nilly, with the 'vices' of popular leisure. The physical context of entertainment itself is a context of people enjoying themselves, of drink and casual sex and violence. Rock musicians play in pubs, clubs and dance halls; they are surrounded by means of relaxation – alcohol, drugs, sexual partners. Indeed, musicians are themselves the symbols of leisure and escape; their 'glamour' supports their use as sex objects, as fantasies and briefly held dreams. What for them is routine, one night like another, is for their fans a special event, bedecked with the trappings of stardom. In Pete Townshend's words:

Pop audiences and pop musicians are geared to different time structures, they lead different lives entirely. They say it's very difficult to go and see a group and feel totally in with what they're doing because they're on a different time trip. They are doing one gig out of a hundred gigs, whereas to the fan this is a very important occasion, like this is the only chance he's gonna get to see, say, The Cream and never again in his life.[23]

This relationship of musician and fan is not just a matter of stars and glamour but is rooted in the rock musician's role at all levels of success. Simply by being at work when other people are at play, all professional rock players, whatever their origins and however close their ties to a particular audience, are distanced from their listeners' lives. Bohemianism is the musicians' 'natural' ideology; the values of leisure – hedonism and style – are elevated above the conventions and routines of 'normal' society.

Discussing this point with respect to the black jazz musician, Newton has argued that even if he was separated from the daily life of his community the musician's mode of behaviour was, nonetheless, determined by his origins and role in that community:

if he was often bohemian in his ways, it was not on the pattern of the standard bohemia of the nineteenth-century arts, which is at bottom the scale of the values of the lower middle-class turned inside out, but on the pattern of the unskilled labourer magnified . . . for the star was what every slum child and drudge might become: the king or queen of the poor, because the poor person writ large.[24]

Newton distinguishes pre-war jazz bohemians from nineteenth-century literary bohemians in three respects. Firstly, jazzmen were not frightened of manual work and, indeed, often had to do it; secondly, the values and way of life of the jazzmen came less from a deliberate reversal of the respectable values of clerks and shop-keepers than from an exaggeration of the values of casual workers, of their thriftlessness and swank and indulgence; thirdly, jazzmen were not contemptuous of their audiences but felt themselves to be part of them.

Such distinctions between petit-bourgeois and proletarian bohemianism are less easily applied in rock. The professional rock musician is a member of a highly individualistic occupation which is built on ambition and the belief in opportunity. Rock, no less than any other branch of show business, is a willing repository of petit-bourgeois values. 'Here,' suggests the blurb on Cliff Richard's autobiography, 'is a fascinating story of what could happen to anyone with talent and determination in this wonderful age of opportunity.' 'You can get money if you want it,' suggests Johnny Rotten of the Sex Pistols seventeen years later. 'You can get whatever you want. It's called effort. It doesn't take much, just a lot of guts – which the majority of the general public seems to be lacking.'[25]

When rock musicians began to distinguish themselves ideologically from the 'hacks' of show-biz, they retained their craft pride, but their hip values did express a contempt for clerks and shopkeepers, and if rock musicians attempted to shock the bourgeoisie they sneered equally at manual work. The ideology of rock contains all the petit-bourgeois fears of organisation – of big business and capital (including that of 'bureaucratic' record companies), of unions (even the MU), of the state. A contempt for the masses is a sustaining force for many unsuccessful rock bands, who can blame their failures on the cloth ears and conventional habits of their audiences, and the 'rebellious' politics of rock bohemians rest on a totally aesthetic reaction to the social conditions of capitalism. Individualism is dominant, and it is not much of a move from hipster to tax exile, as Mick Jagger takes his place with Tom Jones, Tony Jacklin, and the rest.[26]

This brings us to the contradiction at the centre of rock performers' ideology. In the last section I argued that although rock musicians experience the same pressures as other professional players, their solutions to the tensions between art and commerce are different because of the history of rock as a medium and because of rock musicians' special audience, youth. But we have now seen that we cannot interpret rock performers' relationship with their audience in folk terms – the musicians are not part of a youth community. In terms of both origin and occupation rock performers are detached from class cultures; their bohemianism is individualistic and rooted in petit-bourgeois rather than proletarian indulgence. There is a contradiction between rock musicians' claims as youth spokesmen and the reality of their separate life-style and outlook. On the letters pages of the music press this contradiction is usually blamed on success – 'selling-out' is seen less in terms of sacrificing art to commerce than of sacrificing community to commerce – whether the community of street kids left behind by tax exiles, or of hippies betrayed by rock-star capitalists. But this is to misinterpret the problem. Success confirms musicians' distance from their audience but it doesn't cause the separation. Keith Richard has commented on the peculiarities of life on the road:

When you're canned up – half the time it's impossible to go out, it's a real hassle to go out – it was to go through a whole sort of football match. One just didn't. You got all you needed from room service, you sent out for it. Limousines sent tearing across cities to pick up a little bag or this or that. You're getting really cut off.[27]

But long before the Stones reached international superstar status, Keith Richard was part of the isolated community of musicians. John Lennon remembers life when the Beatles first came to London:

> That was a great period. We were like kings of the jungle then, and we were very close to the Stones. I don't know how close the others were but I spent a lot of time with Brian and Mick. I admire them, you know. I dug them the first time I saw them in whatever that place is they come from, Richmond. I spent a lot of time with them, and it was great. We all used to just go around London in cars and meet each other and talk about music with the Animals and Eric and all that. It was really a good time, that was the best period fame-wise. We didn't get mobbed so much. It was like a men's smoking club, just a very good scene.[28]

At the time when the Beatles and Stones most clearly articulated 'youth' culture, they were already living in the privileged confines of 'a men's smoking club'. Where, then, did their self-identification with 'ordinary' youth come from? Their answer was their music. Central to these musicians' ideology was the argument that if they played youth music then they must represent youth culture.

In some respects this argument was both cynical and circular. 'Teenage' songs and styles, 'teenage' lyrics and rhythms can be routinely turned out to meet (and manipulate) a perceived demand; the makers of such music no more speak for youth than the people who write the stories in *Jackie* or make denim jeans – the youthfulness of their products is simply a marketing phenomenon. But the claim can be made sincerely. Many rock musicians do believe their music to be dependent on their relationship with their audience. In the words of Pete Townshend:

> We all share the simultaneous experience of forgetting who we are at a rock concert, losing ourselves completely. When the music gets so good, and the audience are so relaxed and free and happy, the music isn't just good music it's also *dance* music – it makes you want to dance. Everybody for a second forgets completely who they are and where they are, and they don't care. They just know that they are happy, and that now is now and life is great. And what does it matter if you're a big star – you just know that you

are one of a crowd of people. If you have experienced that enough times, it starts to become something that you strive for, because it is so sweet.[29]

Problems remain. Peter Townshend's membership of the rock community depends on his experience of performance. It is live rock which binds audience to musician, which creates the ties symbolised by rock festivals, the Spirit of Woodstock, etc. The difficulty is to relate this argument to the reality of the rock business – its basis in records. The tensions in the rock role are less those between the freedom of art and the demands of commerce than those between lonely strivings in the studio and the collective constraints of a public performance.

Most rock performers begin their career on the assumption that their live shows prove their understanding of the youth audience (such proof supports them in their struggles with record companies for control of the means of record production); recording is simply a technical device for bringing their music to the greatest possible number of potential fans. Many bands, indeed, continue to make music on this basis long after their commercial success has become dependent solely on record sales. The claims to rock greatness of the Stones, the Who, Led Zeppelin and all the other bands who continuously ply America's huge rock stadiums (and Europe's smaller ones) are still rooted in these live shows rather than in their platinum albums, which, at best, simply provide hints and reminders of the *ultimate* Stones or Who or Zeppelin experience, their performance.

For these musicians every post-album tour (which for their record companies is a simple matter of promotion) is a crucial musical test – songs created in studio isolation are now given their chance to draw meaning from the *real* rock relation. But this is an ideal. In practice, bands, especially successful ones, face the pressure to recreate the same live show for ever. There is a contradiction between their own impulses to experiment and self-expression and the crowd's demand for the collective confirmation of past joys. Bands are faced with a choice: to act out a fixed rock role for the length of their careers or to retreat into the studio, to make music with reference only to their own artistic concerns (or according to a commercial formula). The choice made depends, to a large extent, on the sort of rock involved. Rock musicians tend to a stylistic conservatism – their musical values are rooted in their *past* experiences as listeners (they are remarkably uninterested in the music of their peers); in the end, their ideological commitments are to forms of music. Consider, for example, Pete Townshend's almost mystical belief in rock and roll:

That's what rock and roll says to life: it says, you know, I'm hip, I'm happy, forget your troubles and just enjoy! And, of course, this is the biggest thing it has to offer. At the same time it can have content, if one desires content in something as incredible as it is already. The rock and roll songs I like, of course, are songs like 'Summertime Blues', man that's beautiful. It says everything: don't have the blues, it's summertime; summertime, you don't get the blues in summertime! There is no such thing. That's why there is no cure for them.[30]

I will examine the ideological roots of rock's musical forms in the next chapter. I want to conclude this one by making a point which is tangential to this argument but which must be central to any understanding of rock musicians: the musicians' community – whether John Lennon's men's club and Keith Richard's hotel rooms (with their 'dumb chicks'), or the mythical rock'n'roll brotherhood – is a man's world.[31]

Women in rock

Even a superficial survey of rock reveals the lack of women involved in creative roles. There are few female musicians and virtually no back-room girls – producers, engineers, or arrangers (women's only chance here has been as writers). Girls do have a place in rock, but it is almost always as singers, fronting a performance or record, musical abilities confused with visual images and style. Rock ideologues are keen to differentiate their values from those of show business, but their attitudes to women are not much different. The assumption continues to be made that women aren't musical. In the words of singer Billie Davis:

> Audiences don't expect girls to be musical, even singers like Maggie Bell. There's the same problem of communication with musicians. They think: 'She's a girl, she doesn't know what she's talking about.' It's very hard to get a band to do what *you* want to do, all the time they want to do their own thing.[32]

The male chauvinism of rock culture in general is reflected in rock lyrics, which with their assertions of romance, of male supremacy, narcissism and self-pity are hardly 'counter-cultural'. As far as musicians' culture is concerned what is significant is women's exclusion from the heart of the male players' lives, their friendships and work together as comrade craftsmen, in the studio, on the road, in performance. If musicians derive their ideology from their music, they derive their self-esteem from their ability as musicians, from their skills as writers, instrumentalists, performers. Women are usually excluded from this esteem and even their place in the rock audience is played down. The Great Live Rock Experience is often presented as an exclusively male affair; female fans are reduced to sex objects, teeny-boppers, potential groupies.[33]

Women musicians have made it – there are obviously a number of female rock stars – but such individual successes have made little difference to the overall organisation of rock or to its ideology. Many of these stars, indeed, have only made it by working within a man-made notion of how women should sound. If it is clear that female musicians will only take their proper place as rock professionals on the basis of a collective, feminist struggle, the question remains as to whether, in fact, rock's ideological limits are not set by the musical form itself.[34]

10

Rock and musical cultures

Rock, despite the millions of words devoted to it, is seldom subject to musical analysis. In the words of *Rolling Stone*: 'Little rock criticism is concerned with music, because most rock critics are less concerned with sound than sociology.'[1]

Rock critical terms are impressionistic; sounds are described but their effects and functions are treated in purely subjective terms; musicians' most common complaint about rock writers is of their lack of interest in musical purposes and problems. What serious musical criticism of rock there has been (following *The Times*'s analysis of the Beatles) has come from outside rock culture and has little influence on it.[2]

The most obvious reason for this state of affairs is ignorance. Most rock musicians lack formal musical training and so do almost all rock commentators. They lack the vocabulary and techniques of musical analysis and even the descriptive words commonly used – harmony, melody, riff, beat, etc. – are only vaguely understood and applied. As a sociologist I share this ignorance and this vagueness – this chapter will not contribute anything to the musicology of rock.

But rock is a form of music and it must be understood, even from a sociological perspective, as a form of music. One difficulty here is that rock is a song form. There is a temptation to analyse the words at the expense of the music: words can be reproduced for comment with comparative ease, rhymes are better understood than chords; sociologists of popular music have always fallen for the comparatively easy terms of lyrical-content analysis. Such a word-based approach is not helpful at getting at the ideology of rock; the fans know, in Greil Marcus's words, that 'words are sounds we can feel before they are statements to understand'. Most rock records make their impact musically rather than lyrically – the words, if they are noticed at all, are absorbed after the music has made its mark; the crucial variables are sound and rhythm.[3]

There is a paradox here. Rock's cultural significance is as a form of music, rock ideology is not articulated in musical terms – but behind this paradox lies the central musical fact of rock, its eclecticism. Rock doesn't have a unique musical form, it is the result of an ever-changing combination of independently developed musical forms, and if the musicology of rock is notable for its underdevelopment, the historiography of rock is notable for its abundance. The greatest part of serious rock scholarship has been devoted to unravelling its musical strands, and the ideology of rock rests on the claims that can be drawn from its roots – the realism of the blues, the honesty of folk, the sensuality of soul, the politics of reggae, and so on. I haven't the space (or the expertise) to do justice to the details of rock's history or to the range of its eclecticism, but any sociology of rock must examine the significance of its musical sources and that is the purpose of this chapter.[4]

Black music

Rock'n'roll is the blues form of the classes of Americans who lack the 'sophistication' to be middlebrows, or are too naïve to get in on mainstream American taste. (Leroi Jones)[5]

Black musical forms and styles have been an aspect of western popular culture since at least the middle of the nineteenth century, and in many ways the impact of rhythm and blues on youth music in the 1950s and 1960s was only another example of the continuing process through which white popular music is invigorated by styles and values drawn from black culture – styles and values which lose their force and meaning as they pass through the bland wringer of mass music but are rediscovered by each new generation of hip musicians and audiences. Black music has always been central to pop, and rock, in using black musical ideas, has used ideas that were already, in a diluted and distorted form, a part of mainstream mass culture. A good starting point for an understanding of these ideas is Marshall Stearns' definition of jazz, the source of black music's impact on pop in the 1920s and 1930s. Jazz is

a semi-improvisational American music distinguished by an immediacy of communication, an expressiveness characteristic of the free use of the human voice, and a complex flowing rhythm; it is the result of a three-hundred-years' blending in the United States of the European and West African musical traditions; and its predominant components are European harmony, Euro-African melody, and African rhythm.[6]

I want to examine each of the elements of this definition: firstly, *immediacy of communication*.

At the centre of Afro-American music is the performance. Black music is performance music rather than composition music; it is based on melody and rhythm rather than on theme and harmony; it is improvised, spontaneously composed within its rhythmic and melodic structure. The value of black music lies not in its solutions to musical problems, not in its performers' technical expertise in interpreting a formal, written piece of music, but in its emotional impact, in the direct expression of the performing musicians' feelings:

> soul singers get down to the profoundness of their inner self, and bring this up into the tune. It's rare you'll see a live performance done twice the exact same way. This is because the human feeling, the current immediate human feeling has so much to do with this thing called soul. (Black DJ Enoch Gregory)[7]

Black music is immediate and democratic – a performance is unique and the listeners to that performance become part of it. They need no special training or knowledge to appreciate it; the qualities that are valued in spontaneous music-making are emotional rather than technical, musicians are judged for their honesty, sincerity, passion.[8]

Initially, the spontaneous basis of black music limited its pop possibilities – to make black music mass music the qualities associated with performance had to be brought to an audience far bigger than that which could actually be present. The solution to this problem was electrical reproduction – the history of black music as a mass cultural form has been dependent on the development of records and recording, through which a performance can be captured, preserved and responded to long after its original circumstances have been forgotten.[9]

The relationship works in both directions. If a performance-based music has been essential to the history of records as a medium, the development of that medium has had its own effects on the music. The mass-music industry is organised around principles derived from music as composition: American copyright laws protect composers rather than performers and have legitimated a massive exploitation of black artists whose music is often, in a formal sense, composer-less.[10] In fighting for their economic rights, in learning the rules of this commercial game, black musicians have had to adapt to the principles of mass music-making, to the technology of recording. The clearest effect of mass culture on black music has been the shift of emphasis from the performance to the performer as black artists have become part of a star system. This brings us to the second element in Stearns' definition of jazz: *expressiveness characteristic of the human voice.*

The essence of the black musical performance is the direct expression of the performers' own feelings and emotions to the audience, and the possibilities of such expression depend on the music's vocal qualities. In the words of Ian Hoare:

> Even in instrumental jazz, the basic mode of expression lies in imitating the effects of the human larynx. Voices can express inchoate emotion directly by, say, laughing or screaming or moaning or grunting; or they can communicate reactions to the world in the form of description, analysis, evaluation – using the full potential of language, a potential not available to purely instrumental music.[11]

This emphasis on the voice as the source of human expression has a number of musical consequences. Hoare contrasts blues vocal techniques like melisma with the perfect pitch and enunciation of a classical singer; jazz critics describe players' unique 'voices' on their instruments; it was the 'vocal' qualities of the electric guitar developed by black musicians that inspired a generation of white rock stars in the 1960s. In gospel music, voices are used not just to express individual religious emotion but also, through vocal interplay, through the call and response of preacher and congregation, to express communal religious emotion. Such group vocal techniques have enabled black musicians to develop a form that combines individual and collective expression, a form that can be contrasted with white pop, in which the singer appears to direct his message to an individual listener only – the pop ideal is to make mass communication feel like a conversation.[12]

The pressure as black music becomes part of the pop business is for its vocal qualities to be subordinated to the star system. Record companies seek to control expression, to package passion, to sell honesty; Louis Armstrong's voice, for example, was a better pop commodity than his trumpet. The performer's 'soul' is marketed as a gimmick, a sound reproducible at will, so that every live performance can be as interchangeable as every record. Direct communication between artist and audience, in which the performer's music draws its meaning from his shared experience with his listeners, becomes the distance between the star and the consumer, and a tension develops between the artists' concerns, the audiences' demands for reassurance, and the industry's assessments of consumer needs. This tension has emerged most clearly with respect to the third element of black music – its *rhythm*.

Black music's most obvious influence on pop has been rhythmic. It became a mass cultural form as dance music and it is in opposition to such functionalism, to the formal rigour of a steady big band or disco beat, that black musicians most commonly oppose themselves as artists (hence, for example, the avant-garde in jazz). But it is also as dance music that black music has developed its meanings for white users, meanings which are tied up with the significance of dance itself.[13]

The most obvious feature of dancing as an activity is its sexuality – institutionalised dancing, a peculiarly constrained form of male/female physical interaction, is redolent with sexual tensions and possibilities, and one feature of the black musical use of rhythm is its clear expression of such tensions. Whereas Western dance forms control sexuality with formal rhythms and innocuous, pretty tunes, black music celebrates sex with a directly physical beat and an intense, emotional sound. It makes obvious the potential anarchy of sexual feeling; I have already described (with reference to girl culture) how rock's black-based dance forms are heard by moralists as a threat to respectable codes of sexual behaviour. Black music, in short, is a means for the public expression of normally private feelings. The institutions in which it is played consequently acquire an atmosphere of risk and excitement and provide for the young people drawn to them symbols of rebellion, of opposition to mainstream culture, of hipness and cool. In Britain, black music – from jazz to rhythm-and-blues to soul to reggae – has been the background music of the hippest kids for at least three generations.[14]

Black music's intimations of the real needs and forces in society, its hints of the truth behind mass culture's bland images, are not confined to its expressions of sexuality. Afro-American music is not just body music, its arguments have also had a lyrical form. Jazz fans have always contrasted the 'facts of life' of blues lyrics with the 'idealisation/frustration/demoralisation' formula of pop songs, and rock fans too have drawn on the social realism of black words. In the 1960s young white musicians found in the blues a more honest account of the world than that of white pop and a more political one. In Ian Birchall's words:

> rhythm and blues combines an awareness of frustration and oppression with a vigorous rejection of it. With only minor modifications, this style, originating among American negroes, could be transferred to reflect the attitudes and preoccupations of British working-class youth in the early sixties.[15]

The political significance of black music became clear in this period against the background of the changing nature of the black struggle in the USA. The old oblique blues-based social commentary (one aspect of black lyrics is their slyly elaborate use of metaphor) was replaced by a more explicit and assertive expression of black consciousness. Haralambos has shown how the fateful resignation of the secular blues was combined with the promises and collective excitement of gospel to produce music that was explicitly related to black politics. He quotes the soul musician Curtis Mayfield:

> Our purpose is to educate as well as to entertain. Painless preaching is as good a term as any for what we do. If you're going to come away from a party singing the lyrics of a song, it is better that you sing of self-pride like 'We're a Winner' instead of 'Do the Boo-ga-loo!'[16]

Rock ideologists draw from this argument their own claims to community, recognising, in Ian Hoare's words, that

> soul is a music which typically avoids one of the most common weaknesses of pop in general – the apathetic stance which seeks private solutions to public problems. It turns that stance on its head, in fact. 'I'm a Loser' becomes 'We're a Winner'.[17]

And it is as a means of expressing collective feelings that black music has most clearly become a part of rock culture. Pete Townshend's rock'n'roll faith, for instance, is a faith in rock'n'roll's black elements, in its sense of performance, its energy, its directness of expression, its vocal and rhythmic techniques. These are the rock qualities that enable even the most distant superstar to experience a sense of rock communion.

In the mid-sixties heyday of the white use of R & B and soul, letter writers to the *Melody Maker* agonised over a difficult question: can white men sing the blues? Much of the resulting discussion of the quality of, say, Eric Clapton's 'suffering' missed the point. White blues, like rock'n'roll before it, was not being used to express individual angst but to articulate the young's collective feelings of frustration, aggression, rebellion and lust; songs' individual lyrics were less important than their shared musical qualities – rock developed its own forms of inchoate emotion, its own solidary beat, and these continue to be the source of its claims as a youth culture. But not of its claims as art – deeply embedded in rock ideology is the assumption that while black music is valuable as an expression of vitality and excitement, is in other words 'good to dance to', it lacks the qualities needed for individual expression. The progressive rock fans in my Keighley sample were virulent in their contempt for soul and reggae; rock ideologists are currently equally contemptuous of disco.[18]

In the last chapter I described how musicians began to develop an ideology of art as the rock emphasis shifted from live performance to the recording studio, from a collective beat to an individual lyric, from a dancing teenage crowd to an appreciative listening audience. The movement was away from the places and activities from which rock'n'roll and R&B had drawn their meanings. Rock musicians 'progressed' and in their progress they began to emphasise the non-black elements of their music.

Country music

The values of white American country music are similar in several respects to those of black American music – not for nothing is one book on country sub-titled 'White Man's Blues'. Critics have emphasised two parallels in particular. Henry Pleasants, analysing the style of country singer Jimmie Rodgers, comments that:

> Country music and, of course, the blues demonstrate more vividly than any other Afro-American musical styles except gospel the relationship between music and language, or, to put it more dogmatically, music's origin in speech.[19]

The emphasis here is on musical similarities, on the parallel uses of harsh, raw voices and harmonies, of instruments and instrumental techniques which give even non-sung sounds individual vocal qualities. Other critics have focused on the similar lyrical content of black and white country music. In Bill Malone's words:

> It is true that, in the last analysis, the major difference between country and 'popular' songs has been their instrumentation. But apart from the mode of accompaniment, country songs differed in that their lyrics dealt with subjects that other forms of music would not touch. More than any other form, country music became the naturalistic mode of expression within American music, dealing with the problems of drink, divorce, infidelity, marital problems and tragedy. The country song, more than any other [white] American musical expression, dealt with the tragic element in life, and the sad song was the type which prevailed and predominated.[20]

Country music, like blues, is a vocal music concerned with the realistic presentation and appraisal of the problems of the common people, of the workers and oppressed. And country music, like black music, is a source of both secular entertainment and of spiritual uplift; it is music for dance, for collective excitement, for religious

expression. In these respects black and white country musical values
are so similar that when Elvis Presley and the other Southern white
rockabilly singers put the two styles together to make rock'n'roll, the
shock was less musical than social – it was the social intermingling
of black and white in the South that was difficult, musical intermingling had been a fact of Southern life for years.[21]

But there are differences in the ways in which black and white
musics have evolved from their rural roots, and it is these differences
that have been significant in the development of rock as youth
culture. Country music, for all its realism, populism and sensitivity
to injustice and exploitation, is a conservative form carrying a conservative message. Its lyrical emphasis is on people knowing their
place, and the tensions which result – for women, for example – are
treated as tragic but not soluble. It's as if in black music the stoicism
of the blues had never been injected with the hope of gospel. Country
music tells it like it is, but the possibilities of improvement rest on
individuals, on luck, hard work, blessings from God. In the country
tradition there is little of the aggressive political music that has been
developed by black Americans, and if country music acknowledges
and expresses sexual feelings, they are rarely celebrated. Country
music, much more clearly than black music, is a form of family
entertainment; the development of its mass popularity in the 1920s
and 1930s was based on radio, a family medium.

The conservatism of country music is a feature of its form as well
as of its content. Changes in instrumentation have been slow, each
move – to drums, to electric amplification – has been hard fought,
and there is a much greater emphasis than in black music on songs.
Country is a performance form but its focus is less on improvised
creation than on the virtuoso treatment of tried and tested standards,
and country musicians, via their publishing companies, have found
it much easier than black musicians to become a part of the mainstream of American show business. There have obviously been tensions, as home-made music has become big business, as the boys and
girls next door have left their communities to become stars, but
country glamour rarely becomes bohemian, and, more than any other
type of popular entertainer, country performers continue to share the
values of their audiences, to cultivate a direct relationship with their
fans.[22]

The extraordinary popularity of country music in 1970s America
is clearly a result of its conservatism – it can symbolise a past, express
a nostalgia, describe a way of life that the urban masses still value,
even if they'd never actually want to live that way again. This is the
crucial difference between the white and black forms of American
populist music: the white form is just what it says, country music,

while the black form has developed into being the sound of the city. Country music has responded to social change by digging its toes in, emphasising in its ideology rural values and patterns, leaving the mainstream popular-music business to cater for its adherents' city needs; black music has continued to develop organically. Country was an important musical element of rock'n'roll because of the rockabilly singers' own Southern rural origins; today's 'country rock', by contrast, is a deliberately nostalgic form, an attempt by musicians to draw on long-gone (and often non-existent) roots. Country rockers are making an ironic claim to respectability, using country forms to symbolise their adult concerns. The irony is that for young people in the 1950s, including country rock'n'roll singers, the most obviously limiting feature of country music was precisely its maturity. It provided no space for rebellion, no symbols for the social concerns and restlessness of the young; it described the tragedies of life as 'poor white trash' but not its possibilities.

The formula rock'n'roll = blues + country is deeply entrenched in rock history, but whatever its accuracy as a musical description, its sociological significance is not easily assessed. In his book *Mystery Train* Greil Marcus argues convincingly that their country-musical values bound the original rock'n'rollers to the rural culture of the American South and that rock'n'roll was a contradictory form, blending its pride with shame, its celebration with guilt, its anger with acceptance – the contradictions gave a rock'n'roll artist like Elvis Presley his sensitivity and power. From this perspective rock's country elements, its use of fiddle and steel and rhythm guitar, its yearning vocals and rolling beat, its songs of self-pity and self-sufficiency, reflect a much wider form of popular expression – hence country-rock musicians' ambition to take their place in a mainstream of American mass culture. But this argument is not applicable to British rock. Here country music has had little meaning except as a particularly bathetic form of pop. Rural American music reached British musicians not through its country performers but as an aspect of a city-based folk movement.[23]

Folk music

The early days of the American folk 'revival' (via which route folk styles most clearly influenced rock) were bound up with a rural romanticism, with a search for values and ways which could be opposed to urban corruption, to commerce, to mass music – hence, in the late 1940s and early 1950s, the city interest in blues and blue-grass. But this vague utopianism was tempered by other aspects of the folk revival. Singers like Woody Guthrie and Pete Seeger made explicit the working-class values, the latent politics of the folk tradition, and the association of folk and radical politics that had been formalised in the 1930s remained significant in the 1950s. In folk music young whites found a form that could be made directly responsive to their political concerns and that, in this respect, served a parallel purpose to that of black music for its users – the two concerns and the two forms of music came together most obviously in the civil rights struggle.

'Protest' was not confined to specific demonstrations. The music was developed in permanent folk institutions – clubs, coffee houses, festivals – in which the folk 'community' defined itself and its distance from the mainstream of popular music making. In the folk clubs there was little distinction between performer and listener; anybody could, and did, get up and sing. The emphasis was less on technique or skill than on authenticity and honesty; autobiographical truth, political correctness, were more important than musical talent or individual performing styles. In fact, the emphasis, in true folk fashion, remained firmly on the song rather than the singer.[24]

The folk song movement was self-consciously opposed to mass music making and its values were developed in isolation from the usual practices of commercial pop. By the late 1950s this alternative was becoming attractive to an increasing number of young white listeners, as the energy and aggression of rock'n'roll were diffused in the banalities of teenage pop. Folk was a particularly attractive alternative for musicians unwilling to commit themselves to a life of apparent manipulation and exploitation by the pop moguls:

As well as its musical challenge, folk offered something else – a sense of commitment, political or otherwise, and a whole way of life apparently diametrically opposed to the world of *American Bandstand*, the leading pop television show of the era.

Musicians found in folk:

The idea that songs could concern themselves with topics far wider than the conventional love themes, that musicians could approach their work as self-expression, rather than 'giving the people what they want'.[25]

In the 1960s these ideas were introduced 'into the heart of mainstream popular music', as the folk emphasis on songs and lyrics, on the performers' honesty and insight, were adapted to the commercial needs of rock, and as the rock songwriter became the poet, the singer/songwriter the archetypal rock artist – I have already cited Bob Dylan's effect on John Lennon.[26]

There were ironies in this use of folk forms to support artistic claims. Part of rock's appeal as teenage culture had been that anyone could do it – anyone could make such simple music, could write such straightforward songs, no expertise was needed to play rock'n'roll or to dig it. Rock's listeners were active as well as passive – record sales were correlated with instrument sales – and skiffle was only the most publicised example of the continuing inspiration that young people had to make music for themselves. Initially, folk ideology not only confirmed this culture but politicised it: folkies were anti-commercial pop, rejected the star system, were proud of their integration of performer and audience. But as the folk movement fed into the mainstream this argument was subtly transformed. If anyone could play folk rock – the guitar and harmonica techniques, the harsh and muttered vocals, were not difficult to learn – not anyone could play it with *originality*. Bob Dylan was the symbol of a new argument: he was valued for his individual genius, his personal insights, his poetry, his unique voice and style. And the suggestion that not anyone could make good music became the parallel suggestion that not anyone could appreciate it – expertise was needed by the listener as well, a notion which suitably flattered the new 'intelligent' rock market. The letters page of the mid-sixties *Melody Maker* is again a useful archive, this time of the emergence of an elitist notion of rock in which 'progress' was measured in terms of musical, lyrical and emotional complexity, in terms of qualities of 'art' and 'genius' that were taken to differentiate rock from the banalities of mass teenage pop.

The contradictions of folk music's contribution to rock ideology were clear, for example, in the implications for women. Folk rock's emphasis on words, on performing sincerity, opened up chances for female musicians not available elsewhere in white popular music – a generation of female singer/songwriters has been able to establish its musical importance and to confound the sexist assumptions built into most other rock forms and institutions. But these women succeeded as individuals, and were confined within a narrow view of female creativity. The ideology of rock-as-art has only confirmed women's general lack of rock opportunities: if women have been accepted as poets, they have been rejected as instrumentalists. The new ideology of rock simply replaced the sexy boy-next-door as superstar by the long-haired male genius hunched over his electric guitar.

For the musicians who found in folk rock a means to artistic identity the most important feature of the music was its independence of the usual practices of commercial pop. Rock'n'roll rebellion had been vaguely directed against adults but not against adult record companies; only now could a rock culture be developed which explicitly opposed the ideology of mass music making. I will discuss this opposition and its effects in the next chapter; first I must discuss the ideology of mass music itself.

Pop music

Record companies don't much care what forms mass music takes as long as its sources can be organised and controlled to ensure profit, and in some respects the business practices that I described in Chapters 5 and 6 are musically neutral – music and musicians can be packaged and marketed as commodities and stars whatever their styles. But the history of the music business has not left it entirely without principles. Music was a product long before rock'n'roll, and the industry's musical values derive from its origins as a publishing business and from its initial response to recording. Tin Pan Alley was organised around song rather than performance, and while it was transformed in the 1920s – from a system for selling goods for musical creation (sheet music and pianos) to a system for selling goods for musical consumption (records and record players and radios) – the 'bland universal well-made song' remained central to its organisation.[27]

From the 1920s to the early 1950s the music industry aimed its products at the family audience; records reached the public on family radio and on the family phonograph – most homes had only one of each. To be popular a song had to transcend all the differences between listeners: it had to appeal to all ages, classes, races and regions, to both sexes, to all moods, cultures and values. Mass musical taste was built on cheerfulness and uplift, on songs that raised no problems in their lyrics, stirred no untoward emotions in their sounds or rhythms. Such 'nice' music was determined too by the technological limits of early radio and recording. Subtlety of tone, harmony or melody was impossible to reproduce; nothing too long, discordant or intricate could survive the primitive recording techniques; song writers were advised to stick to the notes in the middle range of the piano.[28]

The musical values established in the early days of the record industry have remained dominant – most clearly in the concepts of 'easy listening' and 'middle of the road', in the programming policies of, say, BBC Radio 1 and 2 – and it is with these musical attitudes that the music business has responded to the problems of absorbing rock culture; I have already described how British record companies sought to produce bland well-crafted songs for the teenage market, to groom their performers as teenage entertainers. The aim was to give the new singers the right image, to create teen idols who looked right. The show-biz convention of the 'sincere' performer was applied to a new look – the boy- or girl-next-door, the vulnerable or the cool heart-throb. Rock'n'roll stars were established through films and television programmes, through touring package shows, and such shows meant show-business, involved concepts of entertainment, glamour and gimmick that did little to differentiate teenage stars from any other kind. By the late fifties adult record producers dominated teenage music, records were sold as packages of sound, and the stars simply presented the music they were given, sold their 'personality'.[29]

Charlie Gillett has documented the subsequent 'decline in importance of dance rhythms'. 'Words and sounds became pre-eminent', and those words and sounds were still created along Tin Pan Alley lines. Teenage pop, like adult pop, described a romantic cloud-cuckoo land; making pop songs youthful simply meant filling this land with appropriate teenage references and giving the words to a teenage singer who could present the situation as his own, thus helping teenage listeners identify with the emotions involved. The object was a teenage market, the resulting songs tended to be about finding love rather than losing it, but otherwise there is little formally to differentiate the classic teenage pop songs which emerged from the Brill Building from the similarly well-made love songs that had been pouring out of Tin Pan Alley for decades. David Riesman's 1950 description of the mass-cultural picture of 'adolescence in America as a happy-go-lucky time of haphazard clothes and haphazard behaviour, jitterbug parlance, coke-bar sprees, and "blues" that are not really blue' could have been applied as accurately to teenage music in 1960.[30]

In the 1960s, however, this ideology of adolescence became something new, an ideology of youth; 'The young ones' became 'My generation'. The significance of this change was that although adolescence had always been romanticised in song, although the teenage world had always had glamour, youth had been presented as a period of transition, a stage on the path to adulthood. The essence of the ideology of courtship, for example, was that a time would come, a marriage to the perfect partner, when all emotional and sexual needs would be fulfilled. In the 1960s this false suggestion was replaced by another – that youth was preferable to age and that no one need ever grow old. What was at issue was not chronology but ideology. If youth was the perfect social condition – glamorous, irresponsible, sexually vigorous, emotionally unrestrained; if to be young meant to be free from the narrow routines of maturity, then anyone who lived and thought right, regardless of age, could be 'young'. Teenage culture, in holding up 'irregular, spontaneous, unpredictable, exhibitionist behaviour' as desirable became the basis for a more general ideology in which pleasure was a way of life. The three groups most concerned with leisure – bohemians for ideological reasons, show-business for commercial reasons, and teenagers for social reasons – came together in the cult of youth and youthfulness.

The ideology of youth was reflected in the lyrics of courtship – content analysis reveals the increasing celebration of 'existential choice'. Romance was no longer presented as a once-and-for-all thing, the selection of a partner for life; boy/girl relationships were presented as active creations, valuable even when they ended – the instability of adolescent sexual relationships was another measure of youth's superiority, of its greater freedom, honesty, truth to self and refusal to conform to social conventions.[31]

This ideology of youth reflected the general changes in youth culture that I outlined in Chapter 2 – it was the record companies' response to their newly discovered market – and it had a number of musical effects. Firstly, there was an increasing integration of performer and song. Teenage stars had always been expected to come across sincere, to appear to identify with their material, even when that material was the product of the song-writing assembly line, but now the folk notions of honesty and sincerity were adopted by the music business – I have already described the rise of the singer/song-writer genre, the introduction into rock of the values of self consciousness and truth.[32]

Record companies were equally happy to accept the concept of rock 'progress'. The term tied in with their attempts to differentiate their stars from the mass of pop performers and to service the developing student market: increasing promotional emphasis was placed on musicians' technical skills, on their instrumental artistry, on their willingness to experiment, on their unwillingness to be bound by formulas or conventions. This argument, risky for the usual concern of the business with control and prediction, was a response both to an audience reluctant to choose its idols on the basis of too-obvious manipulation and image, and to musicians reluctant to be so manipulated, to be given such images. The institutions of sixties rock – LPs, stereo, concerts – all supported 'intelligent' musical values – improvisation, virtuosity, stamina, originality.

There was a moment, perhaps, when the music business was bewildered by its market. Musicians gained a measure of control of the production of rock simply because they seemed better able than the established A & R men to predict what would sell; record companies had to experiment because for this new youth market, with its explicit anti-showbiz ideology, there was no convention or tradition to exploit. But in the 1970s Progressive Rock has been bound by its own commercial formulas and clichés, its own versions of show business. The traditional notions of entertainment, of professionalism, of the well-made song, the well-constructed star, have never been far from the surface of rock, and we have already seen their importance for rock musicians. In the end, the only effect of the anti-commercial ideology of sixties rock seems to have been to oblige record companies to use a new set of terms and concepts to justify their activities. But this is to prejudge the issue. The important point is that whatever the musical sources of rock's ideology, its messages have been as a mass medium – the general implications of this will be my concern in the next chapter.[33]

11
Rock and mass culture

The study of rock as a particular medium has been neglected by sociologists, but there is a general literature on the meaning of mass culture from which interpretations can easily enough be drawn. The tone of this literature is gloomy. The products of the mass media are censured by reference to the values and practices of both high art and folk art. Rock criticism itself uses these contrasts: records are valued for their artistic authenticity or for their truth to youth experience, they are condemned for commercialism. The belief in a continuing struggle between music and commerce is the core of rock ideology: at certain moments artists and audience break through the system, but most of the time business interests are in control. Thus, for example, the American critic Jon Landau:

> Rock, the music of the sixties, was a music of spontaneity. It was a folk music – it was listened to and made by the same group of people. It did not come out of a New York office building where people sit and write what they think other people want to hear. It came from the life experiences of the artists and their interaction with an audience that was roughly the same age. As that spontaneity and creativity have become more stylized and analyzed and structured, it has become easier for businessmen and behind-the-scenes manipulators to structure their approach to merchandising music. The process of creating stars has become a routine and a formula as dry as an equation.[1]

This is the critical argument that underpins the rock historians' correlations of competition and creativity, their suggestion that rock progress comes from independent local labels, rock stagnation from the major music corporations, and the assumptions here are obvious. Commercial mass culture is bad; rock music is good only in so far as it is not a business product but an art form, a folk music. In this chapter I want to examine each of these assumptions.

Mass culture

The critical analysis of mass culture is dominated by the (overlapping) approaches of Leavisite literary criticism and Marxist ideological criticism.

The Leavisite approach stems from the comparison of mass-cultural objects – standardised, escapist, effortlessly consumed – with works of art – unique, challenging, instructive. Mass culture is analysed with the tools of literary criticism and condemned accordingly; mass music, for example, is worthless because there is 'nothing essential in the music itself which belongs either to real emotion or to an inner unmistakable vitality.'[2]

What is involved here is not a comparison of the good taste of an educated élite with the bad taste of the uneducated masses, but an assessment of the processes by which different cultural objects are produced. Leavisites celebrate the values of popular art; their argument is that mass culture is a 'corruption' of such art. The key critical concept is 'authenticity'; the argument is that a culture created for commercial profit must lack 'a certain authenticity' even if it 'dramatises authentic feelings'. Mass teenage culture is

> a contradictory mixture of the authentic and manufactured – an area of self-expression for the young and lush grazing ground for the commercial providers.[3]

For Leavisites, mass-cultural production is production to formulas which limit individual creativity; the mass-cultural audience is an audience of consumers making market choices rather than of respondents making artistic judgements; the mass-cultural account of the world is trivial, denying the past and obsessed with fashion and change. Such a culture corrupts feeling; it makes no demands on its users but titillates them with its stars, its flattery of mediocrity, its myth of the mass consumer as the common man.[4]

From this perspective the commercial basis of mass culture explains both its existence and its quality. Mass art is produced for profit and the pursuit of profit determines form and content, is the source of inauthenticity. The problem is to explain cultural consumption, to account for the inexorable replacement of popular art by mass culture. Reference to the power of advertisement, to market manipulation, is not enough: mass-cultural solutions may be 'false' but the needs to which they are a response are real – this, as we have seen, is the argument of the adolescence theorists. It has been applied most vehemently to youth music by David Holbrook, who hears pop as the degradation of art: rock draws on the power of real fears and emotions but instead of dealing with them exploits them. It provides only a 'manic moment of uplift' and plays with the psychological tensions of puberty:

the attitude to sexual love in the 'pop' song is so ugly and mechanical as to seem schizoid, and psychopathological. Exposed as they are to such powerful cultural statements, young people are being encouraged to forfeit genuine commitment in love in favour of depersonalised sexual activity, with an undercurrent of violence, and to take false solutions in which they must deny their deepest needs, by hate.[5]

Holbrook argues that the exploitation of adolescent needs rests on the deliberate commercial creation of youth 'culture', of an ideology designed to separate the young from their families and communities and to make them more vulnerable as consumers. Rock, as a mass medium, is a false art serving a false community.

Holbrook's tone is particularly gloomy, but his argument is commonplace. The assessment of youth culture as inauthentic is widespread among Marxist as well as Leavisite commentators. Charles Parker, for instance, echoes many of Holbrook's points in his comparison of pop and folk music and goes beyond him in rooting rock culture in the political, as well as economic, processes of capitalism: 'This, then, is my thesis, that pop is, in fact, now cherished by a ruling class as a peerless form of social control.'[6]

Parker argues that youth culture has been created for ideological as well as commercial purposes; what is powerful or radical in youth experience is channelled through rock into 'the false community of the cosmopolitan teen-scene where the identity is submerged in a common, conditioned response of the viscera'. Rock – 'this Witches' Sabbath of meaningless orgiastic utterance' – is deliberately used by the power élite to safeguard its political position, to control and divert popular expression.[7]

For Marxists, the commodity form of mass culture is another aspect of the general process through which capital has transformed social relations and analysis can go beyond vague notions of a conspiratorial 'they', corrupting our youth, to focus on the precise ideological content of mass communications. Ever since Marx suggested that the ruling ideas in society were those of the ruling class, Marxists have been concerned to understand how ideology works. The most sophisticated account of mass music from this perspective is that of Adorno. He argues that it is the production of music as a commodity, to be consumed, that determines its cultural quality – popular music has to be something which *can* be consumed, a means (to profit on the one hand, to well-being on the other) rather than an end. The consequent standardisation of musical form is the source of its ideological effect – a soporific social consciousness – and the reduction of culture to commodity and ideology is made possible by the

technology of mechanical reproduction, by the techniques of recording and broadcasting which make cultural consumption an indi-
vidualised and alienating process. The mass-music consumer has no
real relationship with either the music's producers or with fellow-
consumers. Art has become entertainment, cultural choice has become selection in the marketplace, popular creation has become the
commercial attempt to attract the largest possible number of consumers. Mass culture produces both a pseudo-individualism and a
pseudo-collectivism.[8]

Adorno, like the adolescence theorists, draws on psychology to
account for the effectiveness of mass music. This is his 1940s description of pop fans:

> In general they are intoxicated by the fame of mass culture, a fame
> which the latter knows how to manipulate; they could just as well
> get together in clubs for worshipping film stars or for collecting
> autographs. What is important to them is the sense of belonging as
> such, identification, without paying particular attention to its
> content. As girls, they have trained themselves to faint upon hear-
> ing the voice of a 'crooner'. Their applause, cued in by a light-
> signal, is transmitted directly on the popular radio programmes
> they are permitted to attend. They call themselves 'jitter-bugs',
> bugs which carry out reflex movements, performers of their own
> ecstasy. Merely to be carried away by anything at all, to have
> something of their own, compensates for their impoverished and
> barren existence. The gesture of adolescence, which raves for this
> or that on one day with the ever-present possibility of damning it
> as idiocy on the next, is now socialised.[9]

For Adorno the aesthetic basis of art is its 'practically useless,
imaginative element', its utopian protest against reality; art is the
source of human hope, the inspiration to the struggle for social
change. Mass culture, in contrast, settles with reality and so corrupts
its imaginative base and renders its consumers impotent – Adorno
hears 'jazz' (his term for all mass music) as castration symbolism:

> expression, the true bearer of aesthetic protest, is overtaken by the
> might against which it protests. Faced by this might it assumes
> a malicious and miserable tone which barely and momentarily
> disguises itself as harsh and provocative. The subject which ex-
> presses itself expresses precisely this: I am nothing, I am filth, no
> matter what they do to me it serves me right . . . art is permitted to
> survive only if it renounces the right to be different, and integrates
> itself into the omnipotent realm of profane. . . . Nothing may exist

which is not like the world as it is. Jazz is the false liquidation of art
– instead of utopia becoming reality it disappears from the picture.[10]

Adorno's is the most systematic and the most searing analysis of
mass culture and the most challenging for anyone claiming even a
scrap of value for the products that come churning out of the music
industry. The weakest point of his argument seems to be his account
of cultural consumption – the actual use of pop by its fans is scarcely
examined, their passivity is assumed rather than investigated – and
it was this point that was developed by American media sociologists
in the 1940s. They were interested in the 'measurement' of cultural
consumption and their investigations focused on the social structure
in which media use was embedded. Their aim was to show that the
media/consumer relationship was a complex one in which the media
are only several among many sources of meaning; their Cold-War
concern was to provide a positive account of capitalism, to challenge
the concept of 'the mass' – it was argued that as the media were used
by different cultural groups in different cultural contexts, the sociological problem was not to establish a single significance for mass
culture but to describe a plurality of meanings. Mass culture meant
democratic culture.[11]

In the 1960s this argument was made more theoretically respectable
by the interjection of interactionist concepts. It was now argued that
an outside analyst couldn't make sense of cultural symbols even if
he could describe the structure in which they were used – their meanings were as much the creation of their consumers as of their producers. To claim to understand the meaning of a cultural object for
anyone other than oneself was both arrogant and wrong:

A fundamental problem in such studies stems from the long tradition that has regarded artistic productions as *social facts*. By re-
garding such productions as social facts the analyst is relieved of
the burden of demonstrating what meanings these productions
have for the artist and his audience. It is too frequently assumed
that such meanings can be identified by a capable analyst, independent of the interpretations brought to such works by the artist or
his audiences. In my judgement artist productions must be seen as
interactional creations; the meanings of which arise out of the
interactions directed to them by the artist and his audience.[12]

The conclusion is that commodity forms do not determine cultural
possibilities – to decide whether rock is 'inauthentic' or 'corrupt' a
detailed investigation of the audience is necessary. I have already outlined the sub-culturalists' application of this argument to youth

culture. Their approach reflects, too, a similar argument that has developed within Marxism. Even in the 1930s Adorno's sour view of mass culture was complemented by Walter Benjamin's celebration of the positive possibilities of 'the work of art in the age of mechanical reproduction'. Benjamin argued that the technology of mass production was a progressive force, the means by which the traditional authority and 'aura' of art would be broken, by which artists would become democratic producers, their work shared with a community in which everyone would be an 'expert'. The technology of the mass media had changed the relationship of the masses to art and opened up new possibilities for cultural work: creation had become a collective rather than an individual process, the development of socialised means of expression made possible a socialist aesthetics.[13]

In the 1950s the Marxist problem had been to explain the lack of opposition to the capitalist social order, to explain the mass media's ideological effectiveness; in the context of the 1960s cultural conflicts these questions lost their force and Benjamin's points were rediscovered. They were particularly suggestive for popular music – the emergence of the radical youth movement meant that a new assessment had to be made of the ideological effects of rock. Dave Laing, for example, argued that capitalist cultural forms contained liberating as well as oppressive elements; rock was 'squeezed out' of the conflict between commercial machinations and youthful aspirations – if the industry was seeking to exploit a new market, the youth audience was seeking a medium through which to·express its experience and musicians, who were at the centre of this conflict, were able to develop their own creative space. Laing concluded that the mass media were the location not of cultural pluralism but of cultural struggle: if the capitalist organisation of cultural production is not entirely determinant, then both artists and audiences can fight for the control of the meanings of cultural symbols. Benjamin's original point is remade: it is precisely the technological and socialised basis of mass production that makes cultural struggle possible.[14]

This sort of argument lies behind the claims for rock products we have seen to be made by musicians, in the music press, among Keighley's hip kids. The suggestion is that some records, in some circumstances, express something more than the culture of profit, the ideology of passive consumption. The question is how to recognise these special products.

Rock as folk music

The first way to distinguish rock products from the mainstream of commercial pop is to claim them as folk music. The distinction between mass and folk cultures is important for the mass media's critics, who contrast mass and community, fragmented consumption and collective creation, alienation and solidarity, passivity and activity. Folk culture is created directly and spontaneously out of communal experience; it is the culture of the working classes, it expresses the communal experience of work; there is no distance between folk artist and audience, no separation between folk production and consumption. In A. L. Lloyd's words:

> The main thing is that the songs are made and sung by men who are identical with their audience in standing, in occupation, in attitude to life, and in daily experience.[15]

The argument is that this form of popular creativity has been destroyed by the means and relations of artistic production under capitalism. Cultural products are now produced and sold for profit and the consequent processes of taste manipulation and artistic exploitation have been made possible by the recording techniques which enable culture to be mass produced and individually consumed. Folkies celebrate a tradition of live performance in which the performer was not even distanced from his listeners by amplification – Bob Dylan was booed at the Newport Folk Festival simply for playing with electrified instruments.[16]

Undaunted by these arguments, Jon Landau writes of rock'n'roll:

> It was unmistakably a folk-music form. Within the confines of the media, these musicians articulated attitudes, styles and feelings that were genuine reflections of their own experience and of the social situation which had helped to produce that experience.[17]

Critic Greil Marcus suggests that rock'n'roll was a 'secret' that bound a generation and made it culturally independent of its elders; Robert Christgau argues that rock is a source of solidarity. For these writers, it is not so much the lyrical content of rock'n'roll (all those teenage topics that can so easily be faked) that make it a genuine form of youthful expression as its physical content: rock's entertainment value, as dance music, is essential to its folk value of giving symbolic form to the energy and needs of its users – I have already described the importance of rock's black musical elements for its expression of community. From this perspective there is no distance between musicians and fans. In Landau's words:

> There existed a strong bond between performer and audience, a natural kinship, a sense that the stars weren't being imposed from

above but had sprung up from out of our ranks. We could identify
with them without hesitation.[18]

And it is precisely the technology of rock, particularly radio, that
enables it to provide its disparate audience with a shared experience.
As Marcus puts it:

> We fight our way through the massed and levelled collective taste
> of the Top 40, just looking for a little something we can call our
> own. But when we find it and jam the radio to hear it again it isn't
> just ours – it is a link to thousands of others who are sharing it
> with us. As a matter of a single song this might mean very little;
> as culture, as a way of life, you can't beat it.[19]

Rock culture is not confined to ceremonial occasions but enters
people's lives without aura, taking on a meaning there independent
of the intentions of its original creators. The rock audience is not a
passive mass, consuming records like cornflakes, but an active community, making music into a symbol of solidarity and an inspiration
for action. The claim is that the rock audience is not always manipulated but can make real choices; the music doesn't always impose an
ideology but can, in Marcus's phrase, 'absorb events', absorb its
listeners' concerns and values.[20]

The problem of the rock-as-folk ideology (and I have cited only
the most articulate expressions of an argument we have already
seen to be common among rock's makers and users) is its circularity –
the music is folk music because its audience is a real community, but
this community is recognised by its common use of the music. The
way out of the circle is via an independent measure of the rock community, and here we find two rather different arguments. On the one
hand, rock is heard as the culture of adolescence, as the expression
of the community of teenagers; on the other hand rock is heard
as counter-culture, as the expression of specific, vanguard youth
groups.

The first argument need not detain us long. It involves the straightforward derivation of rock meanings from general teenage needs and
values; it assesses rock records as the expressions of teenage fun,
excitement, anxiety and sexiness; it is another version of adolescence
theory. But the problem is not to establish rock's general relevance
for young people, but to establish particular records' expressive
authenticity and, in this respect, the folk claims are not convincing.
If rock is the permanent background music of teenage culture, it is not
usually the focus of much attention and it fails to meet the basic
criteria of a folk form. Youth, as I argued in Chapter 2, is not in

itself a community – rock celebrates leisure rather than work, its per-formers are stars, bohemians, distanced from their audiences in status and power and situation; music is used by teenagers almost exclus-ively as entertainment. Rock's relevance for the young, its meaning as a mass teenage medium, is not as folk culture but as popular culture – I will return to this distinction in the next chapter.[21]

But there is a second and more convincing folk claim that is often wrongly confused with the teenage argument. In 1950, David Riesman identified a minority group among American adolescents which re-jected the image of youth presented for their consumption by the mass media; he added that

> such a 'youth movement' differs from the youth movements of other countries in having no awareness of itself, as such, no direct political consciousness, and, on the whole, no specialised media of communication.[22]

In the 1960s this assessment had to be revised. Rebel youth had become both self-conscious and politically assertive, they had their own media, their own forms of expression; the hippies were the source of a new folk claim: rock as counter-culture. The counter-cultural argument started from the description of a community and only then valued rock as the expression of that community's feelings and experiences. This ideology of rock rested on an analysis of the way music was produced as well as of the way it was consumed. It was important for the counter-cultural position that rock musicians were part of the community for which they made their music, that their art was an explicit expression of communal values – rock was a folk form not despite commercialism but in opposition to it, and musici-ans' claims to represent their communities were seen to be compro-mised by involvement with the capitalist organisation of the record industry.

This argument is important for any assessment of music as the expression of particular youth groups' experiences – it has not been confined to hippies or to hippie records. Its most recent version can be found in the music papers' discussions of whether punk bands can continue to represent the young deprived while signing comfort-able recording contracts. The technology of rock is seen to carry con-trary implications: amplification and recording are the basic means of rock expression but they also enable businessmen to take control. As local live performers, musicians can remain a genuine part of a community, subject to its values and needs, but as recording artists the pressures they experience are those of the market, of 'rock'n'roll imperialists' seeking the biggest possible national and international sales – the musicians' 'community' quickly becomes the purchasing pattern symbolised by the charts.[23]

The implication of this argument is that rock operates as a counter-cultural music briefly and sporadically. If its creative breakthroughs are the musical expressions of needs and changes in real communities, it does not take the industry long to control and corrupt the results. Indeed, the record companies' task has been made easier by the confusion of counter-cultural ideology with the ideology of the teenager. Counter-cultural musicians can legitimate their acquisition of star status by reference to their importance for youth in general, while the rebellious youth groups themselves are diverted by the commercial success of the counter-cultural stars. We have already seen how easily progressive rock became just another form of show business, how quickly the new youth culture of the 1960s became just another market. As Michael Lydon has eloquently argued:

> In fact rock, rather than being an example of how freedom can be achieved within the capitalist structure, is an example of how capitalism can, almost without a conscious effort, deceive those whom it oppresses. . . . So effective has the rock industry been in encouraging the spirit of optimistic youth take-over that rock's truly hard political edge, its constant exploration of the varieties of youthful frustration, has been ignored and softened.[24]

The argument that rock expresses the values of specific counter-cultural communities is, then, only convincing at occasional moments in rock's history. The implication is that rock, far from being a distinct form of mass culture, loses its unique, radical significance precisely in as far as it becomes mass culture, and we are left with the much vaguer assertion that as all forms of popular art must touch somehow on popular concerns, so popular youth music must touch on youthful concerns. The question is how: and in the 1970s, as the counter-cultural argument has lost its force and become a selling technique, the special status of rock's best music has increasingly been explained in terms not of its folk claims but of its power as art.

Rock as art form

The distinction between art and mass culture rests on the distinction between individual sensibility and lowest-common-denominator consciousness, between moral enrichment and escapism, between self-conscious creation and alienated consumption. To claim rock as art is to claim that rock songs and records are demanding individual creations and this claim, as we have seen, began to be made in the late 1960s. Wilfred Mellers, for example, contrasted popular music as entertainment, a substitute for experience, a stimulation and titillation 'without commitment or threat', and rock as art, a complex creation of symbolic forms which related to the reality of the artists' experience. Other critics argued that rock was a form of popular music that, through its lyrics, for the first time put 'youth in touch with serious, intellectual critiques' of Western culture – comparisons of John Lennon and Plato were surprisingly frequent.[25]

The ideology of rock as art raises two problems. Firstly, rock music, like other works of art in an age of mechanical reproduction, is not made by individual creators communicating directly to an audience: record-making (as opposed to music-making) depends on a complex structure of people and machines. Rock critics have had to establish their own version of *auteur* theory – Jon Landau comments, for example:

> To me the criteria of art in rock is the capacity of the musician to create a personal, almost private, universe and to express it fully.[26]

The rock *auteur* (who may be writer, singer, instrumentalist, band, and even, on occasion, record producer or engineer) creates the music with his or her unique experience, skill and vision. Everyone else engaged in record-making is simply part of the means of communication. For many fans it is this process of individual creation that distinguishes rock from other forms of mass music – the fact that the Beatles wrote their own songs freed them from Tin Pan Alley culturally as well as economically – and, as Greil Marcus has pointed out, these days it is routine to equate art and personal confession. Self-consciousness is the measure of a record's artistic status; frankness, musical wit, the use of irony and paradox are musicians' artistic insignia – it is such self-commentary that reveals the *auteur* within the mass machinery of a commercial culture.[27]

The second problem for rock's claims as art is its continuing function as entertainment. Entertainment from this point of view is understood to be neither improving nor instructive, it takes its audience nowhere and comes easy – a true art makes people work. The solution to this problem has been to make rock work too, to complicate its structure (by aping classical music or jazz) and to move it (literally and metaphorically) from dance to concert halls. The listener can then deny that the immediate response to rock exhausts its meaning: rock can't just be consumed, but must be addressed like any other form of art – its tensions and contradictions engaged and reinterpreted as part of the listener's own experience. Such engagement is intellectual and moral, the results are enriching and can be disturbing – this was the rock belief of the sixth-formers in my Keighley sample.[28]

The trouble with the resulting descriptions of rock records as the hard work of rock *auteurs* is that they are not often very convincing. The image of the individual creator, the genius, is too obviously part of the process by which A Star Is Born – this was the feature of sixties rock ideology that was most easily controlled by the business – and the rock star, like any other mass artist, is under constant pressure to confirm his commercial status, his sales popularity, by providing his audience with more of the music that gave him that status in the first place. There is a permanent contradiction between being an artist – responsible only to one's own creative impulses – and being a star – responsible to one's audience's perceived values and needs – and the problem for rock-as-art fans is to explain how their musician-artists can sustain their individual impulses in the face of the market pressures. The conclusion in the music press is that they can't: the folk story of creative breakthrough and commercial retrenchment has a parallel artistic version – the artistic claims of rock are based not on the form itself but on the achievements of a handful of disparate geniuses. Rock musicians' culture as a whole is not really much different from that of any other group of entertainers: their object is to give a particular market what it wants. If that market wants artists then, OK, that's what they'll get. In Robert Levin's words:

> Rock's superiority over previous popular musical forms is simply the result of its existence in a period of expanded and heightened social, political, and psychological awareness, a period which makes possible and necessary a hip and relevant popular music.[29]

We're back to rock as popular culture again, only this time as the popular culture of sophisticated, individualistic sixth-form and student youth. This audience may sneer at the 'mindless pop' of teenage culture, may exchange its pin-ups for illustrated books of lyrics, its dancing shoes for headphones (except at weekends), its communal 45s for personal LPs, but the processes through which its music arrives in the marketplace are not really any different. Manfred Mann once commented that

> Pop music is probably the only art form that is totally dependent for its success on the general public. The more people buy a record, the more successful it is – not only commercially but artistically.[30]

It is this suggestion that I must finally consider.

12

Conclusion

The power of popular music comes, as Manfred Mann suggests, from its popularity. Music becomes a mass culture by entering a mass consciousness, by being heard simultaneously on people's radios and record players, on pub and café juke-boxes, at discos and dances. Mass music is recorded music; records which don't sell, which don't become popular, don't enter mass consciousness whatever their particular artistic claims, their authenticity and interest as music. I began this book by defining rock as music made for a mass market and I must end it by taking this definition seriously. Rock is a mass medium and, in the end, the attempts to claim rock products as folk music or as works of art miss the point. Rocks works as mass culture; records' ideological influence is determined by what happens to them in the marketplace.

The mass-cultural critics claim that he who controls the market controls the meaning, and argue that the mass audience plays no part in cultural creation – even its consumer choices are manipulated and limited. But this does not make sense of rock. The vast bulk of the music that is aimed at the mass market does not reach it, and the music business is organised around the fear of over-production – its daily practices reflect not the problems of creating needs but of responding to them. Few labels have the capital or the courage to risk stirring up new demands; it is enough of a problem to suit existing ones – hence the importance of the charts, of the star system, of the 'reserve army' of rock musicians. These are the peculiar essentials of a business in which many records are issued, but few are chosen.

This account of the record business is confirmed by rock's history. There are a number of versions of the story but their plot is always the same – creative breakthroughs (from artists, audiences, localities, sub-cultures) followed by record-company control and rigidity. The industry has made its money through its response to needs independently expressed; punk rock, to cite the most recent example, was developed as a musical style by musicians and audiences operating outside the usual record-business relationships; it was taken over and exploited by record companies only when its market potential seemed assured. In general terms, the rock business is built on two great market discoveries: the discovery of the working-class teenage audience in the 1950s and the discovery of the middle-class youth audience in the 1960s. The industry had to learn about these audiences and their demands, and the musical results have followed rather than led youthful tastes and choices.

For the mass-culture critics, rock's commercial success reflects its psychological success in *manipulating* adolescent needs. All rock, in other words, has the same psychological function and the choices made within it are insignificant, reflect merely the competitive calculations of the producers and the random irrationality of the consumers. But this argument makes sense of neither the history nor the practice of the record industry, and if the power of popular music lies in its popularity then the particular choices that the people make are important.

This is the source of the distinction between mass culture – its ideology explicable in terms of producer stimulus and audience response – and popular culture – its ideology the result, too, of genuinely popular attitudes and values. Rock is a capitalist industry and not a folk form, but its most successful products do, at some level, express and reflect its audiences' concerns. This is its significance as popular culture.

In *Mystery Train*, the most sustained attempt to analyse rock as popular culture, Greil Marcus argues that rock, like all mass culture, functions to provide a sense of community for an audience fragmented by the experience of competitive capitalism. Most mass culture plays this role safe – American-ness or British-ness is presented as the bland and conventional acceptance of a lie, that the way things are is just dandy. For Marcus, mass culture can only become art if it can carry unconventional visions so powerful that they can't be evaded even by mass consumption. The central worry for popular artists is that

> if you get what you have to say across to a mass audience, that means what you have to say is not deep enough, or strong enough, to really matter.[1]

This is also the worry of the cultural critics, but Marcus goes on to suggest that the mass media can communicate disturbing truths, can be the vehicle for a popular art, if they draw on and respond to the contradictions that are already disturbing and powerful in popular ideology. Rock is a form of popular art in so far as it expresses and deals symbolically with contradictions, and Marcus's particular concern is with American rock's treatment of the ideology of equality, an ideology particularly fraught with difficulty – not only is the ideal of equality contradicted by daily experience, but there are contradictions within the ideal itself: it opposes ambition, the sense of private worth to community and the collective prejudices that support the unequal in their individual failures. It is this contradiction that Marcus finds expressed in the most powerful rock music: on the one hand, ambition and risk-taking, a sense of style and adventure, a refusal to be satisfied; on the other hand, a feeling for roots and history, a dependence on community and tradition, on the acceptance of one's lot. The central image of rock as American popular culture is Elvis Presley, demanding good times and getting them and finding them all too easy. As rock'n'roll became rock and forced its way into the culture of a much wider community of white youth, its tense combination of dissatisfaction and guilt took meaning as a looser contradiction between utopianism – California as the Promised Land – and cynicism – California as the final dead resting-place of alien souls.

Marcus is pointing here to a particular aspect of the central concern of mass culture, its attempt to make a symbolic community out of disparate audiences. Rock, from this point of view, is particularly expressive of the problem of the youth community: it idealises as a permanent experience a state that must inevitably be temporary – young people know well enough that they are growing up. The contradictions of youth 'community' are clear, for example, in sixth-form culture, in which music is used both to express the sense of generation, the general verve and pride and independence of adolescence, and the particular individuality of students on the edge of making their independent ways in the world. Rock becomes the popular art of sixth-form culture in so far as it provides simultaneously the symbols of individual possibility and doubt and the symbols of collective security and comfort.

If sixth-formers value individual as well as group symbols, respond to lyrics and musical complexity as well as to sound and rhythm, spend time listening as well as dancing, theirs is not a completely distinct form of youth culture. I argued in Part I that for the vast majority of young people rock is a background rather than a focus. In analysing its meanings as popular culture we must understand rock use as well as rock content, we must understand rock as leisure. What is involved here is not the autonomous expression of cultural or sub-cultural values, but the different patterns of freedom and constraint experienced by young people in different relationships to production.

The second contradiction that runs through all capitalist mass culture is that between the belief that we work to enjoy leisure and the reality that we enjoy leisure in order to work; leisure is, on the one hand, a source of fun and freedom and pleasure, a necessary counter to alienating labour; but it must be, on the other hand, constrained and controlled and made trivial so as not to interfere with the labour process. This tension is felt particularly intensely by young people, whose 'free' time is freer than that of adults and whose hedonism is therefore 'riskier' – rock is the main symbolic means of expressing these risks. The music has a radical, rebellious edge: it carries a sense of possibility denied in the labour market; it suggests the solidarity of comradeship, the abandon of sensuality, the grace and joy and energy lacking in work.

The essence of rock, then, is fun, a concept strangely neglected by sociologists. Analysts of high art are obliged to respect the autonomy of aesthetic judgements, but sociologists of popular art try to avoid confronting fun and describe the 'irrationality' of mass taste with aloof disgust, as if irrationality were irrelevant for popular culture instead of a vital part of it. Marxists, in particular, have interpreted the fact that people *enjoy* mass culture as a reason for gloom – Adorno, for example, values high art for its imagination, its fantasies, its utopianism, but dismisses the irrationalities of mass culture as psychological disorders. But the power of rock fantasy rests on precisely the same sort of utopianism. In the *Grundrisse* Marx comments that the capitalist, needing producers for his products,

> searches for means to spur workers on to consumption, to give his wares new charms, to inspire them with new needs by constant chatter, etc. It is precisely this side of the relation of capital and labour which is an essential civilising moment, and on which the historic justification, but also the contemporary power of capital rests.[2]

Cultural commodities may support the contemporary power of capital, but they have their civilising moments. Even as the most effortless background music rock is a source of vigour and exhilaration and the good feelings that are as necessary for the next morning's political struggle as for the next day's work. Rock's fun is as much a quality of its use as of its form. The usual theory is that the star is an extraordinary fellow who brings excitement and glamour into the lives of his fans, ordinary people, but the process also works the other way round: stars, dull professionals, are made glamorous by the imagination, wit and excitement of their fans. The basic problem for rock's capitalist producers is, in fact, to control its use – what is at issue is the ideology of leisure. One of the reasons why rock has been the most vital form of popular culture in the last twenty years is that it has expressed so clearly the struggle involved: rock has been used simultaneously as a source of self-indulgence and individual escape, and of solidarity and active dissatisfaction.

In girl culture, for example, rock's significance derives from its expression of the tensions in the girls' preparations for their careers as wives and mothers. At one level the tensions are purely sexual, and rock both expresses girls' denied sexuality and dissolves it in the fantasies of dance, daydream and pin-ups on the wall. More importantly, the best rock also draws on the tensions between the romanticism that sustains girls' commitment to love and marriage and the boy next door and the wry realism with which they pursue marriage as a job and accept that he is, in the end, *only* the boy next door. This argument can be generalised. Rock, as popular culture, expresses a series of contradictions in leisure between freedom and constraint, and girl culture merely reflects the particular problems of women's work and play. But the girl example also makes clear the problems of cultural control. If rock's expression of the contradictions involved in the popular ideology of women is too powerful then those contradictions run the risk of being exploded – hence the common adult fear of rock's sexiness, of its overtly sexual performers. Female musicians, whether through implicit but disturbing images of what a woman could be or on the basis of an explicitly feminist culture, can challenge the safe solutions to the problems of girl culture, the safe symbols of the glamorous star-as-mum. In the end, rock's importance rests on visions and fantasies that appeal (*pace* Adorno) because of their utopian, idealistic versions of reality; the most successful rock (successful commercially and artistically) presents these visions and fantasies so strongly that they do become a critique of reality, and the task for mass-cultural producers, for record companies and for media ideologists is therefore to control such dangerous visions. Girl performers and their images, for example, are controlled by an ideology of sexism which confines female rockers within narrow limits (and the success of which, as Angie McRobbie pointed out to me, is reflected in the instinctive way in which every pupil in my Keighley sample used the term 'poofta' to abuse musicians they disliked).

In the last chapter I showed how Marxist theories of cultural domination became, in the context of sixties rock, theories of cultural struggle; what I have now argued is that rock struggle concerns cultural use as well as cultural content. The ideology of rock depends not only on the relationship of producers and consumers, but also on the success of rock intermediaries' attempts to define rock's meanings by constraining its uses. Rock reaches its audience via other media – radio, television, newspapers, the music press; for most rock consumers these media are the source of their knowledge and interpretations of particular rock styles, stars and sounds. If punk, for example, originated among small, creative youth groups, its meaning for its subsequent fans was derived not just from the music itself, but also from the various punk images and analyses battling it out in the media.

Three processes, in particular, have been central to the struggle for the control of rock use. Firstly, there has been the continuing attempt to confine rock to entertainment, to ensure that its leisure values are limited precisely to leisure, to temporary moments of relaxation. This is the interpretation of rock made by radio, for example: in Chapter 7 I described how Radio 1 drains all the power from music until even the funkiest disco rhythms, the astutest protest lyrics, the most stirring heavy metal sounds get heard as muzak, a cheery accompaniment to the washing up. A similar attitude is obvious in the music press: *Rolling Stone*, for example, developed from a magazine in which the leisure values of rock were taken as the source for a critical commentary on the organisation of politics and production, into a magazine in which rock is understood only as an enjoyable form of consumption – *Stone*, like the rest of the rock press, is now a consumer guide.

Secondly, there has been a continuing effort to freeze the rock audience into a series of market tastes. Record companies themselves, radio programmers, music papers, DJs, critics, all attempt to control musical demands and so ease the process of meeting them. If audiences can be persuaded that a precise style, genre, artist or image meets their needs, expresses the solution to their particular leisure problem, then not only is their commercial exploitation made easier, but rock's disturbing and challenging and instructive elements are transformed into the easy confirmations of well established conventions.

Thirdly, there has been the continuing process through which the anti-work elements of rock-as-leisure have been reduced from their threatening collective forms to the individual indulgences of bohemian hedonism. This is the way in which rock's creative forces are blunted and made to conform to the exigencies of an entertainment industry. Hippie culture, for instance, was thus translated into a commercial ideology, and in Chapter 9 I showed how musicians, the originators of rock's symbolic forms, are confined by craft pride and the star system, and by their own place in the capitalist organisation of leisure, to a petit-bourgeois view of the world. For them leisure is a special sort of work, not an alternative to it, and it is inevitable that rock stars should 'sell out' to individual ambitions, careers and success the hopes of the hard core of hip rock believers who continue to find in music not *just* entertainment, not *just* a confirmed taste, not *just* a piece of instant pleasure, but also the outline of a better life to come.

Rock commentators nowadays argue that whatever the art and power of particular songs and records and styles, the overall struggle to control the use of rock has, for the moment, been lost to the entertainment industry. Whatever its radical cultural possibilities in the 1960s, rock has become, in the 1970s, a culture of predictable market tastes and indulgent superstars, of slick radio shows and standardised sounds; it has become, in short, music business as usual. Rock's eldest fans are now the parents of their own teenagers and their music has been part of the experience of settling down. Rock is, in Sue Sharpe's words, 'just a part of the sound-scene of growing up' and the notion that rock might be the sound of *not* growing up is, it is suggested, silly – record companies are already charting with precision the continuing rock tastes of husbands, wives, parents, teachers and workers; rock, the marketing assumption goes, need no longer be the music of youth.[3]

But it will remain fun and it will remain the source of a power and joy that are disturbing as well as relaxing – witness the contradictions of punk. The industry may or may not keep control of rock's use, but it will not be able to determine all its meanings – the problems of capitalist community and leisure are not so easily resolved.

List of abbreviations

LIR	:	*Let It Rock*
MM	:	*Melody Maker*
MW	:	*Music Week*
NME	:	*New Musical Express*
RB	:	*Retail Business*
RS	:	*Rolling Stone*
WPCS	:	*Working Papers in Cultural Studies*

BMRB	:	British Market Research Bureau
BPI	:	British Phonographic Industry
CSO	:	Central Statistical Office
DES	:	Department of Education and Science
IBA	:	Independent Broadcasting Authority
ILR	:	Independent Local Radio
IPC	:	International Publishing Corporation
JICNRS	:	Joint Industry Committee for National Readership Survey
JICRAR	:	Joint Industry Committee for Radio Audience Research
MSC	:	Manpower Services Commission
MU	:	Musicians Union
NUT	:	National Union of Teachers
PPL	:	Phonographic Performance Ltd
PRS	:	Performing Rights Society

Notes and references

Chapter 1: Introduction

1. In 1973 it was estimated that about 70% of households in the UK owned some form of record-playing equipment. Ownership of record players rose steadily from 38% in 1963 to 55% in 1972; ownership of tape or cassette recorders rose in the same period from 9% to 20%. In 1970, 84% of households owned a radio, a percentage which had remained constant throughout the 1960s, although the number of households with transistor radios rose from 32% to 67%. In this pattern of ownership Britain led a European trend and matched the situation in the USA. Britain accounts for about 8% of the world music market, and in 1974 the British sale of records and tapes was worth £160 million (a rise from £25 million in 1959).

   I've put these figures together from a variety of sources: *The Readers' Digest*'s *Products and People*, 1963, Table 3, and *Survey of Europe*, 1970, 68-9, 104-5, 108-9; IPC's *Marketing Manual of the UK*, 1975, Tables A.4 and B.8.2; CSO's *Annual Abstract of Statistics*, 1975, 212; *Retail Business* 23 (1960), 74 (1964), 98 (1966), 159 (1971), 200 (1974); surveys of the music business in *Time*, 12 Feb. 1973, *MW*, 4 Aug. 1973, *RS*, 6 Dec. 1973 and *Financial Times*, 20 Jan. 1975; UNESCO (1975), 134-6; Stokes, *Star-making machinery*, 4; Chapple and Garofalo, *Rock'n'roll is here to pay*, 186.

2. For a useful summary of the sociological characteristics of mass media see McQuail, *Towards a sociology of mass communications*, 7-10.

3. For these figures see the *RB* reports on gramophone records. For comparative national breakdowns see UNESCO (1975), 137-8, and Bornoff, *Music and the twentieth-century media*, 66.

4. See Tunstall, *The media are American*, passim.

5. For these figures see the *RB* reports on gramophone records and BMRB's *Target Group Index*, 1976, xxxiv. In the USA it has been calculated that teenagers buy 60% of singles and under-25-year-olds 80% – see J. P. Robinson and P. Hirsch, 'It's the sound that does it', *Psychology Today*, Oct. 1969. For Europe see Bontinck, *New patterns of musical behaviour*.

6. British release figures are calculated from *The New Singles* and *The New Records*, published for retailers by Francis Antony Ltd. *Music Week* also keeps a running total of the year's release statistics. For further discussion of singles releases see S. Frith, 'A year of singles in Britain', in Gillett ed., *Rock File 2*. For American statistics see Stokes, 3, Shemel and Krasilovsky, *This business of music*, xvii, and Hirsch, *Structure of the popular music industry*, 17-18, 25.

7. For the importance of the charts for the record industry in its early days see Briggs, *History of broadcasting*, 110–11. For how charts are currently compiled see A. Walker and E. Tiegel, 'How the charts are compiled', in Gillett and Frith, eds., *Rock File 4*.

8. For sales distribution see BMRB's *British Analysis of Record Sales*.

9. For music press readership see JICNRS' *National Readership Surveys* for *NME, MM* and *Sounds*; for Radio 1 see the BBC's Audience Research Dept. reports; for Luxembourg see the statistics reported in *MW*, 27 Jan. 1973.

Chapter 2: Youth

1. MacInnes, *Absolute beginners*, 6; cf. his non-fictional writings on the same subject in *England, half English*.

2. Abrams, *The teenage consumer*; Mays, *The young pretenders*, 51. For similar arguments for America and France cf. Bernard, J., 'Teen-age culture: an overview' in Vaz, ed., *Middle-class juvenile delinquency*, and Morin, *Plodémet*, 132–3.

3. Seabrook, *City close-up*, 150–60. cf. White, D., 'The Young Workers', *New Society*, 1 June 1972, and Harrison, P., 'Growing Up Ordinary', *New Society*, 18 Sept. 1975.

4. Albemarle, *The Youth Service in England and Wales*, 1960. For a socialist response to the report see Ray Gosling's Young Fabian Pamphlet, 'Lady Albemarle's Boys', 1961, and cf. NUT, *Popular culture and personal responsibility*. Conservative quote from Wilson, *The youth culture and the universities*, 168–9.

5. For the history of fears of juvenile delinquency see Gillis, *Youth and history*, 170–5. For fifties fears see Hopkins, *The new look*, 207–8, 426. For an example of the sensation of the ordinary teenager, see the press reactions to National Children's Bureau, *Britain's sixteen-year-olds*.

6. For the distinction between college and corner boys, see Cohen, A. K., *Delinquent boys*. The most important English study in this tradition is Downes, *The delinquent solution*, an extremely sophisticated application to British teenagers of American deviancy theory from Merton to Matza. There is a stimulating discussion of the relationship between deviancy and teenage culture in Cohen, 'Breaking out, smashing up'.

7. MacInnes, *Absolute beginners*, 49; and see Nuttall, *Bomb culture*.

8. Melly, G., 'Didn't I?', *New Society*, 13 June 1963.

9. Hopkins, 429.

10. See, e.g., Kvaracceus, W., and Miller, W. B., 'Norm-Violating Behaviour in Middle-Class Culture' in Vaz.

11. Birnbaum, N., *The crisis of industrial society*, New York, 1969, 165.

12. Rex, J., 'Power', *New Society*, 5 Oct. 1972.

13. Bottomore, T. B., *Sociology as Social Criticism*, London, 1975, 206.

14. The most interesting contemporary argument was Rowntree and Rowntree, 'The political economy of youth'. Their position was that youth were a class because of their roles in the 'absorption' of surplus value (as soldiers, students and unemployed workers) – roles which involved economic exploitation and social alienation. For a useful discussion of the issues see Jacques, 'Trends in youth culture'.

15. For the concept of generation see Mannheim, *Diagnosis of our time*, 35–52 and *Essays in the sociology of knowledge*, ch. 7. cf. Abrams, Philip, 'Rites de passage'.

16. Eisenstadt, *From generation to generation*.

17. See, e.g., Friedenberg, *The vanishing adolescent*, Goodman, *Growing up absurd*, and, for Britain, Musgrove, *Youth and the social order*.

18. Allen, 'Some theoretical problems in the study of youth'.

19. The classic study from this perspective is Cohen, S., *Folk devils and moral panics*.

20. For the American sub-cultural approach see, e.g., Hollingshead, *Elmtown's youth and Elmtown revisited*, and Buff, 'Greasers, dupers and hippies'. For the radical British version, see Cohen, P., 'Sub-cultural conflict and working-class community, Parker, *View from the boys* and wpcs, 7, 1975. For examples of the heights of absurdity which this approach can reach, see I. Taylor, 'Soccer Consciousness and Soccer Hooliganism' in Cohen, S. ed., *Images of deviance*, and G. Pearson, 'Paki-Bashing in a North-Eastern Lancashire Cotton Town' in Pearson and Mungham, eds, *Working-class youth culture*.

21. Abrams, *The teenage consumer; Teenage consumer spending in 1959*. It may be worth stressing that the affluence of Abrams' teenagers wasn't just a demographic phenomenon. The percentage of the population aged 15–24 has steadily fallen this century – from 19·6% in 1901 to 13·1% in 1951. It has stabilised since then at 13–14% but the long-term trend is still down.

22. cso, *Annual Abstract of Statistics*, 1975, pp. 123, 127–8; Gillis, *Youth and history*, 135.

23. Gillis, 189; J. Sandilands, 'Portrait of a Generation', *Observer Magazine*, 12 Sept. 1976; B. Spittles, 'Children at Work', *New Society*, 8 March 1973; Smith, C. S., *Young people at leisure*, ch. 2; des, *Undergraduate income and spending*. For the statistics of the sharp increase in teenage income on leaving school, see the ipc's *Marketing Manual of the UK*, 1975, Table A.8.14.

24. Calculated from the *Dept. of Employment Gazette*, Dec. 1975: 'Young People Entering Employment in 1974', Table 6.

25. See, e.g., the *Donovan Report on Trade Unions*, 1968, 90–2 and Research Paper II; the Finer Report on One Parent Families, 1974, 421–3; the Report of the House of Commons Expenditure Committee on the Employment of Women, 1973.

26. Quote from Joseph, 'A research note on attitudes to work and marriage'. *Cf.* Wilkins, *The adolescent in Britain*, 84. Figures from the *Annual Abstract of Statistics*, 1975, 18. The Dept. of Employment's Manpower Paper 9, *Women and Work*, shows that in 1971 12·8% of the female work force was under 20 (16·3% in 1961) and 7·9% of the male work force (9·2% in 1961).

27. M. P. Carter, 'Teenage Workers: a Second Chance at 18?' in Brannen, ed., *Entering the world of work*, 97; opcs, *Fifth form girls*, 8–10; Spittles in *New Society*, 8 March 1973. For feminist discussion see Sharpe, *Just like a girl*; cf. Eve Figes, *Patriarchal Attitudes*, London, 1970, 169–71.

28. Statistics from Gollan, *Youth in British industry*, 310; *cf.* Roberts, R., *The classic slum*, 222.

29. See Schools Council, *Young school leavers*, 135–58; Phillips, 'Young and unemployed in a northern town', 413–17; Brown, R., 'Attitudes, expectations and social perspectives of shipbuilding apprentices'.

30. Gillis, 118–28; Roberts, R., 157–9. For a contemporary account of the young rough/respectable division see P. Willis, 'Lads, Lobes and Labour', *New Society*, 20 May 1976.

31. C. S. Smith, 'Entry, location and commitment of young workers in the labour force', in Brannen, ed., 23–4.

32. For the statistics see Dept. of Employment, *Unqualified, untrained and unemployed*, 20, 83 and the Manpower Services 1976 *Report*, p. 20. And see Smith, C. S., *The Wincroft youth project*, 82; Phillips, 413–14; Carter in Brannen, ed., 99–101; Marsden and Duff, *Workless*, 82.

33. See, e.g., Ashton, 'The transition from school to work'. For a useful summary of the observed characteristics of 'problem' youth, see Wilkins, 82.

34. Coventry City Centre Project, Research Team Report, 1975–6.

35. See, e.g., Venables, *The young worker at college*, 87; W. Liversidge, 'Life Choices', in Williams, W. M. ed., *Occupational choice*, 74. Carter, in Brannen, ed., 104–5, 108.

36. For theories of entry into work see K. Roberts, 'The Entry into Employment', in Williams, W. M., ed. For unemployment and the unskilled, *cf.* P. Brannen, 'Industrial and economic change and the entry into work', in Brannen, ed.

37. Dept. of Employment, 25–6. *Cf.* M. Church, 'Bleak Prospect for the Unskilled', *TES*, 11 June 1971; MSC's 1976 *Report* pp. 9–11. For the 1945–68 boom in youth employment see Gillis, 204–5.

38. See the MSC's 'There's Work To Be Done', 1974; P. Venning: 'Doubts About Job Prospects', *TES*, 5 July 1974; J. Hughes: 'Employing the Young', *New Society*, 14 Oct. 1976. For training and stability see Swift, 'Job orientations and the transition from school to work', and Roberts in Williams, W. M., ed. The use of training as discipline was revealed in a series of interviews with personnel managers that have been conducted for the Coventry City Centre Project by Kevin Buckley. For the ideology behind this development see a number of articles in *Industrial Society*: E. McLeod and H. Adamson, 'Starting Work', March 1972; J. Marsh, 'Investing in Youth', July 1973; D. Allcock, 'Why Youth Training', Oct. 1973; and *cf.* V. Ahier, 'Work Experience', *TES*, 8 March 1974. This change in labour demand can be linked to the simultaneous Great Debate on education and to the various arguments that schools should turn out young workers with 'skills' more relevant to industry.

39. Mr Stanley Dixon, quoted in the *Guardian*, 1 June 1976, p. 4.

40. Quoted in Gollan, 178. *Cf.* Robert Rodwell, 'Labour Gains', *Guardian*, 13 Oct. 1975, for the MSC's similar ideology.

41. For the 'work experience programme' see the MSC's *Reports*, and *cf.* M. Adeny, 'Working their way to the dole?', *Guardian*, 20 Dec. 1976. Earnings figures from the Dept. of Employment's *New Earnings Survey*, 1975, Part E, Table 124.

42. For dole-queue rock see, e.g., P. Marsh, 'Dole-Queue Rock', *New Society*, 20 Jan. 1977. For teenage income and the family see Gillis, 123 and Roberts, R., 52. Cyril Smith makes the point that youth culture could only emerge when family income was sufficient to allow individual rather than family ownership of radios, record players, etc. – Smith, C. S., *Young people at leisure*, 27.

Chapter 3: Youth and music

1. Rowntree and Lavers, *English life and leisure*, 280, 282. Ch. X has a general discussion of dancing as a form of leisure; for case histories of young people see pp. 108–21. For post-war sociology of youth see Logan and Goldberg, 'Rising eighteen in a London suburb', and note the lack of any reference to music in Stewart, 'The leisure activities of grammar school children'.

2. See Gillis, 61–6, 128–31, 138–48; Roberts, R., 155–6; *The new survey of London life and labour*, vol. IX, 140–61, 195–217, 295–6. For the development of dance halls after the First World War see Rust, 89–93. For jazz as young music see Leonard, *Jazz and the white Americans*, 54–5, 68 and Newton, *The jazz scene*, 229–51.

3. See Hopkins, 426, 431–3. For 'Swoonatra' see Pleasants, *The great American popular singers*, 182; for teds, Rock and Cohen, 'The teddy boy', 289; for dancing, Rust, 117–18; for youth and records, the BBC research cited in Belson, *The impact of television*, 38–45; for sociology, Venness, *School leavers*, 118 (her research was done in 1956).

4. Abrams showed that teenagers spent £2m annually on records – only 2% of their total expenditure but 42·5% of the total expenditure on records. This was easily the biggest domination of a consumer market by teenagers, and more than 25% of Abrams' 16–24 year olds had been to a dance at least once in the previous week, compared with 4% for the rest of the adult population. For American adolescents and music see Coleman, *The adolescent society*, 4, 22. For Britain see Venness – she discusses how record and music listening had become a 'regular pastime' in the previous decade; Carter, *Home, school and work*, 306; Jephcott, *Time of one's own*, 59–66, 69, 91. Willmott's contemporaneous study of adolescent boys in London doesn't have an explicit discussion of the teenage use of music, its presence was taken for granted – see Willmott, *Adolescent boys of East London*, e.g., 22.

5. D. White, 'The young workers', *New Society*, 1 June 1972, 460; C. S. Smith, 'Adolescence', Smith, M. A., ed., *Leisure and society in Britain*, 154. And see Sugarman, 'Involvement in youth culture', and Brown and O'Leary, 'Pop music in an English secondary school system'.

6. Carrick James Market Research, *National survey among teenagers and young adults, aged 11–24*, Nov. 1974. And see the IPC's *Marketing Manual*, 1975, Table A.8.15 and BMRB's *Target group index*, 1976, vol. 34. For Europe see Bontink, ed., *New patterns of musical behaviour*. Countries with post-1962/3 youth musics include Finland, Hungary, Poland, Denmark, Yugoslavia, Austria, Sweden and Belgium. For

German youth see UNESCO, *Music and tomorrow's public*, vol. II, pp. 168–179.

7. Jephcott, 59–60.
8. My sample was 105 pupils from one of Keighley's two comprehensive schools and was representative of the school's social and academic mix. In the town as a whole only upper-middle-class children were creamed off to direct-grant or public schools. I also talked to pupils' friends who were at the other comprehensive school or had already started at college and university.
9. In a small survey of teacher trainees in Bradford in 1971 (36 students) Paddy Rogers found that the majority (23) stressed music's importance as a source of relaxation. Only 10 students preferred listening to dancing (most enjoyed both equally), the majority went dancing regularly, and of the 30 who thought pop 'valuable' half saw it as a source of escape and only 12 stressed its 'positive' effects. (private communication)
   An article in *Music Week*, 25 May 1974 ('Record industry backs out of student campaign') suggests that record companies had been over-promoting 'heavy' rock on campuses at the expense of the 'entertainment' music that students really wanted.
10. For a useful survey of the adolescence literature see Smith, M. A. ed. For the emphasis on peer groups see e.g., Coleman, Jephcott and Willmott.
11. C. Fletcher, 'Beats and gangs on Merseyside', Raison, ed., *Youth in New Society*, 158. This is not quite the picture of Liverpool that comes through in Williams, A., *The man who gave the Beatles away* – he suggests that the beat groups complemented the gangs and, if anything, increased their violence.
12. Quoted in Hamblett and Deverson, *Generation X*, 20.
13. 14 year old girl quoted in the West Riding County Council Education Committee's *Schools Bulletin*, July 1971. *Cf.* a contemporary American comment from a junior high school boy: 'freaks always wear Lees, greasers wear Wranglers, and everyone else wears Levis.' – quoted in Alison Lurie, 'The dress code', *New York Review of Books*, 25 Nov. 1976.
14. Quote from a fifth form girl in my Keighley sample.
15. See the pictures of Slade and Faces fans in Gold, ed., *Rock on the road*.
16. Orlando Patterson, 'The dance invasion', *New Society*, 15 Sept. 1966. For a brilliant description of the dance as an institution see G. Mungham, 'Youth in pursuit of itself', Pearson and Mungham, eds. and *cf.* Leigh, *Young people and leisure*, 139.
17. For an early statement of such angst see Ray Gosling, 'Dream Boy', *NLR*, 3, 1960 and *cf.* Jephcott and Leigh.
18. Quote from P. Harrison, 'Growing up ordinary', *New Society*, 18 Sept. 1975, 633.
19. Murdock and Phelps, *Mass media and the secondary school*, and *cf.* G. Murdock and R. McCron: 'Scoobies, skins and contemporary pop', *New Society*, 29 March 1973.
20. For America see J. Robinson and P. Hirsch: 'It's the sound that does

it', *Psychology Today*, Oct. 1969, 43 and, for differences by class and race within a student population, Skipper, 'How popular is popular music?'. For the 'randomness' of pop tastes see Corrigan, *Schooling the Smash Street kids* – he found that pupils apparently similar in their class backgrounds and academic abilities but in different schools, had diametrically opposed musical tastes, one group preferring heavy rock, the other traditional pop singers like Tom Jones.

The JICNRS *National Readership Survey* for 1976 reveals the following readership patterns for July 1975–June 1976:

	Social Group										
% of group reading											
	A		B		C1		C2		D		E	
	m	f	m	f	m	f	m	f	m	f	m	f
NME	3	3	3	2	5	2	4	2	4	2	2	1
MM	4	3	4	2	5	2	4	2	4	2	2	1
Sounds	1	1	2	1	2	1	2	1	2	1	1	–
Fab 208	–	–	–	1	–	1	–	1	–	1	–	1

These figures have been roughly the same since 1970.

BBC Audience Research figures suggest that age differences are much more significant than class differences in determining listening habits. Most shows reach similar percentages of middle-class and working-class listeners – the only slight trend being for the day-time strip shows to reach a slightly higher proportion of the working-class audience. There is a pattern of working-class listeners listening to more hours of Radio 1 per week, but not to different programmes and *Top of the Pops* (20·6%/22·0%) and *Old Grey Whistle Test* (2·7%/2·4%) reach very similar proportions of the middle- and working-class audiences. These figures cover October 1976, but this pattern of media use has been observed since the mid-sixties.

For expenditure patterns see BMRB's *Target Group Index*, 1976, vol. 34. Detailed market research conducted for IPC into the readership of the music press suggested that the most significant differences in musical preferences and habits within the general youth market depended on age (15–17-year-olds *vs* 21–24-year-olds) and sex – see Taylor, Nelson and Associates Ltd., *Final Stage of the Research into the Market for 'Pop Music' Magazines*, ms, January 1973.

21. Rock and Cohen, 310–11, 316–17; Jefferson, 'The ted'.
22. Pidgeon, *Rod Stewart and the changing Faces*, 9 and *cf.* Herman, *The Who*, 19–27.
23. For mods as hooligans see P. Barker, 'The Margate offenders', Raison, ed.; for mods as consumers see Wolfe, *The Pump House gang* and Twiggy, *Twiggy*, 16–19; for mods as sub-culture see S. Cohen, *Folk devils and moral panics*, ch. 6 and D. Hebdige, 'The meaning of mod', WPCS, 7, 1975.
24. Quote from *The Paint House*, 12; for skinheads as sub-culture see Clarke, 'The skinheads and the study of youth culture'.

25. We can expect the current moral panic about punks to produce in due course sub-cultural readings of safety pins, hennaed hair and the Sex Pistols, although one novel feature of the punks is their readiness to be their own sociologists – see the ideology of the punk fanzine, *Sniffin' Glue*, for example.

26. For the football argument see Pete Fowler's stimulating and influential 'Skins Rule', Gillett, ed., *Rock File* and Chris Lightbown's 'Kids, soccer and pop', *New Society*, 11 July 1974. For a shoddy and misleading application of the argument see I. Taylor and D. Wall, 'Beyond the skinheads', Pearson and Mungham, eds. For football symbols entering rock see S. Frith, 'Cum on feel the noize', Gold, ed. Although sub-culturalists claim to be able to read the symbols of youth culture only one has 'read' music with any subtlety or depth – see Willis, *Profane culture* and *cf.* Monod, 'Juvenile gangs in Paris'.

27. For useful critiques of sub-cultural assumptions see G. Murdock and R. McCron, 'Consciousness of class and consciousness of generation' in WPCS, 7, 1975, 203–6 and 'Youth and class: the career of a confusion', Pearson and Mungham, eds., 24–6.

28. Young, *The drug takers*, 147 and *cf.* his 'The hippie solution', Taylor I. and Taylor, L., eds., *Politics and deviance*, 188. For hippie ideology see Neville, *Play power* and S. Hall, 'The hippie: an American moment', Nagel, ed., *Student power*.

29. Mills, *Young outsiders*, 123–41.

30. See, for example, Ian Walker's interview with the Derelicts in *The Leveller*, 2, 1976: 'Music [after the revolution] would play that role of binding people together, enabling them to communicate at a rare and high level: the replacement of individualism by collectivism.'

31. Fyvel, *The insecure offenders*, 71–81, 240.

32. Willmott, 175–6 and *cf.* Newton on jazz fans, 223–5. For a good description of the working-class drop-out coffee-bar hippie see T. O'Brien, 'Young Nick', *New Society*, 17 Feb. 1972, and *cf.* Willis, Nuttall, *Bomb culture*, Rapoport and Rapoport, *Leisure and the family life cycle*, 144–70.

33. See B. Rogers, 'Rock around the years', *S. Telegraph Magazine*, 28 Nov. 1976, on British Elvis fans; A. Bailey, 'Apple scruffs come to dinner', *RS*, 24 Dec. 1970, on Beatles fans; P. Fowler, 'Fighting off the Martians', *LIR*, Oct. 1975, on Bowie and Ferry fans.

34. For 'weird scenes' *cf. MM*'s 1974 series – e.g., 'Nashville cats', 18 May, on country clubs and 'Where Irish eyes are smiling', 1 June, on Irish clubs. For music, as opposed to star, fans see R. Katz, 'Behind a painted smile', *Sounds*, 27 July 1974, on the Tamla Motown fan club, and L. Henshawe, 'When a fan club is not a fan club', *MM*, 27 July 1974.

   A fanzine is a privately published non-profit-making magazine devoted to a particular genre and circulating among that genre's devotees. There are 50–100 such magazines in Britain, covering everything from old time music to punk.

35. Quotes from Northern Soul fans interviewed by Dave Godin for *Black Music*'s special feature on 'The strange world of northern soul', June

1974, 13. See also *Black Music* January and November 1975 and Gordon Burns, 'A hard week's night', *Sunday Times Colour Supplement*, 29 Feb. 1976, and *cf.* the brief Southern disco cult in 1975–6 for forties music and dress.

One group with an interesting 'deviant' use of music is young blacks. In material terms black youth are like *lumpenproletariat* white youth, only more so – marginal in terms of their lack of jobs and training and low social status – but their music, reggae, has emerged from the politics and culture of Jamaica and expresses a racial and political consciousness which is neither youthful nor British. The use of reggae by Britain's black youth involves contradictions not explicable in terms of sub-culture, though for an attempt see Hebdige, 'Reggae, rastas and rudies'. For black youth see 'The black youth speak', *Race Today*, April 1975; for black youth and music see Carl Gayle, 'The reggae underground', *Black Music*, July 1974 and C. McGlashan, 'From Babylon to Brixton' in Gold, ed.

Chapter 4: Music and leisure

1. Quoted in the West Riding County Council Education Committee's *Schools Bulletin*, July 1971.
2. Quoted in Hamblett and Deverson, 132.
3. For a good introduction to an analysis of girl culture see Angela McRobbie and Jenny Garber, 'Girls and Subcultures', wpcs, 7, 1975. For statistics of staying in see, e.g. Tables IV–V in Crichton 'Youth and leisure in Cardiff' – only on Saturday nights were an equal number of boys and girls out; one consequence of this pattern is that boys spend a considerable part of their leisure time with a group of only their own sex. *Cf.* Barker, 'Spoiling and keeping close', 582–4.
4. *Cf.* Barker; Sharpe, 219; Smith, C. S., *Young people at leisure*, 15–16, 24–6.
5. The circulation of *Music Star*, which rose to a peak of 634,000 in September 1973 on the basis of its coverage of Cassidy and the Osmonds, was down to 160,000 little over a year later – see 'Bopper power', *NME*, 14 Dec. 1974. For the final death of *Music Star* and *Music Scene* and the merging of *Melanie* with *Fab 208* and of *Valentine* with *Mirabelle* see 'More pop papers debut', *MW*, 19 Oct. 1974. All these magazines had lost circulation drastically – *Melanie* fell 200,000 in less than a year. *Cf.* Alderton, *Magazines teenagers read*.

   It's worth noting that of the major teenybopper musical idols of recent years, the Monkees, David Cassidy (the Partridge Family) and the Osmonds all came out of carefully aimed TV shows, and the Bay City Rollers' success depended on a clever and exhaustive use of guest spots on the various children's TV programmes. Even non-teeny-aimed TV stars can become idols – David McCallum in the 1960s, Starsky and Hutch more recently.
6. See Simon Frith, 'Cassidy at Wembley', *LIR*, May 1973. Among the abusive letters I got in response to this piece ('Maybe his suit was tight

fitting but he has some balls to show. I'm sure you haven't. An ever-loving David Cassidy Fan. Aged 15 yrs 7 months'.) was this comment: 'You were moaning about Donny Osmond fans having to put up with David everyday in the 'Sun' (which by the way is a lie). What about David's fans having to put up with Donny Pouf Osmond and Marc Pouf Bolan rosettes being sold outside David's concerts? How dare you put Donny Osmond in the same column as David Cassidy'.

7. For a brilliant account of girls' responses to the Rolling Stones see M. Geddes, 'Roll over and rock me baby', *Spare Rib*, May 1973 and *cf.* Sharpe, 112–16. For magazine readership see JICNRS 1976 readership profile, which revealed the following ratio of men to women in the readership of the music press: *NME*: 66/34; *MM*: 66/34; *Sounds*: 67/33; *Fab 208*: 16/84. *Let It Rock*'s Readers Poll in 1974 had 261 responses, of which only 16 were from women.

The BBC Audience Research Department found the following male/female ratios in audiences in October 1976: John Peel: 87·6:12·4; Alan Freeman: 55·3:44·7; Tony Blackburn: 40·3:59·7; *Old Grey Whistle Test*: 65·7:34·3; *Top of the Pops*: 43·9:56·1.

Market research carried out by Carrick James in 1974 found that when 15–24-year-olds were asked what type of music they particularly liked far more boys than girls said 'hard rock' – girls were more likely to say 'Top 30 Pop'. (*National survey among teenagers and young adults*, Table 12A.)

For the heavy male dominance of the 'hi-fi' equipment market, see BMRB's *Target group index*, 1976, vol. 34. And *cf.* Newton, 229 for the masculinity of jazz fans.

8. Alderton, 48; G. Rowntree, 'New facts on teenage marriage', *New Society*, 4 Oct. 1962. For the equally dramatic fall in female record buying after marriage *cf.* BMRB's *Target group index*. In what follows on the dance I shall draw extensively on the insights of Mungham in Pearson and Mungham, eds.

9. For statistics of girls' expenditure on clothes and cosmetics, see e.g., IPC's *Marketing manual of the UK*, 1975, Tables A.8.14 and 15.

10. From an unpublished report on youth leisure in Coventry by Kevin Buckley, research worker on the Coventry City Centre Project, 1975.

11. *ibid.*

12. *ibid.* For the claims of a steady boy friend on a girl's leisure time *cf.* Table V in Crichton. Tina Myers, research worker on the Coventry City Centre Project found the same pattern in leisure diaries completed by day release students at Coventry Tech. in 1976.

13. For an astute observation of the importance of the seaside and the fairground for working-class youth culture see the film *That'll Be The Day*. The special importance of holidays for girls has not, to my know-ledge, been analysed by sociologists, though there are common images in the mass media of the easy pickings from package holidays for Latin romeos, and of the sex-lives of Redcoats and beach photographers. *Cf.* Pradeep Bandyopadhyay, 'The holiday camp', Smith, M. A., ed., 250. For fairs *cf.* Duncan Dallas, 'The gaff lads', *New Society*, 4 Nov.

1971. Sexual panic is most obviously a characteristic of Mary White-house and her followers. For the sexuality of pop *cf.* Geddes in *Spare Rib*, May 1973. For the importance of visiting pop stars as a source of consequence-free sexual pleasure *cf.* Greene, *Billion-dollar baby*, 259–65.

14. Olivia Records, for example, is a record company controlled by feminist musicians, engineers and technicians.

15. *College Event*, the magazine which serves college promoters of live rock was founded in 1968. For the importance of the college circuit to the rock industry, see, eg., *MW*, 15 Nov. 1975, where it is suggested that colleges subsidise rock to the tune of £600,000 per year – that's what they lose on their promotions; *cf.* Lindsey Boyd, 'Campus blues', *LIR*, January 1973. For Virgin and students, *cf.* Nick Powell, head of Virgin Retail, on their first stores, which opened in 1969: 'we aimed at students and the rock market because that was where our expertise lay and also because that was where the majority of album sales were.'; and on the situation in 1976: 'I'm still very keen to maintain what I call the sort of leader market, which happens at this time to have a large number of students in it . . .' – quoted in 'Stock more, or sell less', *Music Business*, November 1976.

16. For student leisure before the rock era *cf.* Marris, *The experience of higher education*, 93–4, 119.

Chapter 5: Making records

1. See Hirsch, *The structure of the popular music industry*, Part 1. By far the best account of how the industry works in practice is Stokes, *Star-making machinery*, the case study of the production of a Commander Cody LP. For British 'over-production' of singles *cf.* the Rock File League Tables of Record Companies in Gillett, ed., *Rock file*, vols 2, 3, 4.

2. The values of professionalism were preached every week on the ATV talent show, *New Faces*. They have been organised into book form by panellist Tony Hatch, *So you want to be in the music business* – the quote is from page 12.

3. For the number of groups and 1973 costs see Tom Tickell, 'The long and costly road to screaming weenies', *Guardian*, 20 Oct. 1973 and *cf.* Hatch, 24, 36. For Pink Floyd see Wale, *Vox pop*, 134, 139. *Cf.* Mark Plummer, 'The life and hard times of a semi-pro band', *MM*, 20 Feb. 1971; Godbolt, *All this and 10%*, 13–14.

4. Hal Carter, manager and promoter, quoted in 'Revival of the fittest', *MM*, 30 March 1974.

5. 'Artist vs label, part II', *MW*, 17 Nov. 1973.

6. Hatch, 115–18.

7. For the standard recording contract see Shemel and Krasilovsky, *This business of music*, 401–3.

8. Terry King (agent/manager/producer) quoted in 'Royalties – a case of live now, play later?', *MM*, 3 April, 1971.

9. For the following description see S. Frith, 'The A&R men', Gillett

and Frith, eds., *Rock File 4*. For the A & R strategies of particular companies see Davis (1974) for CBS; Wale, 94–112 for EMI and 113–17 for Charisma; R. Partridge, 'Leahy's dozen keep ringing up the sales at Bell', *MW*, 9 June 1973 and 'Bell, ringing in the new pop', *MM*, 1 June 1974 for Bell; Gillett, *Making tracks* for Atlantic; Frith in Hoare, ed., *The Soul Book* for Motown; 'The Trojan story', *MW*, 30 Dec. 1972 for Trojan; Chapple and Garofalo, *Rock'n'roll is here to pay*, ch. 5 for American A & R policies in general. For a survey of record companies' approaches to reggae, a genre based on independent producers, see V. Goldman, 'The reggae merchants', *Sounds*, 24 Jan. 1976.

10. '. . . RCA President confirmed that [Wilson] Pickett had been signed: "You stole him from Atlantic?" another executive was asked. "Right," came the answer. "How'd you do it?" The reply, this time accompanied by a blood-and-feathery grin: "Money." ' – 'Pop records: moguls, money and monsters', *Time*, 12 Feb. 1973, 35.

11. 'The glitter thing passed us by', *MM*, 19 Oct. 1974.

12. 'You're what's known in the business as a company freak. What does that mean? Well, a kept hippie, mediating between the turtle-necked titans of the record industry and the unpunctual, crazy monsters called musicians.' – Danny Fields, 'Who bridges the gap between the record executive and the rock musicians? I do.', Eisen, ed., *The age of rock, 2*, 153.

13. Hatch, 73 and 110–14, and see the series 'Artists vs label', *MW*, 10, 17, 24 Nov. 1973.

14. Quoted in Wale, 224. For the manager as source of capital see the interview with John Coletto, co-manager of Deep Purple, 214–18. For the conflicts that can arise see 'To protect an investment', *NME*, 3 August 1974 – on the dispute between Edgar Broughton and World Wide Artists Ltd. For a graphic account of manager as financial negotiator see the discussion of Allen Klein, then manager of the Beatles, in McCabe and Shonfield, *Apple to the core*, ch. 7.

15. Quoted in Wale, 236.

16. For the manager as image creator see Michael Watts, 'Bowie's Main-Man', *MM*, 18 May 1974 (on Tony De Fries). Albert Grossman was the star of *Don't Look Back*, Peter Grant of *The Song Remains The Same* – and *cf*. Michael Watts, 'Led Zeppelin: strategies of a supergroup', Gold, ed. The best accounts of the job of management are Stokes on Joe Kerr, manager of Commander Cody – *passim* but esp. 70–1; and Greene on Shep Gordon, manager of Alice Cooper – *passim* but esp. 168–78. And see Chapple and Garofalo, 131–7.

17. Colin Irwin, 'Pop in the supermarket', *MM*, 23 March 1974. The reality is not so very different and can make for problems if the created group acts stroppy – *cf*. the case of the group Kenny and its creators, Phil Coulter and Bill Martin, which reached the courts (*MW*, 22 May 1976). For a good account of a manager vs musician conflict see Lorraine Alterman, 'Fleetwood Mac Flak', *Rolling Stone*, 28 Feb. 1974. Clifford Davis, then manager of Fleetwood Mac, explained why he was presenting a band as Fleetwood Mac that did not have one member of the group previously seen on stage or heard on album:

'I want to get this out of the public's mind as far as the band being Mick Fleetwood's band. This band is my band. This band has always been my band'.

18. See Frith, in Gillett and Frith eds., *Rock File 4*, 27–8. Hirsch estimated that there were about 300 independent producers in the USA, the same as the number of A&R men, for whom they act as a safety net.

19. Quoted in Wale, 188.

20. Quoted in Roy Carr and Andrew Tyler, 'Leaders of the pack', *NME*, 3 Nov. 1973. *Cf.* Greg Shaw, 'Brill building pop', Miller, ed., *The Rolling Stone illustrated history of rock and roll*. For commercial song writing in Britain see the interviews with Les Reed and Elton John in Wale.

21. For the role of publishers see Hatch, ch. 9; Wale, ch. 6; Stokes, ch. 8.

22. Quoted in 'The creators', *MM*, 12 Dec. 1970.

23. Bob Johnston quoted in Wale, 62; Gus Dudgeon quoted in 'The creators', *MM*, 12 Dec. 1970.

24. For the importance of the arranger see Charlie Gillett, 'All for one: a study in frustration and black organisation', *Cream*, September 1971 – an account of arranger Harold Battiste. For the job of session musician see Wale, ch. 7; for tape-operating as the bottom rung of the production career ladder see, e.g., 'Chairmen of the board', *MM*, 28 April 1973.

25. Quoted in Wale, 67 – see the whole interview for an excellent account of the engineer's job. For studio technology see Hatch, ch. 11; for studio costs see 'Recording studios', *MM*, 22 Jan. 1972, Anthony Holdcroft, 'The bigger recording studios sound happy', *Financial Times*, 20 Jan. 1975, and by way of contrast, S. Frith, 'Holy ground: a recording studio in Wakefield', Gillett, ed., *Rock File*.

26. 'The producer and engineer is now every bit as important as the artist', Mickie Most, quoted in 'The creators'. For the rapid increase in the importance of engineers see 'The engineers', *MM*, 3 July 1971.

27. Johnston quoted in Wale, 60–3; Smith quoted in 'The creators'; Most quoted in Rob Finnis, 'Mickie Most, people's producer', *LIR*, June 1973, 23. The best accounts of such producers at work are Stokes on producer John Boylan and engineer Paul Grupp, and Greene, chs. 3–5, on producers Jack Douglas and Jack Richardson.

28. For Phil Spector and American teenage production in the sixties see Williams R., *Out of his head* and Finnis, *The Phil Spector story*. For British pop producers see Simon Frith, Profits without honour', *LIR*, Nov. 1973; the interview with Jonathan King in Wale; and 'All that glitter turned to gold for Mike Leander', *MW*, 7 July 1973.

29. For manufacturing costs and developments see *RB* 159, 1971 and 200, 1974; Phil Hardy, 'A pressing problem', *LIR*, January 1974; Rob Partridge and Laurie Henshaw, 'Records: what price quality?', *MM*, 24 Aug. 1974; 'Manufacture', in the *BPI Year Book*, 1976.

30. For the history and significance of sleeve design see *MM*, 24 Oct. 1970; Stokes, 130–3; Hipgnosis, *The album book album*.

31. Colin Irwin, 'Pop in the supermarket', *MM*, 23 March 1974. Hirsch estimated that American companies can spend $50,000 on a big promotional campaign. The best account of how the whole process

works is Stokes, chs. 24–30. For Britain *cf.* Charlie Gillett, 'The promised land . . . and how to get there', *NME*, 21 Dec. 1974 and 'Single file', *NME*, 29 Nov. 1975.

32. For women in press offices see Marion Fudger, 'Women in music', *Spare Rib*, 16, 1973; 'The personal touch', *MW*, 3 Feb. 1973. For press office use of such promotional tools as fan clubs see 'They still want to be in the club', *MM*, 26 Feb. 1972.

33. For the work of publicists see Wale, ch. 12; Taylor D., *As time goes by*; Pete Erskine, 'Les, it's Mick', *NME*, 23 Aug. 1975, on publicist Les Perrin; 'The adrenalin industry', *MM*, 6 March 1971, on publicist Tony Brainsby.

34. For America see Hirsch, 43–51; for Britain see 'Field promotion, a new art', *MW*, 6 and 13 Oct. 1973, and 'Selwood's love-hate relationship with the music business', *MW*, 6 Nov. 1976.

35. *RB*, 159, 1971, 32.

36. For an extended discussion of promotion and airplay see Gillett and Frith, eds., *Rock File 3*. Throughout the 1960s record companies spent little on TV advertising and the bulk of their promotional budget went to Radio Luxembourg – in 1970, for example, EMI spent £100,000 for twelve hours' needletime a week, arguing that 'pops come and go too quickly to need advertising beyond air time on Luxembourg and the BBC programmes'. In the 1970s, however, this picture changed dramatically, as record companies spent £9,000 on TV ads in 1971, £2·2m. in 1974 and £4·6m. in 1975. But what is noticeable about this sudden and successful (indicated by the number of TV albums in the charts) use of TV is that it was pioneered not by record companies but by specialists in TV selling ('demonstrators') turning their skills to records. What they have done is repackage and remarket previous hits. Even when record companies themselves moved into TV promotion they mostly sold greatest hits albums this way – few new products are advertised on television and it is unclear whether TV promotion of previously unheard sounds is successful. See *RB*, 74, 1964; 98, 1966; 159, 1971; 200, 1974; and *MW*, 28 Feb. 1976. For TV promotion see 'How to sell 1½ million records to people who don't buy records', *MM*, 4 Nov. 1972; 'Levene spills the beans', *MW*, 19 May 1973; Phil Hardy, 'Battle of the box', *Music Business*, Nov. 1976.

37. For Luxembourg see '40 years of Radio Luxembourg', *MW*, 9 Nov. 1974. For pirate radio, see Harris, *When pirates ruled the waves* – record companies paid the pirates £100 for 30 plays of a record and often, in addition, a broadcast fee every time a record not in the stations' idiosyncratic charts got broadcast. Some stations even demanded the publishing rights on singles' B-sides – see page 59, and *cf.* 'The progress of the offshore pirate stations', *MW*, 8 Feb. 1975.

38. For Radio One's play-list policy see the interview with Derek Chinnery, station boss, in *MW*, 5 June 1976.

39. For pluggers see Wale, ch. 14; Michael Watts, 'The record pluggers', *MM*, 24 June 1972. For the lack of payola in the British industry *cf.* 'No bribes at the Beeb?', *MM*, 30 Jan. 1971.

40. I was on Phonogram's DJ mailing list for a while and this is a typical

example of a press release – from 1975. For ballroom DJs see Saville, *Love is an uphill thing*; for the importance of discos for promotion see Frith in Gillett and Frith, eds., *Rock File 3*, 22–37.

41. From an unpublished interview with Charlie Gillett and myself in 1973. For the rise of discos see 'Have discothèque – will travel . . .', *MM*, 24 April 1971; Geoff Brown and Laurie Henshaw: 'Goin' to a go-go', *MM*, 14 Sept. 1974.

42. For the world of the DJ see Rosko, *Emperor Rosko's dj book*.

43. Quoted in Wale, 254 and see chs. 9–10. *Cf.* Hatch, 109–18; Mick Gold, 'Mel Bush: the man who hired the world' in Gold, ed.; Godbolt, ch. 13; for America, Chapple & Garofalo, 124–31, 137–54.

44. Dave Laing, 'Weak link in the chain', *Time Out*, 6 Nov. 1975. *Cf.* 'The godfathers of rock', *MM*, 3 March 1973, on American promoters; Roy Carr, 'You only give me your funny paper', *NME*, 6 July 1974, on promoter Harvey Goldsmith; and *MW*, 5 April 1975 and 10 Aug. 1976, on live music in Britain.

45. James Fox, 'It's only rock'n'roll – but it's expensive', *Sunday Times*, 25 April 1976.

46. *Cf.* 'Keeping out the touts', *MW*, 31 Jan. 1976. There are various vivid accounts of the experience of touring – e.g., Greene, Greenfield, *Stones touring party* and Pidgeon, *Rod Stewart*, ch. 4; and *cf.* Wale, ch. 11.

47. One intriguing statistic of record sales is their seasonality. Over the year LPs outsell singles, but in the summer singles outsell albums and the sale of the latter is heavily concentrated into the three months before Christmas. See *RB*, 159, 1971.

48. For the development of record retailing see *The Hulton retailer reader-ship studies*, 7, 1948; *RB*, 74, 1964; 98, 1966; 159, 1971; 200, 1974; Colin Handley, 'Marked changes in the retail side' and Colin Inman, '. . . And budget share grows', *Financial Times*, 20 Jan. 1975; *MW*, 12 April 1975; Phil Hardy, 'Covering the market', *Time Out*, 26 March 1976.

49. See Gary Herman, 'Hold the fort – I'm off to the hypermarket', *Music Business*, Dec. 1976. For parallel American developments see Jules Malamud, 'The merchandising of music', *Popular Music and Society*, 2, 1973 and Shemel and Krasilovsky, Charts I–IV. For specialisation *cf.* Simon Frith, 'Change down in Coventry', *Music Business*, Dec. 1976; and Denise Hall and Tony Cummings, 'Selling their souls', *Black Music*, Feb. 1976.

50. *Cf.* Dave Marsh, 'A conversation with Avery Fisher, America's original baron of high fidelity', *Rolling Stone*, 23 Sept. 1976.

51. For the effect of records on instrument sales see Bornoff, *Music and the twentieth century media*, 55 and Hirsch, 16.

Chapter 6: Making money

1. Roth, *The business of music*, 50–1; Rogers, *Tin Pan Alley*, 50.

2. Dick Leahy was then head of Bell Records in the UK – quoted in R. Partridge, 'Leahy's dozen keeps ringing up the sales at Bell', *MW*, 9 June 1973.

T.S.O.R.—H

3. Quote from *RB*, 159, 1971, 34. For a development of this argument see Frith in Gillett, ed., *Rock File 2*; for America see Hirsch, 11, 68–9.

4. Dates taken from Bornoff, 9. *Cf.* Hirsch, 3 and Malone, *Country music USA*, 245.

5. Quoted in Rogers, 36.

6. Newton, 160–1; for America *cf.* Malone, 244–6.

7. For the history of youth cultural media in Britain see Murdock and Phelps, ch. 8.

8. Quoted in Rogers, 139. Such a quota policy has been successfully applied in Canada. For the history of the British record industry see the EMI 75th Anniversary Supplement to *MW*, 1 Dec. 1973; Gillett, *The sound of the city*; 'Big noise from across the water'. The basic histories of Tin Pan Alley are Goldberg, *Tin Pan Alley* and Ewen, *The life and death of Tin Pan Alley*; for the history of the American record business see Chapple and Garofalo, chs. 1, 2.

9. Rogers, 139, 157.

10. See Rogers, 167; Mabey, *The pop process*, 50–5; MacInnes, *England, half English*, 17.

11. This model has been presented in most detail for the rise and fall of rock'n'roll in the 1950s – see Gillett, *The sound of the city*; 'Big noise'. For the general argument see Peterson and Berger, 'Entrepreneurship and organisation' and Peterson, 'Cycles in symbol production'. For the argument applied to jazz see Leonard, 100–30; Newton, chs. 10–11; R. A. Peterson: 'Market and moralist censors of a black art form: jazz' in Denisoff and Peterson, eds., *The sound of social change*.

12. *RB*, 74, 1964, 51, 53 and see Gillett, 'Big noise', 12–13.

13. *RB*, 98, 1966, 27 and 159, 1971; Readers' Digest's *Survey of Europe*, 1970, 68–9.

14. See Gillett, 'Big noise', 27. A useful summary of the underground enterprises flourishing in 1967 is included in Mabey, 99–103. For the majors' hip labels see P. Phillips, 'Underground – the industry was left at the station', *MW*, 6 Jan. 1973.

15. Quoted in R. Partridge, 'Island of dreams', *MM*, 4 May 1974 and see B. Blevins, 'Island: beatniks make it rich', *RS*, 15 April 1971. For Charisma see Wale, 113–17; for artist labels see R. Partridge, 'After the Ball', *MM*, 20 July 1972. The best account of Apple is McCabe and Shonfield.

16. Quoted in Harris, 2.

17. See Frith in Gillett, ed., *Rock File* and, for a useful survey of 'alternative music' in the early seventies, J. Hoyland, 'Up against the business', *LIR*, May and July, 1973.

18. An interesting, if irritatingly coy, account of how a major company (CBS) adapted to the promotional and financial needs of the new youth market is Davis, *Clive* and see Stokes, 8–9. For a general history of the American record business in the 1960s see Chapple and Garofalo, ch. 3.

19. For an extended version of this argument see Frith in Gillett and Frith, eds., *Rock File 3*, 25–8. *Cf. RB*, 159, 1971; 'Why the British music

boom still doesn't echo in the US', *MW*, 27 July 1974; 'The black explosion', *MW*, 21 Sept. 1974. There are still independent companies formed for musical rather than financial reasons – Stiff, Oval, Chiswick for example, and the 1977 rash of punk concerns – but their existence is precarious and dependent, at least for any sort of mass sales, on the help of larger concerns.

20. For the statistics of American radio see Leonard, 92–3. A similar 'symbiotic' relationship links the record industry and the music press – their ends may be different, record sales vs circulation figures, but both depend on the successful promotion of records. Again, I will explore this relationship in a separate chapter.

21. In 1976 the *Mirror* claimed 160,000 members for its pop club and vied with the *Sun* in its use of record competitions and ticket and poster offers – see *MW*, 6 March 1976. An interesting account of TV's use of rock is Stephen Barnard, 'In a week, maybe two, we'll make you a star', in Gillett, ed., *Rock File 2*. For advertising and records see Hirsch, 14 and Laurie Henshaw, 'Jingle bells', *MM*, 20 Feb. 1971.

22. For the American origins of juke boxes see Malone, 162–3, 182, 192–3. In Britain there are currently 65,000 juke boxes, more than half in pubs and many hired out by one firm, Associated Leisure – the number is still growing at 10–15 %/year – see *BPI Year Book*, 1976. For the United Biscuit Network and Hospital radio see Rosko, ch. 20. For working men's clubs see Taylor, J., *From self-help to glamour*, ch. VI. For commercial clubs see Michael Watts, 'Weird scenes', *MM*, 25 May 1974 and Geoff Brown, 'Beside the seaside', *MM*, 6 July 1974.

23. For basic guides to copyright see Hatch, 63–5, 129–42 and *BPI Year Book*, 1976, 41–5; for its history see Peacock and Weir, *The composer in the market place*.

24. For the campaign for a mechanical royalty rise see 'The case for increasing mechanical royalties', *MW*, 25 Sept. 1976.

25. Quoted from the PRS 1976 pamphlet, 'Membership of the Performing Rights Society', 5.

26. Figures from Derek Chinnery, 'The Music Policy of Radio 1', *Music Business*, Dec. 1976; Sheila Black, 'How music to remember earns £12½m in a year between the supermarket and the Albert Hall', *The Times*, 14 Aug. 1974; Clifford Hanley, 'Sonata for cash register', *Daily Telegraph Magazine*, 30 May 1975. Other countries have similar schemes – America has two collecting organisations ASCAP and BMI, with rather different methods of distribution (see Malone, 186–8) but the copyright laws are much the same and have, in fact, just been updated – see *Billboard*'s special bicentennial issue, 4 July 1976.

27. See note 25.

28. PPL data and see Peacock and Weir; Roth, 107. For other countries see UNESCO, vol. II, 148–56 and Bornoff, 104–5. For America see R. Serge Denisoff, 'The evolution of pop broadcasting – 1920–1972', *MW*, 10 Nov. 1973 and Passman, *The Deejays*, 80–1.

29. PPL data. For the BBC/PPL agreement see John Qualen, 'Taking care of business', *LIR*, April 1973.

30. Performers as such are not protected by copyright, although there are

Performers' Protection Acts to prevent the reproduction and un-authorised use of performances, whether live or on record.

31. *New York Times*, 23 Feb. 1957, quoted in Jahn, *Rock from Elvis Presley to the Rolling Stones*, 69. For the Osmonds fan club see 'Tony Stewart meets a mother to 60,000 gym slips', *NME*, 13 Oct. 1973.

32. Beatles' pillow story cited from Hunter Davies's official biography by Jahn, 150. For Beatle finances see Phil Hardy, 'Showing the flag', *LIR*, Sept. 1973; *The Times*, 5 Feb. 1964, 16; and MacCabe and Shonfield, 149, 187.

33. *MW*, 10 July 1976. For the effect of the teenybop boom on *MM* and *NME*, not teenybop papers, see the ABC figures for 1971–5: all the weekly music papers reached a circulation peak in 1973, as they had in 1964.

34. Stokes, ch. 2. He estimates that Warners and CBS had more than 50% of the US record market in 1974; the handful of other majors had 40% and the independents could only claim 5–10%. And see Chapple and Garofalo, ch. 6.

35. See 'WEA to distribute', *Music Business*, Nov. 1976. *The Financial Times*, 20 Jan. 1975, estimated that in 1974 25% of all UK records and tapes were distributed by EMI, 17% by CBS, 16% by Phonodisc and $10\frac{1}{2}$% by RCA – see Antony Thorncroft, 'The strengths of the majors' and *cf.* Colin Handley, 'Marked changes on the retail side' and Brian Mulligan, 'Good year for independents'. And *cf. RB*, 159, 1971 and 200, 1974; Dept. of Industry, *Business Monitor*, June 1972. For the different sorts of distribution deal available see Gillett, ed., *Rock File 2*, 47–54.

36. The ATV/Beatles battle is excellently described in ch. 8 of McCabe and Shonfeld. For the other take-overs see the series on music publishers in *MW*, 24 March–12 May, 1973; Terry Dodsworth, 'Publishing world houses a variety of talents', *Financial Times*, 20 Jan. 1975.

37. See John Graham, 'Sales fight not all left to giants', *The Times*, 29 Nov. 1968.

38. EMI, *Report and Accounts, Chairman's Review, 1969*, 11. For discussion of the range of EMI's interests *cf. The Times*, 6 March 1968; R. Milner and John Bell, 'EMI: The pop singer that became a brain surgeon', *Sunday Times*, 7 March 1976. There are ironic possibilities of conflict within this complex organisation. The Sex Pistols, for example, signed to EMI's record division, shocked the nation on Thames Television, EMI's TV company, getting both into trouble.

39. For a general discussion of the state of the entertainment industry in Britain see Murdock and Golding, 'For a political economy of mass communications'; for the development of the American entertainment industry in the 1920s–30s see Leonard, 102–6; Goldberg, 313–14; Ewen, 322–33; Chapple & Garofalo.

40. For Saga (which recently took over Trojan) see Carl Gayle, 'Reggae explosion', *Black Music*, Oct. 1975 and 'Reggae business', *Black Music*, Oct. 1976. For a general survey of the independents see the *Financial Times'* special survey of the record industry, 20 Jan. 1975. For B&C see *MM*, 30 Dec. 1972.

41. *Cf.* Hirsch, 22; Gillett and Frith, eds., *Rock File 4*, 34–5.
42. See EMI's semi-annual reports. For US sales and profit figures see Chapple and Garofalo, 191–2.
43. See Newton, 172–3; *RB*, 23, 1960; Wale, 115; Davis, *passim*; Stokes, 24–6; Milner and Bell, *S. Times*, 7 March 1976. Chapple & Garofalo, 174, suggests US breakeven sales of 85,000 (LPs) and 25,000 (singles).
44. See the Rock File League Tables in Gillett, ed., *Rock File* vols. 2, 3, 4. The figures for singles are confirmed by Tony Jaspar's 'The great Top 50 single debate', *MW*, 15 May 1976. He used a different year (Jan–Dec) and looked at the whole of the top 50. There seem to be more singles issued now than there used to be but the hit/release ratio has remained much the same – see 'The sound of leisure', *The Times*, 29 Nov. 1968, and *RB*, 159, 1971. Hirsch, 32, has figures suggesting that in America only $23\cdot7\%$ single releases are played more than once on American radio – $61\cdot6\%$ new releases are never played at all! My albums figures were reached by the same methods as used in the Rock File League Tables, but applied to the Top 30. In 1976 in Britain, there were 9 Platinum LPs (£1m. sales = c300,000 units), 32 Gold LPs (£250,000 = c70,000 units) and 1 Silver LP (£100,000 = c30,000). That leaves 158 Top 30 albums selling less than 30,000, and it seems fair to assume that most of the albums that did not reach the Top 30 did not break even (at least over this year). In the singles market there were 2 Platinum Singles (1m. unit sales), 6 Gold (500,000) and at least 42 Silver (250,000) – BMRB data reported in *Sounds*, 8 Jan. 1977.
45. *RB*, 159, 1971, 26.
46. Walter Ridley, EMI Middle Market Manager, quoted in *MW*, 1 Dec. 1973. *Cf.* Roth, 121; 'TV promotion – how long before the bubble bursts?', *MW*, 12 May 1973.
47. The long-term strategy available to a major record company is very evident in Davis.
48. *Cf.* Davis and Wale, 14. Dandelion information from an unpublished interview with John Peel by Dave Amory.
49. For star studio costs see 'Why are we waiting', *MM*, 9 June 1973. For royalty rises, e.g. McCabe and Shonfeld, 149, 187.
50. For McCartney, McCabe and Shonfeld, 173. *Cf.* Jerry Hopkins, 'A piece of the rainbow', *Rolling Stone*, 2 Dec. 1976, for the complex exploitation of Jimi Hendrix that continues after his death.
51. Antony Thorncroft, 'The lucrative business of pop', *The Director*, May 1974, 220. *Cf.* Wale, ch. 13.
52. *Cf.* 'The L.s.d. of rock', *MM*, 21 Nov. 1970; 'Life at the bottom', *NME*, 7 April 1971; 'Rock inflation', *MM*, 6 July 1974; 'Eat your heart out', *MM*, 7 Dec. 1974.

Chapter 7: Radio

1. Blackburn quoted in 'The Radio Hams', *MM*, 31 March 1973; King quoted in Wale, 90.
2. American independent record label boss, Hy Weiss. For general accounts of the history of American music radio see Passman,

Denisoff, 'The evolution of pop broadcasting', Barnouw, *The history of broadcasting in the United States*, and Chapple and Garofalo, 54–64.

3. For contemporary Top 40 radio see Hirsch, 61–5; Peterson and Davis, 'The contemporary radio audience'; Stokes, ch. 25; Paul Gambaccini, 'American radio today' in Gillett and Frith, eds., *Rock File 4*; Rosko, ch. 22; Chapple and Garofalo, 98–107.

4. Barnouw, vol. 3, 303–4. For FM radio see Chapple and Garofalo, 107–22.

5. For the origins and history of Radio Luxembourg see Briggs, *The golden age of wireless*, 351–65; Dick Tracy, '208 – a short history', *NME*, 17 April 1976.

6. Barnouw, vol. 3, 303–4. Pirate stations still survive or, at least, still appear and disappear. The marine based stations have, since 1967, mostly focused on Europe as a whole, and particularly on Holland (until its laws were tightened up in 1975). Britain, meanwhile, is served by a lunatic fringe of local 'free' radio operators, engaged in a constant battle of wits with the GPO and rarely heard by anyone else.

7. See Tracy, *op. cit.*; the listener statistics in *MW*, 27 Jan. 1973; '40 years of Radio Luxembourg', *MW*, 9 Nov. 1974.

8. See Briggs, Part II.

9. Rowntree, and Lavers, 271–2.

10. The 1977 *Report of the Committee on the Future of Broadcasting* (the Annan Report) took such attitudes for granted: its chapter on broadcasting and the arts confined its attention to 'serious' music – Radio 1's trivial purpose was unquestioned. See ch. 21 and pages 84–5. For the MU argument see the *Report of the Committee on Broadcasting* (the Pilkington Report), 1960, vol. II, 798. For an interesting account of BBC workers' attitudes to their programmes and their audiences see Burns, 'Public service and private world'.

11. For the resulting confusions at the beginning of the Radio 1 service see the interview with Tony Blackburn in Wale, ch. 15.

12. The first Radio 1 chief, Robin Scott, quoted in 'Radio One – swinging or just plain square?', *MM*, 2 March 1968.

13. Scott's successor, Derek Chinnery, quoted in 'Derek Chinnery – putting on the style for Radio One', *MW*, 20 April 1974. But the fact that the records on Radio 1's play-list are hits 'proves' that the station is succeeding in its purpose of mass entertainment. Record sales are as satisfying for Radio 1 producers and DJs as for record companies.

14. American programme director, Bill Drake, quoted in Stokes, 165.

15. Derek Chinnery, quoted in *MW*, 20 April 1974.

16. *ibid.* For Radio 1 DJs' special appeal to housewives see Marion Fudger, 'Women in music', *Spare Rib*, 18, 1975 and Mileva Ross, 'Radio' in King and Stott, eds., *Is this your life?*

17. Derek Chinnery, quoted in *MW*, 20 April 1974. One result of the BBC's policy is an increasing amount of music which, like most jazz and avante-garde rock, being neither 'cultural' nor popular, never gets heard on the radio at all. See Ian Carr, 'Down in the cultural ghetto something stirred', *Creem*, July 1972.

18. Derek Chinnery, quoted in *MW*, 20 April 1974.

19. Quoted in *MM*, 2 March 1968.
20. Christopher Chataway, the Minister of Posts and Telecommunications who introduced the legislation, quoted in Robin Thornber, 'Ear say', *Guardian*, 22 Jan 1975. The phrase 'pop and prattle' is also used in the Annan Report, 207–8.
21. Independent Broadcasting Authority, *Annual report and accounts, 1975–6*, 34–8. For play-lists see the weekly magazine *Radio and Record News* and 'MW report on radio unveiled', *MW*, 16 Oct. and 23 Oct. 1976. For ILR and Radio 1 listening overlap see IBA Audience Research Dept., *Capital Radio. Audience attitudes and patterning of listening*, July 1975, and *Radio Clyde. Audience attitudes and patterns of listening*, June 1976.
22. The quotes come from a number of programme plans – they are included in the IBA annual reports from 1972–3 onwards.
23. IBA, *Annual report, 1975–6*, 40–1 and see the Audience Research Dept. reports on Capital and Clyde. 'ILR gets it all together', *Campaign*, 8 July 1977, quotes the following JICRAR figures:

ILR'S weekly reach		*Listening for*
13·6 million adults (15+)	(49%)	12·4 hours
7·0 million men	(52%)	11·8 hours
6·6 million women	(46%)	13·0 hours
5·2 million housewives	(42%)	13·4 hours
2·2 million housewives with cn	(50%)	15·3 hours
4·6 million ABC1 adults	(45%)	10·5 hours
9·0 million C2DE adults	(51%)	13·4 hours

ILR percentage reach by age	*Men*	*Women*
All adults (15+)	52% (11·8 hours)	46% (13·0 hours)
Age 15–24	71% (11·7 hours)	68% (12·2 hours)
Age 25–34	63% (13·9 hours)	51% (14·9 hours)
Age 35–54	49% (10·8 hours)	46% (13·6 hours)
Age 55+	35% (11·3 hours)	30% (11·5 hours)

Chapter 8: The music press

1. For the history of the music press see Dave Laing, 'Yesterday's papers', *Time Out*, 15 August 1975; *NME* 21st Souvenir History, 10 March 1973; *MM* 50th anniversary special issue, Spring, 1976.
2. *NME*'s Alan Smith, quoted in Millar, *Pop! Hit or miss?*, 2.
3. See the *NME*'s 1964 *Annual* for an example of how the Beatles were incorporated into 50s pop assumptions.
4. On Helen Shapiro see, for example, Colin MacInnes, 'Socialist impresarios', *New Statesman*, 15 June 1962. One of the most interesting sources of early serious writing on rock was *Axle*, a 'vigorous and entertaining quarterly on themes of the moment', two of whose three editors were Oxbridge students Alan Blaikley and Ken Howard, who went on to be the extremely successful pop writing/production team of

Howard and Blaikley. William Mann's 'What songs the Beatles sang . . .' was in *The Times*, 27 Dec. 1963.

5. See John Burks, 'The underground press', *Rolling Stone*, 4 Oct. 1969.
6. Quoted in Flippo, 'The history of *Rolling Stone*', 163.
7. For the history of *Rolling Stone* see Flippo; Chapple and Garofalo, 158–66.
8. Flippo, 162.
9. *ibid.* 163, 176, 180–1, 286; Davis, 311–12.
10. Howard Bloom of Famous Music, quoted in Flippo, 278.
11. *MM*, 27 Sept. 1969 and see 2 Sept. 1968 and 30 March 1968.
12. *MM*, 6 Feb. 1971 and see 19 Sept. 1970.
13. For teeny-bop magazines see Margaret Safranek, 'The Donny Bird boom', *Guardian*, 29 Aug. 1973. In 1972–3 IPC alone launched 7 similar 'weeny-bopper' magazines and achieved a total circulation with them of 2·4m.; other companies' equivalent magazines claimed a total of five million readers.
14. I got this description from an IPC marketing man but it obviously relates to the opinion leaders in my Keighley 6th Form sample. For the buying habits of music press readers see BMRB, *Target group index*, vol. 34, 1976.
15. For America see Flippo, 281–97 and Stokes, ch. 30.
16. Rob Townshend of Family quoted in Laing, *Time Out*, 15 Aug. 1975, 13 and *cf.* Stokes, 217.
17. For an interesting discussion of these problems see Robert Christgau, 'Yes, there is a rock-critic establishment (but is it bad for rock?), *Village Voice*, 26 Jan. 1976.
18. See Flippo, 281–97.
19. For a survey of British fanzines see Michael Watts, 'Read all about it' *MM*, 20 March 1976.

Chapter 9: Rock musicians

1. Cliff Richard, *It's great to be young*, 116; 'The Rolling Stone Interview: John Lennon', *Rolling Stone*, 7 Jan. 1971, 34.
2. Newton, 219.
3. The literature on rock musicians is now so vast (the most recent phenomenon is the instant paperback biography) that I can only cite a very select list. The most sensitive accounts of rock musicians as musicians are Lydon, *Rock folk* and Guralnick, *Feel like going home*; the best inside account is Hunter, *Diary of a rock'n'roll star*; the best collections of interviews are the *Rolling Stone Interview Books*. For 1950s rock stars see, e.g., Richard, and Kennedy, *Tommy Steele*; for the new bourgeois rockers of the 1960s see, e.g., Simon Frith, 'Keeping the '67 faith: homage to Kevin Ayers', *Let It Rock*, Feb. 1974. For the relationship of showbiz and rebel images it is interesting to compare The Rolling Stones' *Our own story* with Greenfield. For life at the top and at the bottom of the rock pile compare Greene on Alice Cooper and Idris Walters, 'A walk on the B-side', *Street Life*, 20 March 1976 (on a band called North Star).

4. The ideology of musician as entertainer pervades Hatch. For an example of musicians entertaining in working men's clubs see J. Taylor, 79–89.

5. For the Musicians' Union see 'State of the Union '68', *MW*, 30 March 1968; 'Is the MU out of time?', *MM*, 4 Dec. 1971; and the union's own journal, *Musician*.

6. MU Assistant General Secretary, quoted in *MW*, 30 March 1968.

7. See Laurie Henshaw: 'Are discos killing off bands?', *MM*, 19 Oct. 1974.

8. Union General Secretary, John Morton, quoted in *MM*, 4 Dec. 1971. For a scathing attack on the MU's policy see Godbolt, 51–9.

9. Faulkner, *Hollywood studio musicians*, 157–8, 181–2.

10. Richard, 69.

11. Howard S. Becker, 'The professional jazz musician and his audience', in Denisoff and Peterson, eds., 254.

12. *Musician*, Autumn 1973, 22. *Cf*. Faulkner, 174–80.

13. 'Tommy Steele: "the story of ambition" ', *The Listener*, 10 Oct. 1974.

14. The Rolling Stones, 13, 187.

15. 'Peter Townshend: "a bit of dreamland" ', *The Listener*, 10 Oct. 1974.

16. Yardbird Paul Samwell-Smith quoted in Pidgeon, *Eric Clapton*, 43.

17. 'The Rolling Stone Interview: John Lennon', *Rolling Stone*, 4 Feb. 1971, 28.

18. Simon Frith, 'Hello, hurray – the super sane world of Arthur Brown', *Creem*, May 1973.

19. See James T. Coffman, 'So you want to be a rock and roll star' in Denisoff and Peterson, eds., and *cf*. Kofsky, *Black nationalism and the revolution in music*, 26.

20. 'The Rolling Stone Interview: Keith Richard', *Rolling Stone*, 19 Aug. 1971.

21. For session men as 'failures' *cf*. Faulkner, *passim*. For rock stars' obsessions *cf*. Simon Frith, 'Everybody's in show-biz, everybody's a star', *Creem*, Dec. 1972.

22. Richard, 89.

23. 'The Rolling Stone Interview: Pete Townshend', *Rolling Stone*, 28 Sept. 1968, 14. For good accounts of the relationship between the musicians' work and the audiences' leisure see George Melly's account of his years as a British jazz singer – *Owning up* – and Michael Braun's account of a Beatles tour – *Love me do* – and *cf*. Hunter and the *Rolling Stone* special issue on groupies, 15 Feb. 1969.

24. Newton, 199–200. Edward Lee makes a similar point about popular music enabling white working class kids to become rich and successful without being alienated from the values or attitudes of their class – Lee, *Music of the people*, 254.

25. Andrew Stephen, 'Johnny Rotten is nice!', *Observer*, 19 June 1977. *Cf*. this comment from an MU official: 'Musicians are craftsmen, members of the petit-bourgeois class, traditionally cautious and reactionary,' quoted in Ian Walker, 'Whole lotta shakin' goin' on', *The Leveller*, July/August 1977. And for the petit-bourgeois values of 'hip' bands see, e.g., The Rolling Stones; Hunter; Walters in *Street*

Life, 20 March 1976. The royalty system of rewarding musical services is clearly central to rock's petit-bourgeois ideology (see ch. 6).

26. For an extended version of this argument applied particularly to the Rolling Stones see Simon Frith, 'Let's drink to the hard working people', *Creem*, April 1973.

27. 'The Rolling Stone Interview: Keith Richard', *Rolling Stone*, 19 Aug. 1971, 28.

28. *Rolling Stone*, 7 Jan. 1971.

29. *The Listener*, 10 Oct. 1974. *Cf.* Frith in Gold, ed.

30. *Rolling Stone*, 14 Sept. 1968.

31. For an expanded version of this argument see Simon Frith, 'Girls don't make it in rock . . .', *Cream*, October 1971 and *cf.* Marion Meade, 'The degradation of women', in Denisoff and Peterson, eds. There is a wide ranging discussion of women and rock in the *Let It Rock* special issue, July 1975.

32. Quoted in Simon Frith, 'Billie Davis: woman in pop', *Let It Rock*, Sept. 1973.

33. Rock musicians are rarely written about as *musicians* but for the male world of music making see, e.g., James Fox, 'Sound of the Stones', *Sunday Times*, 14 Oct. 1973, and George Chandler, 'Anatomy of a soul record', *Black Music*, Nov. 1976. There is a good analysis of the sexism of rock lyrics by Terri Goddard *et al.*, 'Popular music' in King and Stott, eds.

34. See Marion Fudger, 'Yeah, he plays with real mammary', *Spare Rib*, 21, 1974.

Chapter 10: Rock and musical cultures

1. Dave Marsh, 'The critics' critic', *RS*, 16 Dec. 1976.

2. The most systematic musical analysis of rock is Mellers' book on the Beatles, *Twilight of the gods*. For an attempt to come up with a suitable critical language for rock as music see the brief flurry of articles in *New Left Review* – Chester/Merton, 'For a rock aesthetic', Beckett/Merton/ Parsons (reprinted in Eisen, ed., *The age of rock*). And *cf.* R. Durgnat, 'Rock, rhythm and dance', *British Journal of Aesthetics*, 11, 1971.

The gap between the 'serious' musicology of rock and its practitioners' own understandings is well illustrated by the following comments on the Animals' record 'I'm Crying'. Richard Middleton, musicologist: 'In "I'm Crying" ostinato and modal harmony are again used in a similar way, but they are organised within an overall 12-bar blues pattern (so that the ostinato is treated in fact as a riff). A refrain of modal vocal harmony is then added. The resulting cultural mixture is one typical of R&B. The cross relations in the ostinato (which is melodic and harmonic) are the equivalents of blue notes, arising from a similar conflict between melodic and tonal implications. The modal melodic movement of the ostinato, with its minor thirds, clashes with the tonal need for major triad imposed by the 12-bar blues structure. The cross relations are symptomatic of the harmonic complexity of the song, in which a modal/blue ostinato is placed in the overall context of a tonal, but stable and repetitive blues form, given a passionately blue vocal and followed by a refrain of triadic but modal "organum" (i.e., parallel triads). The resulting tension, similar in type and effect to that of city blues even though slightly different in cultural make-up, is only partly assuaged by the tribalising role of the ostinato and the universalising, depersonalising effect of the "organum".' (*Pop music and the blues.*)

Alan Price, Animal: 'Eric [Burdon] and I wrote "I'm Crying" together. We did it in the back of a van. I wrote the music and Eric did the words and we just threw it together in rehearsal in Blackpool on the North Pier on a Sunday afternoon. We just stuck it together and recorded it and by chance it was successful. We didn't set out to do anything much, we just had to do it, you know.' (From an interview in May 1973 with David Robson to whom I am grateful for pointing out this comparison.)

3. For a critique of the use of content analysis in the sociology of popular music see Denisoff and Levine, 'The one dimensional approach to popular music'.

4. The best detailed history of rock is Gillett, *The sound of the city*. For an excellent brief account see D. Rogers, 'Varieties of Pop Music', Vulliamy and Lee, eds., *Pop music in schools.*

5. Jones, *Blues people*, 223.

6. Stearns, *The story of jazz*, 282. And *cf.* Leoi Jones, 'The changing same (R&B and new black music)' in *Black music.* The best sociological account of black music is Keil, *Urban blues.* For soul music see Hoare ed.

7. Quoted in Haralambos, *Right on*, 106. And see Pleasants, *Serious music and all that jazz*, 167, and G. Vulliamy, 'Definitions of serious music' in Vulliamy, and Lee eds., 37–9.

8. *Cf.* Stearns, 280, 305; Newton, 254.

9. See Stearns, 190–1.

10. For the exploitation of black musicians see Walton, *Music: black, white and blue*, 65–6. Walton argues that: 'Technology under such circumstances sacrifices the natural, organic, creative process of music for the artificial, simulated, canned musical pollutants.' (142).

11. I. Hoare, 'Mighty, mighty spade and whitey: black lyrics and soul's interaction with white culture' in Hoare, ed., 152.

12. See Hoare ed., 152–7; Stearns, 266; Newton, 261. For gospel music see Heilbut, *The gospel sound.*

13. For black music and dance see O. Patterson, 'The dance invasion', *New Society*, 15 Sept. 1966; Davitt Sigerson *et al.*, 'Dance and discomania', *Black Music*, Jan. 1976.

14. For the hipness of black styles see, e.g., C. McGlashan in Gold ed.: 'In the youth clubs, the black teenagers had what the girls wanted: not super-sexuality, but style, social confidence, and music you could dance to. Out of that equation came the skinheads, London's white Rudies; their music was reggae.' (56).

For reggae and white culture *cf.* Kallyndyr and Dalrymple, *Reggae:*

a people's music and Dalrymple, *Bob Marley*; for the hipness of jazz *cf.* Stearns, 298, 303; for soul Hoare, ed., 156–84, 190–4.

15. Ian Birchall, 'The decline and fall of British rhythm and blues' in Eisen, ed., *The Age of Rock*, 96. *Cf.* Pleasants, *Serious music*, 179 and see Hoare ed., 149; S. I. Hayakawa, 'Popular songs vs the facts of life', Rosenberg and White eds., *Mass culture*.

16. Quoted in Haralambos, 123–4 – see the whole book for the general argument. *Cf.* Newton, 254–6; Stearns, 306–7; Hoare, ed., 198–209.

17. Hoare, ed., 209. *Cf.* Middleton's description of soul as 'basically a social music, a music of action, a music for dancing. It is primarily concerned with social relationships and community character. It plumbs few emotional depths; it is interested in the nature of social rather than personal experience.' (Middleton, 220.)

18. For an extended version of this argument see Frith in Hoare, ed., 51–6.

19. Pleasants, *The great American popular singers*, 121. *Cf.* Karl Dallas on British folk music, the musical source of country:

    'We can observe certain characteristics of folk instruments: the penetrating "vocalised" sound, the use of drones, the adaptation of instruments intended for simple major or minor scales into the unique scales of the folk tradition.' (Laing, ed., *The electric muse*, 112.)

    The best books on country music are Malone; Grissim, *Country music*; Green, D. B., *Country roots*. And see Green, A., 'Hillbilly music'.

20. Malone, 229–30.

21. For an interesting documentation of this point see Russell, *Blacks, whites and blues*.

22. See Grissim, *passim*.

23. See 'Presliad' in Marcus, *Mystery train*.

24. Much of this argument is taken from R. Shelton, 'Something happened in America', Laing, ed. For a useful (and polemical) collection of articles on the American 'folk-song revival' and its meaning see DeTurk and Paulin, eds., *The American folk scene* and *cf.* R. Serge Denisoff, 'Evolution of the protest song in America' in Denisoff and Peterson, eds. For similar developments in Britain *cf.* Laing, ed., 85, 142.

25. Dave Laing, 'Troubadours and stars' in Laing, ed., 48, 78–9.

26. *ibid.* p. 79. *Cf.* the essays by Dallas and Deneslow in the same book.

27. Whitcomb, *After the ball*, 97.

28. *Cf. ibid.*, 111. For analysis of the lyrics of the well-made song see Hayakawa in Rosenberg and White, eds. and *cf.* Ira Gershwin's ironic response – *Lyrics on several occasions*, 112–13. Also R. A. Peterson and D. G. Berger, 'Three eras in the manufacture of popular music lyrics' and H. F. Mooney, 'Popular music since the 1920s: the significance of shifting taste' – both in Denisoff and Peterson, eds.; Mooney, 'Just before rock'. For the development of crooning as the most appropriate style for the broadcasting and recording of such songs see Gillett, *The sound of the city*, 4–5.

29. For the most cynical image maker in British rock'n'roll, Jack Good,

see Whitcomb, 248–52; for the rise of the record producer see Gillett, *The sound of the city*, 236; for the packaging of the Beatles as teen idols see Braun.

30. D. Riesman, 'Listening to popular music', Rosenberg and White, eds., 410. For analysis of lyrics in the 1950s see Horton, 'The dialogue of courtship in popular songs'; Cole, 'Top songs in the sixties'; J. T. Carey, 'Changing courtship patterns in the popular song', Denisoff and Peterson, eds. *Cf.* Mark Abrams' report to NUT, *Popular culture and personal responsibility.*

31. See Carey in Denisoff and Peterson, eds., 211.

32. *Cf.* Peterson and Berger in Denisoff and Peterson, eds., 290 and Belz, *The story of rock*, 209–19.

33. For a good account of the ideology and the commercialisation of Cream, the most influential progressive rock group, see Pidgeon, *Eric Clapton*, ch. 4.

Chapter 11: Rock and mass culture

1. Landau, *It's too late to stop now*, 40 and *cf.* Chapple and Garofalo, ch. 9 ('The Cooptation of Rock') and S. Frith, 'The day the music died', *LIR*, April 1975. For the general argument of this chapter see Frith, 'Rock and popular culture'.

2. D. Hughes, 'Recorded music', Thompson ed., *Discrimination and popular culture*, 154. *Cf.* Hughes' contribution to NUT, *Popular culture and personal responsibility.*

3. Hall and Whannel, *The popular arts*, 276, 280–1.

4. The clearest statement of these arguments (and of their application to teenage culture) is *ibid.*, 365–70.

5. Holbrook, 'Pop and truth', 154. The equation of corruption and commercialism is consistent with the general Leavisite critique of industrial capitalism, but does make difficulties for cultural critics who reject mass culture while believing in market principles. The most amusing solution to this problem can be found in the right-wing American criticism of rock (as 'drugs, sex and revolution') which rejects the notion that rock is the result of market forces and instead attributes its development to a communist conspiracy – see Gary Allen, 'More subversion than meets the ear' and Susan Hush, 'The great kid-con' in Denisoff and Peterson, eds. For a British version of this approach see A. Lejeune, 'Singing the wrong song', *Weekend Telegraph*, 7 Nov. 1969.

6. Parker, 'Pop song: the manipulated ritual', 139. If Holbrook's approach can be traced back to nineteenth century reactions to industrial culture, Parker's analysis has an equally long pedigree. This for, example, is Robert Blatchford in 1894:
   'A few centuries ago the English were a musical people. Part-singing was very popular. The majority of people could read music, and sing at sight; and the English glees and madrigals of the period are unsurpassed. But how many of our Lancashire workers can read music or sing it today? How many of them would prefer a correct rendering

of "Since I First Saw Your Face" to a noisy howling of "The Man
That Broke The Bank At Monte Carlo"? Amongst the many Lancashire operatives who have pianos in their houses, how many tasteful
and correct players are there? Look at the music in their houses, and
see how much of it is real music, and what proportion the quantity of
real music bears to the quantity of Moody and Sankey, and tin-pot
comic song, and sloppy ballad, and see-saw waltz.' – *The Labour
Prophet*, July 1894.

7. Parker, 160–7. For a more subtle and better informed version of this
   argument see Fisher, *We're only in it for the money* and *cf.* Finkelstein,
   Jazz: a people's music.
8. Adorno, 'A social critique of radio music'. For a general version of the
   argument see Marcuse, *One dimensional man.*
9. Adorno, 'Perennial fashion-jazz', 128.
10. *ibid.*, 130–2.
11. See, e.g., P. Lazersfeld and R. K. Merton, 'Mass communication,
    popular taste and organised social action', Rosenberg and White, eds.
    The book as a whole is a good anthology of the fifties media arguments.
12. Denzin, 'Problems in analysing elements of mass culture'. For the
    shift from pluralist to interactionist analyses of mass culture see, for
    example, Gans, 'Popular culture in America'. For the argument
    applied particularly to rock see Hirsch, 'Sociological approaches to
    the pop music phenomenon' and *cf.* Lutke, 'Recorded music and the
    record industry'.
13. See Benjamin, 'The work of art in the age of mechanical reproduction';
    'The author as producer'.
14. Laing, *The sound of our time*, 189–91. *Cf.* Graham Murdock:
    'Of course it is true that, in the final analysis, pop records are com-
    mercial products which are made to make money, but this fact in itself
    does not necessarily rule out the possibility that they may also provide
    genuine means of expression for performers and audiences.' – 'Pop
    Music', *Teaching London Kids*, 4, 1974.
    For the general argument see Enzensberger, 'Constituents of a
    theory of the media'.
15. Lloyd, *Folk song in England*, 346.
16. For the general argument see Lloyd; for a typical folkie put-down of
    Dylan see P. Wolfe, 'Dylan's sellout of the left', Denisoff and Peterson
    eds.
17. Landau, 130. *Cf.* the sociologist Norman Birnbaum: sixties music was
    'made by the people (or some of them) rather than for them; absolute
    domination of this cultural market by the sellers changed into a frantic
    pursuit of the new tastes of the new buyers. This movement spread to
    different class levels; the Beatles in England, the young *chansonniers*
    like Antoine in France, the folk singers like Bob Dylan and Joan Baez
    in America, had this in common: they spoke not only of immediate and
    private concerns, but they gave these general accents. They dealt with
    parents, with bosses, with the atomic bomb, with politicians . . .' 'The
    Staggering Colossus' in Nagel, ed., 158–9.
18. Landau, 21. For Marcus's concept of the 'secret' see 'Rock-a-hula

clarified', *Creem*, June 1971. *Cf.* Christgau, *Any old way you choose it*, 279.

19. Marcus, *Mystery train*, 115. *Cf.* Mellers, 86: 'the long-playing record is a more radical innovation than we once realised. It transplants ritual from temple or theatre into any place where two or three may gather together, including the home or commune, as well as club or discothèque.'

20. The most true believers in the 1960s of rock's ability to absorb a genuine youth culture were the veteran American jazz critics Ralph Gleason and Nat Hentoff. See Gleason's 'Like a rolling stone' and Hentoff's 'Something's happening and you don't know what it is, do you Mr. Jones?' in Eisen, ed., *The age of rock* and Gleason's 'A cultural revolution' in Denisoff and Peterson, eds. *Cf.* Belz: one of the first of the academic treatments of rock it is based on the premise that the music had become a folk form and that it was this that had made it both interesting and important.

21. The wisest as well as wittiest analysis of rock as teenage culture remains Cohn, *Pop from the beginning* – Cohn is well aware of rock's ultimate insignificance.

22. D. Riesman, 'Listening to popular music', Rosenberg and White, eds., 410.

23. For this argument see, e.g., John Sinclair, 'Motor city music', Sinclair and Levin, *Music and politics*, 24–5. For the importance of local musical communities for British rock see 'Back to the roots', *NME*, 17 Jan. 1976.
    The literature on rock as counter-culture is extensive and the most interesting discussions were those of the American left. For positive assessments see Piccone, 'From youth culture to political praxis'; Andrew Kopkind, 'Woodstock nation' in Eisen, ed., *The age of rock 2*; Joe Ferrandino, 'Rock culture and the development of social consciousness', Lewis, ed., *Side-saddle on the golden calf.* For the counter argument that this culture represented nothing more than an easily manipulated 'community' of shared market tastes see Sol Stern, 'Altamont: Pearl Harbour to the Woodstock nation' in Lewis, ed. The best discussion of the issues raised by this debate is Tom Smucker's 'The politics of rock: movement vs groovement' in Eisen, ed., *The age of rock 2.*

24. M. Lydon, 'Rock for sale', Eisen, ed., *The age of rock 2,* 56, 60. For a stimulating British version of this argument see Melly, *Revolt into style.*

25. Mellers, 186–7; Robert Rosenstone, 'The times they are a-changin': the music of protest', Lewis, ed. For Lennon and Plato see, e.g., Palmer, *Born under a bad sign,* 66 – Palmer was the doyen of the late sixties rock-as-art critics, *cf.* 117–22.

26. Landau, 15.

27. See Laing, *passim*; Carl Belz, 'The relationships between the popular and fine arts – recent developments', Bentinck, ed.; the discussion of the Rolling Stones in Eisen, ed., *The age of rock,* 109–20.

28. The most obvious analogy is with literary criticism – see, for example, Michael Gray's treatment of Bob Dylan in *Song and dance man.* For an

attempt to develop a non-literary aesthetics of rock see Chester/Merton and the intriguing (but for me incomprehensible) Meltzer, *The aesthetics of rock*.

29. R. Levin, 'Rock and regression: the responsibility of the artist' Sinclair and Levin, 131.
30. Quoted in Palmer, 145.

Chapter 12: Conclusion

1. Marcus, *Mystery train*, 132.
2. Karl Marx, *Grundrisse*, London, 1973, 287.
3. Sharpe, 112 and see 'NARM: analysing the future adult market', *MW*, 17 April 1976.

Bibliography of major sources cited in the text

Abrams, Mark, *The teenage consumer*, London 1959
——, *Teenage consumer spending in 1959*, London 1961
Abrams, Philip, 'Rites de passage. The conflicts of generations in industrial society', *Jnl. Contemporary History*, 5, 1970
Adorno, T. W., 'A social critique of radio music', in *Reader in public opinion and communication*, eds., Berelson, B., and Janowitz, M., Glencoe 1953.
——, 'Perennial fashion – Jazz' in *Prisms*, London 1967
Albemarle, *The youth service in England and Wales* (The Albemarle report), London 1960
Alderton, Connie, *Magazines Teenagers read*, London 1968
Allen, Sheila, 'Some theoretical problems in the study of youth', *Sociological Review*, 16, 1968
Ashton, D. N., 'The transition from school to work', *Sociological Review*, 21, 1973
Barker, Diana, ' "Spoiling and keeping close" in a South Wales town', *Sociological Review*, 20, 1972
Barnouw, Erik, *The history of broadcasting in the United States*, 3 vols, New York 1966, 1968, 1970
Belson, W. A., *The impact of television*, London 1967
Belz, Carl, *The story of rock*, New York 1969
Benjamin, Walter, 'The work of art in the age of mechanical reproduction', in *Illuminations*, London 1970
——, 'The author as producer' in *Understanding Brecht*, London 1973
Berger, Bennett M., 'On the youthfulness of youth culture', *Social research*, 30, 1963
Bontinck, I., ed., *New patterns of musical behaviour*, Vienna 1974
Bornoff, J., *Music and the twentieth century media*, Florence 1972
Brannen, P., ed., *Entering the world of work*, London 1975
Braun, Michael, *Love me do*, London 1964
Briggs, Asa, *The history of broadcasting in the United Kingdom: the golden age of wireless*, London 1965
Brown, Richard, 'Attitudes, Expectations and Social Perspectives of Ship-building Apprentices' in *Sociological Theory and Survey Research*, ed., Leggatt, T., London 1974
Brown, R. L., and O'Leary, M., 'Pop music in an English secondary school system', *American Behavioural Scientist*, 14, 1971
Buff, Stephen, 'Greasers, dupers and hippies: three responses to the adult world', in *The white majority*, ed. Howe, L. K., New York 1970
Burns, Tom, 'Public service and private world', *Sociological Review Monograph*, 13, 1969

Carter, M. P., *Home, school and work*, London 1962

Chapple, Steve, and Garofalo, Reebee, *Rock'n'roll is here to pay: the history and politics of the music industry*, Chicago 1977

Chester, Andrew, and Merton, Richard, 'For a rock aesthetic', *New Left Review*, 59, 1970

Christgau, Robert, *Any old way you choose it*, Baltimore 1973

Clarke, John, 'The skinheads and the study of youth culture', *CCCS Occasional Papers*, 23, Birmingham University 1973

Cohen, A. K., *Delinquent boys*, London 1956

Cohen, Phil, 'Sub-cultural conflict and working class community', *Working Papers in Cultural Studies*, 2, 1972

Cohen, Stan, ed., *Images of Deviance*, London 1971

——, *Folk devils and moral panics*, London 1973

——, 'Breaking out, smashing up and the social context of aspirations', *Working Papers in Cultural Studies*, 5, 1974

Cohn, Nik, *Pop from the beginning*, London 1969

Cole, Richard R., 'Top songs in the sixties', *American Behavioural Scientist*, 14, 1971

Coleman, James S., *The adolescent society*, New York 1961

Corrigan, Paul, *Schooling the Smash Street Kids*, London 1978

Crichton, A., *et al.*, 'Youth and leisure in Cardiff, 1960', *Sociological Review*, 10, 1962

Dalrymple, Henderson, *Bob Marley: music, myth and the rastas*, London 1976

Davis, Clive, *Clive*, New York 1974

Denisoff, R. Serge, and Levine, Mark, 'The one dimensional approach to popular music', *Jnl. Popular Culture*, 4, 1971

—— and Peterson, R. A., eds., *The sound of social change*, New York 1972

——, 'The evolution of pop broadcasting, 1920–1972', *Music Week*, 10 Nov.–22 Dec. 1973

Denzin, Norman K., 'Problems in analysing elements of mass culture: notes on popular songs and other artistic productions', *Amer. J. Sociology*, 75, 1970

Dept. of Education and Science, *Undergraduate income and spending*, London 1976

Dept. of Employment, *Unqualified, untrained and unemployed*, London 1974

De Turk, David A., and Paulin, A., Jr., eds., *The American folk scene*, New York 1967

Downes, David, *The delinquent solution*, London 1966

Eisen, J., ed., *The age of rock*, New York 1969

——, *The age of rock 2*, New York 1970

Eisenstadt, S. N., *From generation to generation*, New York 1956

Enzensberger, Hans Magnus, 'Constituents of a theory of the media', *New Left Review*, 64, 1970

Ewen, David, *The life and death of Tin Pan Alley*, New York 1964

Faulkner, Robert R., *Hollywood studio musicians*, Chicago 1971

Finkelstein, Sidney, *Jazz: a people's music*, New York 1948

Finnis, Rob, *The Phil Spector story*, London 1975

Fisher, Trevor, *We're only in it for the money*, Birmingham 1972
Flippo, Chet, 'The history of *Rolling Stone*', *Popular Music and Society*, iii, 1973–4
Friedenberg, Edgar Z., *The vanishing adolescent*, New York 1959
Frith, Simon, 'Rock and popular culture', *Socialist Revolution*, 31, 1977
Fyvel, T. R., *The insecure offenders*, London 1963
Gans, Herbert, 'Popular culture in America', *Social Problems*, ed., Becker, H., New York 1966
Gershwin, Ira, *Lyrics on several occasions*, London 1977
Gillett, Charlie, *The sound of the city*, London 1970
——, ed., *Rock file*, London 1972
——, *Making tracks*, New York 1974
——, ed., *Rock file 2*, London 1974
——, and Frith, Simon, eds., *Rock file 3*, London 1975
——,   *Rock file 4*, London 1976
——, 'Big noise from across the water – the American influence on British popular music', paper to Smithsonian Conference on *The United States in the world*, Washington, 1976
Gillis, John R., *Youth and history*, New York 1974
Godbolt, Jim, *All this and 10%*, London 1976
Gold, Mick, ed., *Rock on the road*, London 1976
Goldberg, Isaac, *Tin Pan alley*, New York 1930
Gollan, John, *Youth in British industry*, London 1937
Goodman, Paul, *Growing up absurd*, London 1961
Gray, Michael, *Song and dance man*, London 1973
Green, Archie, 'Hillbilly music: source and symbol', *J. Amer. Folklore*, 78, 1965
Green, Douglas B., *Country roots*, New York 1976
Greene, Bob, *Billion dollar baby*, New York 1974
Greenfield, Robert, *Stones touring party*, London 1974
Grissim, John, *Country music: White man's blues*, New York 1970
Guralnick, Peter, *Feel like going home*, New York 1971
Hall, Stuart, and Whannel, Paddy, *The popular arts*, London 1964
Hamblett, Charles, and Deverson, Jane, *Generation X*, London 1964
Haralambos, Michael, *Right on: from blues to soul in black America*, London 1974
Harris, Paul, *When pirates ruled the waves*, London 1968
Hatch, Tony, *So you want to be in the music business*, London 1976
Hebdige, Dick, 'Reggae, rastas and rudies', *CCCS Occasional Paper*, 24, Birmingham University 1974
Heilbut, Tony, *The gospel sound*, New York 1975
Herman, Gary, *The Who*, London 1971
Hipgnosis, *et al.*, *The album book album*, London 1977
Hirsch, Paul, *The structure of the popular music industry*, Michigan 1970
——, 'Sociological approaches to the pop music phenomenon', *American Behavioral Scientist*, 14, 1971
Hoare, Ian, ed., *The soul book*, London 1975
Holbrook, David, 'Pop and truth' in *English in Australia now*, Cambridge 1973

Hollingshead, A. H., *Elmtown's youth and Elmtown revisited*, New York 1970

Hopkins, Harry, *The new look*, London 1963

Horton, D., 'The dialogue of courtship in popular songs', *Amer. J. Sociology*, 62, 1957

Huizinga, J., *Homo ludens*, London 1970

Hunter, Ian, *Diary of a rock'n'roll star*, London 1974

Jacques, Martin, 'Trends in youth culture', *Marxism Today*, Sept. 1973

Jahn, Mike, *Rock from Elvis Presley to the Rolling Stones*, New York 1973

Jefferson, Tony, 'The ted: a political resurrection', *CCCS Occasional Paper*, 22, Birmingham University 1973

Jephcott, P., *Time of one's own*, Edinburgh 1967

Jones, Leroi, *Blues people*, New York 1963

——, *Black music*, New York 1967

Joseph, Joyce, 'A research note on attitudes to work and marriage of six hundred adolescent girls', *Brit. J. Sociology*, 12, 1961

Kallyndyr, Rolston, and Dalrymple, Henderson, *Reggae: a people's music*, London, n.d.

Keil, Charles, *Urban blues*, Chicago 1966

Kennedy, John, *Tommy Steele*, London 1959

King, Josephine, and Stott, Mary, eds., *Is this your life? Images of women in the media*, London 1977

Kofsky, Frank, *Black nationalism and the revolution in music*, New York 1970

Laing, Dave, *The sound of our time*, London 1969

——, ed., *The electric muse*, London 1975

Landau, Jon, *It's too late to stop now*, San Francisco, 1972

Laurie, Peter, *Teenage revolution*, London 1965

Lee, Edward, *Music of the people*, London 1970

Leigh, John, *Young people and leisure*, London 1971

Leonard, Neil, *Jazz and the white Americans*, London 1964

Leslie, Peter, *Fab. The anatomy of a phenomenon*, London 1965

Lewis, George H., ed., *Side-saddle on the golden calf*, Pacific Palisades, 1972

Lloyd, A. L., *Folk song in England*, London 1975

Logan, R. F., and Goldberg, E. M., 'Rising eighteen in a London suburb', *Brit. J. Sociology*, 4, 1953

Lutke, Heinz Otto, 'Recorded music and the record industry', *International Social Science J.*, 20, 1968

Lydon, Michael, *Rock folk*, New York 1973

Mabey, Richard, *The pop process*, London 1969

McCabe, Peter, and Schonfeld, Robert D., *Apple to the core*, London 1972

MacInnes, Colin, *Absolute beginners*, London 1959

——, *England, half English*, London 1961

McQuail, Dennis, *Towards a sociology of mass communications*, London 1969

Malone, Bill C., *Country Music USA*, Austin 1968

Mannheim, Karl, *Diagnosis of our time*, London 1943

——, *Essays in the sociology of knowledge*, London 1952

Marcus, Greil, ed., *Rock and roll will stand*, Boston 1969
——, *Mystery train*, New York 1975
Marcuse, H., *One dimensional man*, Boston 1964
Marris, Peter, *The experience of higher education*, London 1964
Marsden, Dennis, and Duff, Evan, *Workless*, London 1975
Mays, J. B., *The young pretenders*, London 1965
Mellers, Wilfred, *Twilight of the gods*, London 1973
Melly, George, *Owning up*, London 1965
——, *Revolt into style*, London 1970
Meltzer, Richard, *The aesthetics of rock*, New York 1970
Middleton, Richard, *Pop music and the blues*, London 1972
Millar, Gavin, *Pop! hit or miss?*, London 1963
Miller, Jim, ed., *The Rolling Stone illustrated history of rock and roll*, New York 1976
Mills, Richard, *Young outsiders*, London 1973
Monod, Jean, 'Juvenile gangs in Paris', *J. Research in Crime and Delinquency*, 4, 1967
Mooney, Hugh, 'Just before rock: pop music 1950–1953 reconsidered', *Popular Music and Society*, 3, 1974
Morin, Edgar, *Plodémet*, London 1971
Murdock, Graham, and Phelps, Guy, *Mass media and the secondary school*, London 1973
——, and Golding, Peter, 'For a political economy of mass communications', *Socialist Register, 1973*, London 1974
Musgrove, Frank, *Youth and the social order*, London 1964
Nagel, Julian, ed., *Student Power*, London 1969
National Children's Bureau, *Britain's sixteen-year-olds*, London 1976
National Union of Teachers, *Popular culture and personal responsibility*, London 1960
Neville, Richard, *Play power*, London 1970
The New Survey of London Life and Leisure, *Vol. IX: Life and leisure in London*, London 1975
Newton, Francis, *The jazz scene*, London 1961
Nuttall, Jeff, *Bomb culture*, London 1970
Office of Population Censuses and Surveys, *Fifth form girls: their hopes for the future*, London 1975
Paint House, The, *The Paint House*, London 1972
Palmer, Tony, *Born under a bad sign*, London 1970
Parker, Charles, 'Pop song: The manipulated ritual' in *The Black Rainbow*, ed., Abbs, P., London 1975
Parker, Howard, *View from the boys*, Newton Abbot 1974
Passman, Arnold, *The deejays*, New York 1971
Peacock, Alan, and Weir, Ronald, *The composer in the market place*, London 1975
Pearson, Geoff, and Mungham, Geoff, eds., *Working-class youth culture*, London 1976
Peterson, Richard A., and Berger, D. G., 'Entrepreneurship and organisation: evidence from the popular music industry', *Admin. Science Quarterly*, 16, 1971

Peterson, Richard, A. and Davis, R. B. jnr, 'The contemporary radio audience', *Popular Music and Society*, 3, 1974

——, 'Cycles in symbol production: the case of popular music', *Amer. Sociological Review*, 40, 1975

Phillips, D., 'Young and unemployed in a northern town', in *Men and work in modern Britain*, ed. Weir, D., London 1973

Piccone, Paul, 'From youth culture to political praxis', *Radical America*, 3, 1969

Pidgeon, John, *Eric Clapton*, London 1976

——, *Rod Stewart and the Changing Faces*, London 1976

Pleasants, Henry, *Serious music and all that jazz*, London 1969

——, *The great American popular singers*, New York 1974

Raison, T., ed., *Youth in New Society*, London 1966

Rapoport, Rhona and Robert, *Leisure and the family life cycle*, London 1975

Richard, Cliff, *It's great to be young*, London 1960

Roberts, Robert, *The classic slum*, London 1973

Rock, Paul, and Cohen, Stanley, 'The teddy boy' in *The age of affluence, 1951–1964*, eds., Bogdanov, V., and Skidelsky, R., London 1970

Rogers, Eddie, *Tin Pan Alley*, London 1964

Rolling Stone, *Rolling Stone interview book*, 2 vols, New York 1971, 1973

Rolling Stones, *Our own story*, London 1964

Rosenberg, B., and White, D. M., eds., *Mass culture*, New York 1957

Rosko, Emperor, *Emperor Rosko's DJ book*, London 1976

Roth, Ernst, *The business of music*, London 1969

Rowntree, B. S., and Lavers, G. R., *English life and leisure*, London 1951

Rowntree, John and Margaret, 'The political economy of youth', *Our Generation*, 6, 1968

Russell, Tony, *Blacks, whites and blues*, London 1970

Rust, Francis, *Dance in society*, London 1969

Saville, Jimmy, *Love is an uphill thing*, London 1975

Schools Council, *Young school leavers*, London 1968

Seabrook, Jeremy, *City close-up*, London 1971

Sharpe, Sue, *'Just like a girl'*, London 1976

Shemel, S., and Krasilovsky, M. W., *This business of music*, New York 1964

Sillitoe, K. K., *Planning for leisure*, London 1969

Sinclair, John, and Levin, Robert, *Music and politics*, New York 1971

Skipper, James S., jr, 'How popular is popular music?' *Popular Music and Society*, 2, 1973

Smith, Cyril S., *Young people at leisure*, Manchester 1967

——, *et al.*, *The Wincroft Youth Project*, London 1972

Smith, Michael A., *et al.*, eds., *Leisure and society in Britain*, London 1973

Stearns, Marshall, *The story of jazz*, London 1970

Stewart, M., 'The leisure activities of grammar school children', *Brit. J. Educational Psychology*, 20, 1950

Stokes, Geoffrey, *Star-making machinery*, Indianapolis 1976

Sugarman, Barry, 'Involvement in youth culture, academic achievement and conformity in school', *Brit. J. Sociology*, 18, 1967

Swift, Betty, 'Job orientations and the transition from school to work', *Brit. J. Guidance and Counselling*, Jan. 1973

Taylor, Derek, *As time goes by*, London 1973

Taylor, Ian, and Taylor, Laurie, eds, *Politics and deviance*, London 1973

Taylor, John, *From self-help to glamour – the working men's club, 1860–1972*, Oxford 1972

Thompson, Denys, ed., *Discrimination and popular culture*, London 1964

Twiggy, *Twiggy*, London 1976

UNESCO, *Music and tomorrow's public*, ed., E. Helm, Paris 1975

Vaz, E. W., ed., *Middle-class juvenile delinquency*, New York 1967

Venables, Ethel, *The young worker at college*, London 1967

Veness, Thelma, *School leavers*, London 1962

Vulliamy, Graham, and Lee, Ed, eds., *Pop music in schools*, Cambridge 1976

Wale, Michael, *Vox pop*, London 1972

Walton, Ortiz, *Music: black, white and blue*, New York 1972

Whitcomb, Ian, *After the ball*, London 1973

Wilkins, Leslie T., *The adolescent in Britain*, London 1955

Wilson, B., *The youth culture and the universities*, London 1970

Williams, Alan, *The man who gave the Beatles away*, London 1975

Williams, Richard, *Out of his head*, New York 1972

Williams, W. M., ed., *Occupational choice*, London 1974

Willis, Paul, *Profane culture*, London 1978

Willmott, Peter, *Adolescent boys of east London*, London 1969

Wolfe, Tom, *The Pump house gang*, New York 1968

Working papers in cultural studies, 7, *Resistance through rituals*, Birmingham 1975

Young, Jock, *The drug takers*, London 1971

Index